Istwa across the Water

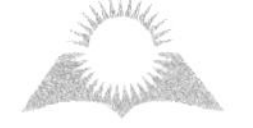

UNIVERSITY PRESS OF FLORIDA

Florida A&M University, Tallahassee
Florida Atlantic University, Boca Raton
Florida Gulf Coast University, Ft. Myers
Florida International University, Miami
Florida State University, Tallahassee
New College of Florida, Sarasota
University of Central Florida, Orlando
University of Florida, Gainesville
University of North Florida, Jacksonville
University of South Florida, Tampa
University of West Florida, Pensacola

ISTWA ACROSS THE WATER

Haitian History, Memory, and the Cultural Imagination

TONI PRESSLEY-SANON

University Press of Florida

Gainesville · Tallahassee · Tampa · Boca Raton

Pensacola · Orlando · Miami · Jacksonville · Ft. Myers · Sarasota

Publication of this work made possible by a Sustaining the Humanities through the American Rescue Plan grant from the National Endowment for the Humanities.

First cloth printing, 2017
First paperback printing, 2022

27 26 25 24 23 22   6 5 4 3 2 1

Library of Congress Cataloging-in-Publication Data
Names: Pressley-Sanon, Toni, author.
Title: Istwa across the water : Haitian history, memory, and the cultural
   imagination / Toni Pressley-Sanon.
Description: Gainesville : University Press of Florida, 2017. | Includes
   bibliographical references and index.
Identifiers: LCCN 2016049597 | ISBN 9780813054407 (cloth) | ISBN 9780813068619 (pbk.)
Subjects: LCSH: Haiti—History. | Haiti—Social life and customs. |
   Memory—Social aspects—Haiti. | Vodou—Haiti. | Haiti—Religious life and
   customs. | Creole dialects, French—Haiti.
Classification: LCC F1921 .P93 2017 | DDC 972.94—dc23
LC record available at https://lccn.loc.gov/2016049597

The University Press of Florida is the scholarly publishing agency for the State University System of Florida, comprising Florida A&M University, Florida Atlantic University, Florida Gulf Coast University, Florida International University, Florida State University, New College of Florida, University of Central Florida, University of Florida, University of North Florida, University of South Florida, and University of West Florida.

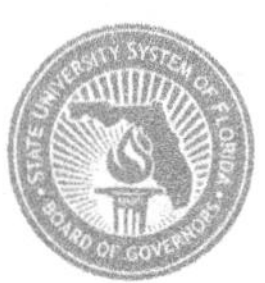

University Press of Florida
2046 NE Waldo Road
Suite 2100
Gainesville, FL 32609
http://upress.ufl.edu

To my own *marasa*, my beautiful young man, Reuben.
Without you there would be no me.

For Max G. Beauvoir and Margaret Mitchell Armand.
May you rest well with the ancestors.

Contents

Figures

Acknowledgments

I am deeply indebted to numerous souls, both seen and unseen, who have contributed to the realization of this project. First among them is my mother, Lucille Pressley, whose warm, protective hand still holds mine, and my Aunt Mary Jackson, who continues to offer wise counsel. My Ruby who has shown me worlds and taught me about the possibilities; I am so grateful that you chose me. I thank my sister, Mona Pressley, whose love and generosity knows no bounds, and my brother, Jeffrey Pressley, who always knows how to make me laugh. I cannot thank enough my dear sister-friend, Nazalima Durham, and her amazing family for always providing me with a home away from home, full of laughter and a good meal—or at least a way to get one. You have been there from the beginning, always a guiding light of love, peace, and acceptance. I am infinitely grateful for the presence of my dear sister-friend, Ama Clarke, who came into my life when we were but babes and who knows me inside out.

I am very fortunate to have been a graduate student at The New School for Social Research, where I was introduced to the genius of M. Jacqui Alexander. I am grateful to Andrée-Nicola McLaughlin, who sent me to her. The Department of African Languages and Literature at the University of Wisconsin–Madison was the perfect place for me to deepen my appreciation and passion for cultural production of and from Africa and its diaspora. There was a level of expertise concentrated in one place that could not be beat. I am grateful to Tejumola Olaniyan as well as James H. Sweet, Aliko Songolo, Harold Scheub, and Deborah Jenson for their support and guidance. As project assistant for the African Diaspora and Atlantic World Research Circle that Teju and Jim directed, I amassed a wealth of experience that would have been impossible otherwise. I also need to thank Alberto Vargas, director of the program in Latin American,

Caribbean, and Iberian Studies, who showed an incredible level of interest and support for my work. Thanks to Dean Makuluni, whose door was always open for chats about everything from the latest African and Caribbean novels to football (soccer) and everything in between. I am also grateful to Henry Drewal, whose boundless energy and pursuit of integrity in researching the visual arts of Africa and its diasporas has inspired me. I also thank him for setting me up with Martine de Souza in Ouidah.

A Fulbright Research Fellowship made it possible for me to spend that all-important year in Ouidah, and the Tinker Nave Short Term Travel Grant allowed me to return to Haiti after being away for much too long.

In Benin Republic, Martine de Souza's strength and ambition was wonderful to witness. Parfait Nago, a brilliant drummer and artist, was a confidante and constant travel companion to the neighboring villages, where I learned more than I could have imagined. I was fortunate to have had Fay and Simon Akindes as well as Yanique St. Jean as fellow Fulbrighters the year that I was in Benin. I am grateful to them for providing my boy and me a place for rest and refuge from time to time as well as their continuing friendship. I also am grateful to Leonie Tossa, my Fongbe teacher, who traveled all the way from Cotonou to Ouidah several days a week to give us language lessons.

At the University at Buffalo, Glendora Johnson-Cooper was an amazing source of support and friendship—and continues to be. Alexis De Veaux's commitment to fostering sisterhood continues to be a beacon of light and an inspiration. The Baldy Center under the direction of Errol Meidinger and Laura Wirth hosted the manuscript workshop that was invaluable to shaping this text. I am especially grateful to Patrick Bellegarde-Smith and LeGrace Benson for saying yes to the invitation to offer their expertise and encouragement. I am deeply grateful to Hershini Young, who read the manuscript with thoughtfulness and sensitivity and offered invaluable suggestions and comments.

I can't begin to name all the people in Haiti who made my "work" so joyous. Carla and Ron Bluntschli have always provided a sanctuary for me in their beautiful home in the mountains, countless cups of super-sweet, rich black coffee, and endless stimulating conversation around their kitchen table. I am eternally grateful to Sean Reubens Jean Sacra (Serge), who was right alongside me traveling out to provinces, using any means possible and sleeping wherever we found space. I wish to thank Francky Joseph and his band, Chay Namn, for their commitment to keeping roots music alive in Haiti and beyond, and for their illuminating spirits, sense of humor, and willingness to share their knowledge with me. I thank Pè Michel and his wonderful partner, Rosalenn, for their guidance at the perfect time. André Eugene has always made me feel "*alez*" at his atelier. He is truly a special spirit, just hanging out with the rest of us for a time, teaching. I thank Leah Gordon and Myron Beasley for organizing the first Ghetto Biennale that introduced me to the talented group of artists known as Atis Rezistans, and to Leah for lending an understanding ear when Haiti was kicking my ass! I am especially grateful for the time, however limited, that I got to spend with the talented and incredibly generous Louko. To my dear brother, Claudel Casseus: thank you for your kind and gentle spirit and your willingness to walk with me. I cannot convey adequately my gratitude to Max Gesner Beauvoir, who took time to share a bit of his vast wisdom with me. You are greatly missed.

Lovalerie King, who headed the Africana Research Center at Penn State University, made my year as a postdoctoral fellow and research associate in the Departments of Comparative Literature and African and African American Studies immensely productive in all kinds of ways. She provided the funds for me to travel to Haiti just a few months after the earthquake to see and talk with my loved ones and hear their stories. My time with Solsiree Del Moral at Penn State, with whom I shared many a phở, will always be cherished.

At Eastern Michigan University, I'd like to thank my colleagues for their commitment to the next generation. EMU's Provost's Research Support Award made possible the inclusion of the two nkisi images from the Smithsonian Museum of African Art as well as the indexing of the manuscript. Thanks to Wade Tornquist for his guidance.

I also wish to thank several scholars who planted the seeds for my intellectual paths, with all of their many twists and turns: Andrée-Nicola McLaughlin and M. Jacqui Alexander; Claudine Michel, Patrick Bellegarde-Smith, and LeGrace Benson (the *marasa twa*); Karen McCarthy Brown, Donald Cosentino, Lizabeth Paravisini-Gebert, Carole Boyce Davies, Joan Dayan, Simone Schwarz-Bart, and Maryse Condé. Gina Athena Ulysse's courageous scholarship and generosity kept me going. I am grateful for her presence in the world. The endlessly creative debauchery of my dear brother-friend Mūkoma wa Ngũgĩ has been a gift. I celebrate KOSANBA for working tirelessly to bring to light the countless lessons that Vodou holds for us all.

At the University Press of Florida, I am grateful to Erika Stevens, who had faith in the project from the beginning, and Stephanye Hunter, who confidently helped steer the project through sometimes choppy waters. I wish to thank Marthe Walters and Patricia Bower for helping shape the work into its final form. Dr. Jean Herskovits came through in the nick of time with grace and generosity. Mèsi anpil!

Finally, I must give thanks to the *lwa*, who have always been there with me, even when I didn't recognize them.

A Note on Spelling

I follow the standard orthography established for Haitian Kreyòl by the Haitian government in 1978. The area of the Kôngo throughout the text refers to the Central West African kingdom that existed prior to European colonization. When quoting other writers, I retain their spellings in all cases. Kreyòl does not use *-s* to pluralize words. I have followed this practice throughout the text.

Groundings

Tidalectics, Marasa, and *Istwa*

Twa fè, twa rasin o
Jete bliye, ranmase sonje.
(Three leaves, three roots, oh
Throw away to forget, pick up to remember.)
—Haitian Vodou song

It is relatively common knowledge that one of the initial acts of Gen. Jean-Jacques Dessalines as the first leader of the newly liberated nation of Hayti was to tear the white from the tricolor flag of the former French colonizer. The color blue in the original flag is believed to have represented Saint-Domingue's black inhabitants; red, the mulatto class; and white, the white population. The removal of the white strip symbolized not only the extrication of the colonial power but also the unification of the two subaltern groups.[1] While this story and explanation are commonly found in history books, there is a parallel "secret" history that is not so widely known. According to Patrick Bellegarde-Smith, the colors of that resultant flag transcend the profane and hold another parallel and equally important and sacred meaning for those who serve the spirits or *lwa* of the Haitian spiritual belief system, Vodou. That bi-color flag, found in most *ounfò* (inner sanctuaries) and *wogatwa* (personal and family altars) also bears the colors of the two *lwa* who were invoked most strongly during the Haitian Revolution: Ezili Dantò and Ogou Feray. The dark blue of Ezili Dantò "represents maternal love and collective welfare" while dark red, the color of Ogou Feray, invokes his "iron will necessary in warfare."[2] The prolific artist and *oungan* (Vodou priest) André Pierre also articulates the centrality of Ogou and Dantò to the nation's foundations when, in an interview with Donald Cosentino, he "testifies" to the presence of Guinea spirits at Haiti's birth, saying "Ogou returned with a red and blue flag. And the woman saint brought the Kongo packet. Ogou took away the white, and left a bi-color. He changed the country. He took the white away from the French flag. He said, 'I am giving this land back to you, and I am coming home.'"[3]

Dessalines is the one that history records ripping the white from the French flag and declaring Haiti's independence. However, as both Bellegarde-Smith's and Pierre's assertions attest, Dessalines was not alone as he stood before those who had fought hard to win their freedom. He was being ridden by the *lwa* Ogou, and it was he who made the pronouncement through his horse.[4] Ezili Dantò was by his side, holding the *pakèt kongo* (kongo packet)[5] that would heal the spiritually wounded warriors both above and below the earth, a healing that was facilitated by Danbala, *lwa* of the earth and sky, and Simbi, the *lwa* that straddles both worlds. But there was one other *lwa*, or rather, family of *lwa* who were present on the battlefield, showing up even if they were not purposely invoked or invited, just as they do in contemporary Vodou ceremonies: the Gede. As the *lwa* who preside over the domain of life and death, they moved among the men and women who fell under bayonets while fighting to create a new life for themselves and their progeny, some of whom were undoubtedly conceived on the battlefield. I agree with Leah Gordon's suggestion that this less performative Gede than the one that manifests today "pervaded the struggle as the invisible army of the ancestors that mirrored the insurgents. The spirit manifested as the healer that stalked the injured on the battlefield, tending to his beloved flesh—be it torn, diseased, or rotting—and finally he was there laughing back at the enemy in the form of the bones and skulls kept as macabre souvenirs of victory by the rebel leaders."[6] In fact, it is appropriate that the Gede were there, for they signify rebirth in the midst of death. As Leslie Desmangles relates, "Gede, the master of Ginen, is lord not merely of death but of life as well. That is why Haitians often identify him with his regenerative rather than with his destructive powers. Even in his official capacity as lord of death, Vodouisants use such appellations for him as the Giver of Life and the 'Rising Sun.'"[7] Indicative of the balance that Vodou as a belief system based in nature strives for, Gede helped restore life in the midst of death, having a bit of fun in the process, as he is wont to do.

There is another aspect of Pierre's pronouncement that is equally intriguing: that is, that in Ogou taking the white from the flag, he declared that he was giving the land *back* to those who had fought to liberate themselves and coming "home." We may ask ourselves to whom was he speaking and to which home was he returning? Perhaps it was not only the African and African-descended people who were readily identifiable among the insurgents but also the Taíno, those who originally inhabited the land and who, in solidarity with African captives, fought to the death to liberate themselves and their land from the colonial oppressors. I would also suggest that the "home" to which Ogou refers is not limited to the geographical space of Ayiti, as the original inhabitants named the land, but the ancestral and spiritual homes of the diverse group of insurgents. Many of the enslaved originated from the West African region of Dahomey and the Central West African area of the Kôngo Kingdom. As such, "home" consists of the Old World and the New, both of which are physical and metaphysical sites of origin for contemporary Haiti.

In fact, we can trace the spirits that led the fight on the battlefield even further back than the revolution. They were there from the beginning in the belief systems of Ayiti's indigenous populations as well as with African captives on the middle-passage voyage. They were also constant companions in the enslaved person's life in Saint-Domingue when, as Madison Smartt Bell avers, "labor conditions . . . were so cruelly severe that the slave population could not reproduce itself. Premature death, suicide and infanticide were so common that an importation of some 200,000 slaves from Africa were deemed necessary between 1789 and 1791, simply to keep the work force stable. . . . In *Vodouisant* terms, the fact that so many people died on the ground meant that the reservoir of *Les Morts et Les Mystères* was brimful and unusually turbulent."[8] Many of the enslaved Africans who arrived in Saint-Domingue during that period time came from the Kôngo, victims of the surge in wars that the transatlantic slave trade engendered. According to John K. Thornton, "The European beneficiaries of this great surge were French merchants who fixed their operations along the coast north of the Zaire River, but regularly visited the Kongo coast as well. In the 1780s, French ships carried a total of over 116,000 slaves from this coast, mostly to Saint Domingue, while their closest competitors, the English exported only 25,000."[9] This means that many of those exported to Saint-Domingue during those years were also warriors and contributed their military skills to the revolution that gave birth to the nation of Hayti. They also brought their spiritual belief systems across the water. Those who were already subjected to the colonial system not only joined in the physical world with those captives who arrived in later years but also in the spiritual realm, to create new systems of existence that recalled their former lives but also accounted for their new conditions of enslavement. This joining together resulted in the reservoir of "brimful and unusually turbulent" *Les Morts* and *Les Mystères* (the dead and their spirits) that Bell suggests populated the colony on the eve of the revolution.

The fate of *Les Morts* and *Les Mystères* has always been inextricably tied to those who serve them. I propose that, following the success of the revolution, they continued to manifest, speaking to the living through Dessalines' secretary, Louis Félix Mathurin Boisrond-Tonnerre, who, on the eve of Haitian independence, famously pronounced, "To prepare the independence act, we need the skin of a white man for parchment, his skull for a desk, his blood for ink, and a bayonet for a pen."[10] Regarding Boisrond-Tonnerre's speech, Sibylle Fischer argues that, "if slavery deprived people of color of their personhood and humanity, the declaration of Haitian independence reduces the slaveholders to an assemblage of exploitable body parts: bones, blood, skin"—again, the domain for the Gede.[11] She further remarks that while the Haitian declaration looks back to the colonial power in wresting writing away from the former master, the act of writing one's own name—Hayti—reduces the former master to a bag of body parts.[12] Thus, in addition to the physical manifestations of the Gede's domain found in "the bones and skulls kept as macabre souvenirs," the turning of the slaveholders into "exploitable body parts" and the act of those formerly enslaved inscribing their names in effect rendered the former master impotent; again the domain of the Gede.

Furthermore, in returning the name of the island nation to that bestowed by its original inhabitants, the new leaders symbolically cut Europe out of the island's future, basing their rule on their memory and a celebration of a time before the Spanish invasion. It also looked forward to the writing of a "completely new script"—one where blacks would control their own destinies.[13] In this dual conceptualization of the nascent nation, the new leaders reclaimed its distant past while simultaneously disavowing its recent history as a requisite for the imagining of a liberated future.

Vodou, History, and Memory

More than a religion, Vodou has been central to Haitian history from the first moments of the nation's inception. While the Haitian Revolution was in no sense a religious war, Sidney Mintz, in his introduction to Alfred Métraux's *Voodoo in Haiti* (1972) argued that Vodou played a critical role in, not only the resistance of the enslaved to their colonial masters but also other would-be colonizers who vied for control of the "immensely profitable colony."[14] Furthermore, Jean Price-Mars' writing that "*1804 est issu du Vodou*" (Vodou is responsible for the revolution of 1804) also reflects the impossibility of disentangling Vodou from the sociopolitical history of the country.[15] Finally, the spiritual underpinnings of Haiti's history and destiny are also made clear in Bellegarde-Smith's assertion that "the engagement of Vodou in Haitian temporal affairs and history has been constant [with] the many revolts of the enslaved [being] efforts toward freedom and liberation writ large, from within an ethos that, at the outset had incorporated similar elements from diverse African"[16]—and I would add, indigenous—ethnicities. This intimate relationship between the revolutionaries' spiritual beliefs and their commitment to the liberation struggle to which these scholars refer is evidenced in the story about the flag that Dessalines created while declaring Haiti's independence. Cosentino highlights this relationship when he calls Vodou Haiti's secret history.[17]

Taking up M. Jacqui Alexander's proposition that cosmological systems house memory, and that "such memory [is] necessary to distill the psychic trauma produced under the grotesque conditions of slavery," this text seeks to explore intersections between history (even as it is unfolding), memory, and cultural production in Haiti vis-à-vis its secret history.[18] It is conceptualized through three theoretical "anchors": tidalectics, a term coined by Jamaican poet and historian Kamau Brathwaite that is inspired by the ebb and flow of the ocean's waves; the Marasa or Sacred Twins, principal *lwa* that are often saluted at the beginning of Vodou ceremonies after Papa Legba, Master of the Crossroads; and *istwa*, a Haitian Kreyòl term encompassing both history and story and facilitated by memory.[19] The text looks to Africa—more specifically, Dahomey (present-day Benin Republic) and the Kôngo—for historical and cultural "blueprints," in the words of Carole Boyce Davies, as twin influences on Haitian cultural production. But because culture is alive and fluid as those who produce it draw from a multitude of influences including time and space, I propose that beyond blueprints as antecedent, the dialogical relationship between Africa and its diaspora persists and is thus also continually expressed as it evolves.

I am indebted to many scholars on both sides of the water who have investigated the intersections of memory and history with regard to Africa's fraught relationship with its diaspora as a result of the transatlantic slave trade.[20] Many texts from the diaspora perform a task similar to the one that I undertake here. These include full autobiographical and biographical narratives and, more recently, collected testimonies.[21] Other written narratives—fictions, as it were—while not empirically verifiable, offer an important lens through which to view the slave trade and slavery and their impact on the lives of those who were exiled.[22]

Several scholars have contributed to my thinking through this project. They include those who have explored historical African and African diasporic identity formation in multiple ways and through diverse lenses.[23] Some have focused on religious traditions and belief systems within the context of sociopolitical realities.[24] Others have lent their expertise in art history to explore processes of retention and transformation in the black Atlantic through material culture.[25] Some recent scholarship looks to specifically literary and aesthetic manifestations of memory.[26] We will note that many of these studies are edited volumes, signaling the need for a collective approach to the work of healing across both physical and spiritual waters. In my own exploration of history, memory, and Haiti's cultural production, the reader will find the scholarship of M. Jacqui Alexander, Patrick Bellegarde-Smith, LeGrace Benson, Karen McCarthy Brown, Claudine Michel, Leslie Desmangles, Donald Cosentino, Rachel Beauvoir-Dominique, and Joan (Colin) Dayan, to name a few, woven throughout the text. These scholars have contributed a great deal to the field of Atlantic World Studies from rich and constructive points of entry—from the historical to the visual to the anthropological in their work on Vodou's role in world history as well as contemporary reality. It is on their shoulders that I stand as I attempt to bring into relief some of the concepts that they introduce and expand upon in their work. I build on their scholarship from an interdisciplinary perspective that relies heavily on the oral and material culture that emerges from primarily Dahomey / Benin Republic, the Kôngo, and Saint-Domingue/Haiti. As such, I explore how oral and material culture from both sides of the water reflect and comment on history while facilitating memory with the ultimate goal of restoring the balance that Vodou strives for and that I propose would facilitate the individual and collective healing that would result from that restored equilibrium.

I conceive of the traditions that emanate from the three geographical sites as engaging in what Benson characterizes as a "Long Conversation."[27] However, where Benson conceives of this conversation as taking place between Haiti and her two motherlands, Africa and Europe, I conceive of the Long Conversation as one that takes place among two of Haiti's other many motherlands, Dahomey and the Kôngo.[28] This Long Conversation began centuries ago and continues into the contemporary moment, constantly evolving as the conditions of Africa and its diaspora evolve. As Benson avers, "The Long Conversations are the communications aspect of an elaborate ecosystem, always in process, where giver and recipient constantly modify and modulate."[29] I read this Long Conversation from within the belief systems of the populations about which I write.[30] I do so based on my understanding that, whatever earthly preoccupations may motivate the oral and visual art that I discuss herein, there are otherworldly forces that guide and manifest their will through their human charges and are illuminated in cultural production. My project seeks to tease out evidence of those otherworldly influences by privileging the cultural production of those who either lived or had access to these histories. Thus, I deploy history to support the stories—both oral and visual—that people express rather than the other way around.[31]

I conceive of the three—history, memory, and cultural production—as working in tandem, as a relationship that is echoed in my theoretical anchors—tidalectics, Marasa, and *istwa*. These two sites—one of inquiry (history, memory, and cultural production) and the other, theory (tidalectics, Marasa, and *istwa*)—are in turn manifest in both the Old World sites of Dahomey and the Kôngo and in the New World context of Haiti, forming a historical and cultural triad.

Vodou, the *lwa*, and the work of *sèvitè*, those who serve the *lwa*, wind their way throughout the text precisely because, as Desmangles notes, Vodou, as the folk religion of the country, "pervades the framework of Haitian culture."[32] The spiritual belief system "is an expression of people's longing for meaning and purpose in their lives."[33] But more than that, it is, as Joan Dayan, postulates, "thought thinking itself through history."[34] Thus, the historical function of Vodou as the project of thought makes its presence known in and through historical practices and the stories about them that we see in the hi/story of the Haitian Revolution.[35] But if we reflect on Vodou's meaning as "Spirit," then we can see its workings in the cultural production from its sources, two of which I focus on in these pages and which had their own storehouses of Spirit. As I will show, Spirit makes itself known in the oral tradition as well as in the power objects that emanate from these sites and that are often discussed as art forms.[36] With Dayan's insight as a guiding principle, I treat Vodou not as separate from but as integral to my exploration of history, memory, and Haiti's cultural imagination.

The Crossing

The transatlantic slave trade engendered a profound physical and metaphysical rupture. As Ngũgĩ wa Thiong'o asserts in *Something Torn and New*, the European invasion resulted in the fracturing or "dismemberment" of Africa.[37] In the first of what wa Thiong'o calls a two-stage process, the transatlantic slave trade divided "the African personhood . . . into two halves: the continent and its diaspora."[38] In other words, the transatlantic slave trade fractured what was once whole, sending one part into exile in the diaspora and leaving the other part in Africa. This fracturing was in turn facilitated by those who were affected and who forgot or threw away the "wholeness" that they knew before as perhaps a requisite for survival in the after time. This fracturing resulted in a disequilibrium that is antithetical to Vodou's principle objective—that is, as a belief system based in nature to achieve and maintain balance. We find the crisis of disequilibrium and its solution delineated in the Vodou song that serves as the epigraph of the introduction: the fact of forgetting (*bliye*) and throwing away (*jete*) that burdens both the African and the African diasporic experience and is resolved with the remembering (*sonje*) and gathering together (*ranmase*) of the parts to their roots or foundations. The solution to this crisis of burdening lies in re-membering the parts to the whole. As the revolutionary Makandal from Edouard Glissant's *Monsieur Toussaint, A Play* suggests when he declares, "We drag the seas behind us, from Africa to America. We carry them with us, like a woman with child who still toils under the sun," this remembering and gathering together offers hope: a lightening of the fragments' respective and collective spiritual loads.[39]

Tidalectics

My first theoretical anchor, tidalectics, is a concept developed by Kamau Brathwaite and expanded upon by literary scholar Elizabeth DeLoughrey. Brathwaite explicates tidalectics by way of a poetic, fractured story:

> The "meaning" of the Caribbean was in that humble repetitive ritual action which this peasant woman was performing. And she was always on this journey, walking on the steps of sunlit water, coming out of a continent which we didn't fully know how to understand, to a set of islands which we only now barely come to respect, cherish and understand
>
> And so my poem startle to ask the question, what is the origin of the Caribbean? How do we come from? Where do we come from? And why are we as we are? Why are we so leaderless, so fragmented, so perpetually caught up with the notion of hope and still at the same time Sisyphean? Why is our psychology not dialectical—successfully dialectical—in the way that Western philosophy has assumed people's lives should be, but tidalectic, like our grandmother's—our nanna's—action, like the movement of the ocean she's walking on, coming from one continent/continuum, touching another, and then receding ("reading") from the island(s) into the perhaps creative chaos of the(ir) future . . . [40]

According to Brathwaite's poem/prose, the repetitive movement of the Caribbean peasant woman reflects an ancient repetition that began to take shape in the original bonded displacement of the African from her site of origin, facilitated as it was by the Atlantic Ocean and the middle-passage voyage.[41] This displacement was not only physical but metaphysical and has led to the crisis of leaderlessness and fragmentation that Brathwaite questions. The displacement has also resulted in a two-ness that is manifested in many ways, including the hope contrasted with the Sisyphean nature of the Caribbean existence, haunted as it is by that original separation. But it is also in the ritualized repetition where meaning resides. In the back-and-forth movement, the doubling back paradoxically facilitates the peasant woman's movement historically outward from a single site of origin (a continent) to multiple sites (a set of islands and beyond) of destination. That movement continues contemporarily in the peasant's migration from the countryside to the urban landscape and the underclass' migration to other islands and continents, facilitated again by the Atlantic in a cyclical formation that also spirals out.

Brathwaite explains that the "'tidal dialectic' draws upon the movement of the water backwards and forwards as a kind of cyclic . . . motion rather than linear."[42] The term, "tidalectics" engages what he calls an "alter/native" historiography to linear models of colonial progress by invoking the continual movement of the ocean.[43] "As a geopoetic model of history, Brathwaite images the ongoing and palpable heritage of 'submerged mothers' who cross the seas, 'Coming from one continent/continuum, touching another, and then receding . . . from the island(s) to the perhaps creative chaos of the(ir) future.'"[44] What Brathwaite describes in the coming, touching, and receding reflects a bodily epistemology that emerges from the ritual of the repetition.[45] Reflecting on the importance of the ritualized and ritualizing body in Vodou, Karen McCarthy Brown suggests that its revolutionary potential lies not in being able to change the world but in changing "the way we experience it."[46] As such, Vodou ritual inscribes powerful memory on the body that I understand to embody liberatory and ultimately revolutionary potential—potential that is healing, as Alexander proposes.[47] This ability for ritual to change how we experience the world also provides evidence of the healing of the inner body that Alexander suggests we would want to know.[48]

The tide's back-and-forth movement as Brathwaite characterizes it—signifying transition, transformation, and the creative potential of chaos—is in the realm of the *lwa* Legba who, I propose, as Guardian of the Crossroads, oversaw and facilitated African captives' transoceanic voyage into the diaspora, and in the process, transformed from the virile Legba in Dahomey to the old man who needs a crutch to walk in the diaspora.[49]

In addition, tidalectical movement is intrinsic to Vodou in the concept of "*balanse*," which in Haitian Kreyòl "does not mean to achieve equilibrium, but rather to activate or enliven, to dance in a back-and-forth way."[50] As Brown counsels, "Balancing is a way of exposing the true nature of something by bringing it within the forcefield of clashing energies and contradicting impulses."[51] So, while Vodou strives for balance, it also thrives on the back-and-forth movement, humble at times and explosive at others, that allows the true nature of something—in this case, history—to reveal itself.[52] Tidalectics is also the realm of Gede, who, in the midst of death, gives birth, a point that André Pierre makes in talking with Brown about the death of a mutual friend. Upon reflection on Pierre's statement that "Gede te balanse kay sa!" (Gede balanced that house!), Brown came to understand that Death had shaken up the friend's house, enlivening it in the process.[53]

Both tidalectics and its Vodou counterpart, *balanse*, speak to the dynamic back-and-forth relationship or Long Conversation that persists between Africa and its diaspora that I explore within this text. As people on both sides of the Atlantic died to one way of being as a result of their contact with the transatlantic slave trade, they were also born to another way. The cultural artifacts that they produce, both in the oral and in the visual realms, reflect and comment on those transformations that took place both in the physical and metaphysical realms. As such, they are signs in and of history.

The cyclical nature of the tide is also reflected in the Vodou belief system that embraces cosmological unity in which the living, the dead, and the unborn play equally significant roles in an unbroken historical chain.[54] Energies are recycled, enabling those in the invisible world to impact the visible world and vice versa in a never-ending continuum. This cosmological unity, I propose, is responsible for the growing recognition "even within Western cultures that 'the past is not finished and done with, receding ever further into the distance,' but remains 'imperfect,' not just in the grammatical, but also in the ontological sense."[55] This cyclical unity makes it possible for a diviner and, later, a priest to inform the anthropologist Stephan Palmié that he had been driven to do work in Cuba by an elderly African enslaved man named Tomás who had lived and died in nineteenth-century Cuba and who had returned to protect and guide him. It also informs Alexander's delineation of her relationship with Kitsimba, one among many who passed through The Door of No Return in the Kôngo Kingdom headed for the Caribbean circa 1780, "unexpectedly showing up" in her book "unabashedly."[56] Later in the text Alexander makes space for Kitsimba to tell her own version of Alexander's story and is convinced by the end of a day of "being turned inside out" that "Kitsimba's singular desire was not to have [Alexander] author her life, but for her to author [Alexander's] and to make public [Alexander's] guarded secrets."[57] Alexander's narration not only illustrates the reciprocal relationship between seen and unseen worlds but also, as I argue throughout this text, that cyclical unity is also evident in the way that oral and material culture changes and transforms, assimilating and adapting itself to its context whether in Africa or in the Africa diaspora. It did so in ancient history, continues to do in the contemporary moment, and will continue to do so in the future as the metaphysical world strives for balance that is in turn reflected in the physical world. We need only know where to look for evidence of the many workings of Spirit as it travels back and forth across the waters.

In her exploration of tidalectics, DeLoughrey problematizes models of Caribbean identity that are predicated on an uncomplicated opposition between land and sea, nation and diaspora, roots and routes.[58] She instead insists, as other scholars have done, that the interrelatedness of land and sea and diaspora and nation be explored through aquatic metaphors that flow between and thus connect different shores.[59] I agree with Jana Evans Braziel's position that, while it has become a conceptual and theoretical mainstay within African diasporic, black Atlantic, and Caribbean studies to contrast maritime routes with land-bound roots, we must rethink these neat demarcations.[60] Rather, following the natural order of sea touching land and land touching sea, then relatedly, diasporic subjects—past, present, and future—are inextricably linked to those who are left behind.[61] As a result, diaspora stands in a dialectical relationship to both its sites of origin and its "adopting" country.[62] This relationship is not relegated to the contemporary moment but originates with ancient migrations, both voluntary and forced. Moreover, what we witness in the physical realm is also manifest in the metaphysical realm. Thus, rather than being stuck with a conceptualization of land and sea, routes and roots, visible and invisible, or physical and spiritual domains as mutually exclusive, tidalectics as a theoretical framework allows us to reconceptualize the multitude of dialectical relationships that are facilitated by the ocean's back and forth as well as cyclical movements and which exchange energies as it does so. This text explores the exchange of creative energies that is evidenced in the cultural production that emanates from both sides of the Atlantic.

Tidalectics, Liminality, and the Abyss

Edouard Glissant explored the Atlantic Ocean / middle passage as a liminal space—one of death as well as rebirth—in his proclamation in *Poetics of Relation* (1990): "The boat is a womb, a womb abyss."[63] Grace Nichols expresses this concept in her poetry collection, *i is a long-memoried woman* (1983), when she writes of the diaspora as children of the middle-passage womb:

> she came
>> into the new world
> birth aching her pain
> from one continent/to another[64]

Glissant also speaks of the slave ship and, by extension, the ocean as giving birth to a new consciousness that "produces all the coming unanimity" to which Brathwaite refers in his assertion that "the unity is submarine."[65] Thus, while it was an abyss, a place of darkness and death, the Atlantic Ocean and the slave ship that sailed across it was also a generative space where, although the captives were alone in their suffering, they shared their experience of the unknown with others whom they did not yet know. Glissant: "The boat is your womb, a matrix, and yet it expels you. This boat: pregnant with as many dead as living under sentence of death."[66] The "you" in the address is the African diaspora that has gestated in the womb of the slave ship in the larger womb that is both place (the Atlantic Ocean) and process (the middle-passage voyage). That womb has given birth to some while others, twinned in their experience of the occupation of the liminal space, have died—at least in the visible realm.

We may recognize the Atlantic both as conduit and as abyss, a generative space as well as a dead end for the African diaspora. But we should also recognize that the shores from whence people were taken and on which they arrived are also generative as well as destructive. When captives were taken from multiple sites on Africa's shores, they suffered both loss and alienation. During the ocean voyage, while they died to being *of* and *in* one way of being in the world, they were also born *into* and *of* other ways of being. Glissant captures this experience in his guiding idea of a "Poétique de la relation," as a Caribbean identity that moves from African roots to rhizomes, multitudes of branching links.[67] Furthermore, since the relationship between Africa and the diaspora is generative, facilitated as it is by the ocean's waves, both African and Caribbean identities are not static but in flux, moving back and forth among themselves as well as outward to their own diasporas.

Picking up on Brathwaite's conviction that Africa is the "submerged mother of the creole system," I propose that an exploration of Africa in relation to its diaspora is instrumental to the resolution to a metaphysical dilemma that manifests itself physically.[68] It is a dilemma that arises out of the rupture and continuity and the concomitant "forgetting" or "throwing away" that the transatlantic slave trade engendered, facilitated as it was by space and time and the experience of liminality.[69] Glissant invokes the liminality inherent in the rupture and continuity that constitute the African diasporic experience when he writes, "Experience of the abyss lies inside and outside the abyss. The torment of those who never escaped it: straight from the belly of the slave ship into the violet belly of the ocean depths they went. But their ordeal did not die; it quickened into this continuous/discontinuous thing: the panic of the new land, the haunting of the former land, finally the alliance with the imposed land, suffered and redeemed."[70] For Glissant, the unconscious memory of the abyss served as the alluvium for the metamorphoses that birthed the African diaspora.

It would seem that the abyss also gave birth to the unity that underlies Brathwaite's pan-Caribbean vision, as "not just a specific knowledge, appetite, suffering, and delight in one particular people, not only that, but knowledge of the Whole, greater from having been at the abyss and freeing knowledge of Relation within the Whole."[71] Again, while the experience of becoming diasporic is destructive, it is also creative, perhaps even liberating. In the language of the rites-of-passage ritual in which an initiate is exiled, undergoes trials, and returns to the community to be reborn and to which I would compare the middle-passage voyage, "wholeness"—or, perhaps better stated, "completeness"—lies in a movement beyond liminality to the stage of transformation and (re)incorporation into a community that is also, itself, transformed.

Because tidalectics guides this text, there is a strong presence of water throughout. The examples of history, memory, and story housed in oral and material culture explored herein should be seen as shores on which the reader is free to land in order to reflect on the workings of fluidity in African and African diasporic cultural production. The *lwa* Danbala/ Simbi, who join the earth, the sky, and the waters and who are also associated with Legba, facilitate these landings.

The Marasa

This text is also guided by the Marasa and their complement, the Dosu/ Dosa, which together, form Marasa Twa. Again, I see Africa and its diaspora in a twinned relationship, both conjoined and separated by the Atlantic Ocean that facilitated the diaspora's exile in the distant past. I also see Dahomey and the Kôngo in a twinned formation that produced the third element or complement: Saint-Domingue/Haiti. With the separated, fragmented parts striving for remembrance of the other with the ultimate goal of achieving holism or balance, the Marasa Twa facilitates my exploration of the dialectical relationship among the three sites of cultural production.

In Haitian Kreyòl, twins are called *marasa,* and their patron *lwa* are the Marasa. The child born after them is called *dosu* if a boy with the patron *lwa* Marasa Dosu, and *dosa* with the patron *lwa* Marasa Dosa if a girl. These children are believed to be even "stronger" and more in need of placation than the twins themselves.[72] Triplets are regarded as a special category of twins, as they are believed to have spiritual significance and possess powers, and their patron *lwa* are Marasa Twa.[73] According to Harold Courlander, "some Haitians believe that the twins are merely a partial manifestation of the group of three, which is completed on the birth of the *dosu* or *dosa.*"[74] As such, while *marasa* are considered to be strong spiritually, their strength is increased with the addition of the *dosu/dosa.* This strengthening is echoed in the realm of the *lwa,* with the Marasa Twa being extremely powerful.

In Vodou, the Marasa or Sacred Twins are principal deities associated with Legba in their linkage with transitional places like thresholds. Their magical powers are so strong that they can protect those who come to the domain ruled by Papa Legba, the Crossroads. Both Marasa must be invoked before a ceremony can begin, as they have the power to open the spiritual road.[75] As such, the Marasa join Papa Legba where the world of the living and the world of the dead intersect.[76] Represented as petulant, jealous children, when considered alongside Legba, the old man, they signify both ends of the age spectrum in a kind of continuum. Thus, the trio also represents the completeness or continuity in rupture signified by the young Marasa joining with the other end of the temporal spectrum, the Dosu, Papa Legba. The holism embodied in this union is intrinsic to Vodou, in which, as Claudine Michel counsels, "All knowledge presupposes a fundamental holism grounded in the idea of oneness and unity of all forces of nature, in the idea of interdependence and interconnectedness of these forces and in the premise of totality over individuality," a belief that is an expression of "African continuity in the Americas."[77]

The transatlantic slave trade not only facilitated the complementarity of Africa and the diaspora that are joined together in a tidalectical union; it was also instrumental in the disharmony that persists. The tension between facilitation and disruption has resurfaced repeatedly throughout Haitian history. Marasa Twa oversee the potential resolution to the resultant crisis in its remembering and joining together that which has been separated or thrown away and forgotten. It embodies the adages, "the whole is greater than the sum of its parts" or "one plus one equals three."

The Marasa's Roots and Leaves

The Marasa can be traced back to both West and Central West Africa. According to Wyatt MacGaffey, among the Bakôngo of West Central Africa, the specialized gene for twinning occurs with exceptional frequency.[78] Not only are twins regarded as an affliction because they are difficult to nurse and keep alive but also because they are endowed with mystical powers that enable them to bewitch each other and other people who incur their displeasure.[79] Nonetheless, because twins are so common, twin cults are very widespread in Africa. Paul Mercier maintains that in Dahomey the cult of twins is considered sacred precisely because "the notion of twin beings . . . expresses the equilibrium maintained through opposites, which is the very nature of the world."[80] Melville J. Herskovits and Francis Herskovits argue that twins are by far the most prized categories of birth as a sign of an ideology that holds that "complements are necessary to achieve completeness."[81] In Fon cosmology, the Supreme Being, Mawu-Lisa, is a pair of twins with Mawu being the female and Lisa the male counterpart. This complementariness can also be found "in visible and invisible worlds, women and men, *migan* and *meu* (prime ministers), city king and bush king."[82] Thus, in the Dahomean worldsense, the ideal birth is a twin birth.[83] Mercier's proposal that a twin birth's "dual and conflicting nature expresses, even before the world was organized, the complementary forces which were to be active in it" recalls Brown's explanation of *balanse*, the back-and-forth movement that plays with conflict and contradiction or clashing energies and contradictory impulses that the twin beings embody.[84] Not only are energies activated or enlivened in the sense of *balanse* through a twin birth, but equilibrium is manifest because they are considered two parts of one soul.[85]

Even if the twin is not manifest on the physical plane, his or her presence is nonetheless felt. According to MacGaffey, throughout Central West Africa, there is a belief that if a child is born missing a limb or appendage, the missing parts have remained in the other (spirit) world.[86] In the diaspora, it seems that this belief in missing parts resonates in the way that people believe that if someone is born with an extra digit, for example, it is an indication that he or she has "eaten" his or her twin in the womb. The absorbed body makes itself known by showing up as an extra piece of flesh. Rather than staying in the other world, the unborn twin comes through in the one who lives as a lingering presence-in-absence.

The physically manifest twin puts aside a symbolic portion of whatever he or she eats or receives as a present for the one who did not physically manifest or passed away. Melville Herskovits attributes this connectedness beyond the physical realm to the widespread belief in West Africa that twins share a single soul.[87] Their bond traverses the divides between life and death, and between physical and metaphysical worlds.[88] I suggest that this belief in the unbreakable link between twinned subjects is at work in the tidalectical relationship that has persisted across space and time between Africa and its diaspora and that is evidenced in their cultural production.

Marasa Twa: Complementarity and Completeness

The Marasa's composite nature is evidenced in its linguistic sources: both Kikôngo and Fon, which together form Marasa Twa in Haitian Kreyòl. Marilyn Houlberg places Marasa's origins in the Kôngo, asserting that "the Creole word for twins, *marasa*, is derived from the Kikôngo word "*mabassa*," which means 'those who come divided'—thus the one who comes as two."[89] The third element in the Marasa—*dosu* if a boy and *dosa* if a girl—is derived from the Fongbe word (of Dahomey), *docu*, which means a child born after twins.[90] It is in Haiti where these elements manifest fully, spiraling out into Marasa Twa.

MacGaffey notes, "Though there has been intermixture between the West and Central African elements, the striking fact is that in a Haitian context the two have come to be defined in opposition to each other as part of a system of belief and practice that is neither Dahomeyan nor Kôngo."[91] While such a statement may be perplexing and even problematic for those who witness the cross-fertilization that has taken place spiritually in Haiti, it also seems to be the nature of the Marasa and their third element, Dosu/Dosa, that is at play in the way that they are assimilated in the Vodou pantheon. Like all the *lwa*, the Marasa belong to different *nachon* (nations), two of which are Rada (cool) and Petwo (hot). There are Marasa of Ginen, Dahomey, Nago, Ibo, Congo, and so on. There are also Kreyòl Marasa—those born out of "the institution of slavery," in response "to its particular brand of sensuous domination," according to Dayan.[92] The Rada nation of the Marasa are generally considered beneficent and calm when they are properly served. However, the distinctions between Rada and Petwo are not always so neat, for some believe that even Marasa that are classified as Rada have a Petwo side. Furthermore, although the Marasa are generally part of the Rada *nachon*, the Dosu/Dosa, which is inextricable from the Marasa, is more associated with the Petwo *nachon*. In addition, while the majority of the *lwa* can be traced back to Dahomean or Bakôngo origins, there are also several whose origins seem to rest squarely in the African diasporic experience, another manifestation of Dosu/Dosa, whereby these two divergent elements in a new context (the New World) transform, combining to create a third entity; again one plus one equals three.[93] What my reading of history, memory, and cultural production through a Vodou episteme ultimately proposes then, is that, in the realm of Spirit that is always striving for balance, Haiti is the essence of completeness or holism. It expresses the third element—the Dosu/Dosa—in its remembering to remember, as the Vodou song from the epigraph suggests, and bringing that which had been fragmented together or re-membering the parts in the whole both through its spiritual belief system and the oral and material culture that emanates from it. In other words, the disparate elements that compose the Marasa Twa—from the Dahomean tradition and from the Kôngo tradition—come together in a diasporic site, Saint-Domingue/Haiti, birthing spiritual traditions and cultural production that resemble both but that is complete in itself in its incorporation and assimilation of the complementary and contradictory traditions. Thus, like the *marasa* and their *dosu/dosa* of Courlander's explanation, the three sites are like the twins who are "integrally linked to the child born after them who may be considered a delayed triple birth."[94] Regarding Courlander's assertion that "some Haitians . . . believe that the twins are merely a partial manifestation of the group of three, which is completed on the birth of the *dosu* or *dosa*," we may also consider Saint-

Domingue/Haiti as the delayed complete manifestation of the Marasa Twa.

Istwa

The third and final theoretical anchor of this text is *istwa*, a word that means both "history" and "story" but that goes beyond them both to also encompass "memory."[95] *Istwa* is central to my reading of oral and visual culture from Dahomey/Benin Republic, Kôngo, and Saint-Domingue/Haiti because although much has been written about the history from these areas, they themselves are essentially oral cultures. The language of the colonizers and imperialist invaders has never been that of "the people," or *pèp la*. In Haiti, while Kreyòl is recognized as an official language with its own orthography that is still evolving, it remains by and large a dynamic oral culture that constantly incorporates new words into its lexicon. Relatedly, Haiti is renowned for its visual art. As Glissant observes about the connection, "Haitian painting is derived from the spoken."[96] Furthermore, "It is the tightly woven texture of oral expression that is introduced into (and the key to) Haitian painting."[97] I extend Glissant's observation to other forms of cultural production, such as sculpture, that emanate from the Haiti, which I discuss in this text.

Because my study privileges popular cultural expressions, I read "stories" broadly defined to incorporate both oral and visual expression in relation to hi/stories written about the sites and their populations. I am interested in how oral and visual artists traditionally and continually deploy their spiritual belief systems to reflect and comment on history in relation to and against popular memories of it through their use of story.

Paul Connerton advises, in *How Societies Remember* (1989), that in some ways oral histories seek to give voice to what would otherwise remain voiceless, if not traceless by producing "another type of history; one in which most of the details will be different, but also one in which the very construction of meaningful shapes will obey a different principle."[98] In such a case "different details will emerge because they are inserted, as it were, into a different kind of narrative home."[99] These are "truths from below," to borrow Elizabeth Isichei's term. They come from voices that have often been undervalued or ignored, sometimes emerging from a different worldsense than from those who write the dominant narratives. Such narratives from below, while perhaps not empirically traceable, nonetheless speak to and offer insight into the historical actors and systems, both worldly and otherworldly, that have contributed to the systems that we see at work in the world historically and contemporarily.

Isichei explores the importance of reevaluating and excavating the oral tradition in *Voices of the Poor in Africa: Moral Economy and the Popular Imagination* (2002), relating how, initially, while conducting oral history interviews in Nigeria in the 1970s, she was dismissive of stories that seemed "unrealistic" or "irrelevant."[100] It was only after she heard the same stories over and over again that she began to rethink their relevance to the "history" that she was writing. She came to understand that there is a reason that stories persist; they hold meaning for the people who tell them. Indeed, the stories that people kept telling Isichei helped them explain the sources of contemporary poverty that she was reading through a traditional historian's lens. Listening to those stories and contextualizing them as part of a larger historical milieu resulted in a text that discusses a history of various peoples in Africa and the diaspora from the perspective of a sector of the population that is traditionally silenced in the historical narrative. I agree with Isichei when she says that these voices are often articulated in the poetics of memory as "true fictions"—that is, symbolic narratives that "encapsulate, in a condensed form, historical insights" that "find expression, not in abstract or even empirically corroborated statements about society, but in images."[101] Like poetry, which in many ways these sources closely resemble, the images have multiple layers of meaning.[102] I would add that, although shrouded in myth, the stories address a historical truth. Nonetheless, their mythical quality often makes it necessary to look to divergent disciplinary sources in order to interpret them. Reading, hearing, or seeing these poetic representations of memory, very often silenced in the dominant discourse, alongside traditional histories, allow them to resonate more deeply and more broadly.

My approach to history, memory, and story seeks to uncover the interrelatedness of individual and collective narrative practices that span the Atlantic. To that end, I keep in mind bell hooks' definition of the word "remember" (*re-member*) as "the coming together of several parts, fragments becoming a whole" as a directive.[103] In the same vein that one gathers together to remember, I take several scattered pieces—histories, memories, stories (oral and visual)—and gather them all together in a symbolic gesture of "re-membering" Africa to its diaspora and the diaspora to Africa, tidalectically.

Telling Stories / Methodology

"The Sea is History," Derek Walcott declares.[104] The sea is also memory. "Water overflows with memory. Emotional Memory. Bodily Memory. Sacred Memory," writes Alexander.[105] In order to uncover "submerged histories," researchers must be open to exploring outside narrow conceptions of the factual to find them.[106] This opening up of multiple avenues of exploration "involve muddying divisions between documented and intuited, material and metaphoric, past and present so that 'who is remembered—and how—is continually being transformed through a web of interpretive systems . . . collapsing, ultimately, the demarcation of the prescriptive past, present and future of linear time.'"[107] I believe that my consideration of the multiple articulations of memory that at times necessarily double back and fold in on themselves—a kind of written ritual—is critical to a fuller apprehension of meanings of that history in struggling postcolonial societies.[108] As such, I take an interdisciplinary approach to exploring how memory that is anchored in workings of the spirit, to paraphrase Joseph M. Murphy (1994), and history conspire to produce several sites of creativity from Dahomey / Benin Republic, the Kôngo and Saint-Domingue/Haiti, and that comment on their disjunctive and continual relationship.[109]

The sources for the ethnographic portion of my exploration of history and memory are Ouidah, Benin Republic, where I conducted research from April 2005 to March 2006, and Port-au-Prince, Haiti where I conducted research from several weeks to months at a time between the summer of 2007 and the winter of 2012. The strong influence of Kôngo traditions in Haitian thought and practices is too well documented to ignore. Therefore, it, as a second, equally important site of memory, also features heavily in my discussion. My text draws on Dahomean, Bakôngo, and Haitian epistemologies evidenced in their cultural production to explore how they work together tidalectically toward resuturing the fragmented parts that the transatlantic slave trade engendered.

While I explore these particular forms of cultural production from specific vantage points, I do so with the hope that the issues I raise can fuel the work of others who take up other "alter/native" ways of exploring historical and cultural connections that have endured across time and space under seemingly impossible conditions. Again, Brathwaite reminds us that "unity is submarine." Not only is Africa and its diaspora linked by the middle-passage voyage and the millions of souls that were lost to that infamous journey but, as Antonio Benítez-Rojo asserts in *The Repeating Island*, while the individual histories of the Caribbean region are unique, they also share the underlying systems of oppression and the history of slavery in common.[110] As such, similar means of liberating themselves from that history and legacy are viable—that is, through the re-membering.

I envision my text as part of the ongoing work of throwing away and gathering together that is evidenced in the histories and stories in their various articulations that emanate from both Africa and the diaspora by way of the spirits. The chapters should be read tidalectically—that is, reflective of the backward and forward movement of the tides that keep the dialogical relationship between Africa and its diaspora going while discouraging a linear orientation. My argument is circular, as life and history are circular, doubling back as it moves outward. Thus, similar to the way that Dayan notes, the reader may ask: "Why do we have to step in the same waters twice, three times?"[111] I answer that my methodology follows that of the Vodou ritual, whereby "the mindful body" is deployed.[112] In other words, the lessons that are to be learned are transmitted through the ritual, through the repetition of actions that engage the body, the mind, and the spirit, which are brought into communion to facilitate transformation.[113] This is, to me, a viable way of exploring a "complex and perplexing social history that too often gets lost in exposition."[114] I see it as part of the work of the writing of new narratives that Gina Ulysse calls for and which necessitates a lens that resists the Western, racist, linear, materialist one that dominates.[115] Therefore, the repetition "in this narrative is ritual" because, following Vodou ritual, "The more a detail, scene or theme is repeated, the more its meaning is established."[116] Thus, for example, the reader will note that several of the *lwa* return repeatedly in different contexts, sometimes because the work they do in the different contexts that I explore here changes. Likewise, ideas, people, and events return as themes are picked up repeatedly in my effort to present a fuller picture of the back-and-forth exchange that is simultaneously cyclical and that gives way to transformation that is the nature of the relationship between Africa and its diaspora. There is also a ritualistic aspect to the repetition as it serves as an invocation of the very *lwa*—principally the Marasa—that I argue are key to understanding the dialectics of Africa and its diaspora.

Indicative of Dayan's assertion that Vodou is not just a discipline of faith but an epistemology that joins thought to political action—nothing less than a practice of enlightenment through flesh and spirit, this project is undeniably political.[117] It advocates for a turning of our attention to the spiritual forces that have been at work since before the crossing of the water began in their ongoing efforts to reestablish and maintain equilibrium—in other words, to remember and gather the fractured parts together, a perpetual process.

The Chapters

Chapter 1 discusses a story from the oral tradition of Dahomey that Melville Herskovits published in the second volume of *Dahomey: An Ancient West African Kingdom* (1938) as a source for exploring the history and legacy of the slave trade and slavery. The chapter argues that contemporary explorations of such stories from the oral tradition add valuable dimensions to our understanding of the continuities and ruptures that constitute the relationship between Africa and its diaspora. I discuss the protagonist of the story, Bokọfíọ́, in relation to a power object from Dahomey, the *bociọ* sculpture. I read both the story and the power object as complementary sites of memory of the transatlantic slave trade and propose that, conceptualized through a Vodun/Vodou epistemology, they can be understood as reflecting and commenting on the memory of the Dahomean slave-trading past, a task that is facilitated by Legba, Master of the Crossroads, and Dan, the god of creation, two deities who crossed the water with their supplicants from Dahomey to Saint-Domingue and manifest themselves as principal *lwa*. Finally, I argue that, as evidence of tidalectical transfiguration, while in Dahomey *bociọ* offers insight into the transatlantic slave trade, in Haiti, *bòkò* (sorcerers)—transfigured Dahomean *boko*—who use their powers to both hurt and heal, also offer equally revelatory insight into the slave era.

Chapter 2 continues with its exploration of how the history of the slave trade and slavery is built into the cultural production that emanates from Dahomey, the Kôngo, and Haiti. It discusses how the methods and means of sociopolitical control in the form of several cultural artifacts: *bociọ*, *bo*, and *cakatú* in Dahomey and *nkisi* in the Kôngo resonate in Haiti in the *pakèt kongo* and the *zonbi*. The chapter is based on the premise that these forms of oral and material culture embody historically significant memories and continue to be useful in disfranchised people's resistance to contemporary attempts to silence and disempower them.

The *zonbi* may be read as a metaphor for a psychic and social liminal state between remembrance, return, and reconciliation in which African and African diasporic people are locked. However, as I argue, while liminality and the *zonbi* as an embodiment of absence—that is, without kinship ties, memory of a past or home—are usually read as a state to be avoided or passed through as quickly as possible, it is equally important to read it as a creative, transformative, and liberatory space; one of potential that, if read as such, allows for the recognition of multiple liberatory sites found in contemporary Haitian cultural production. Finally, the chapter reads the Haitian *pakèt kongo* in relation to the Kôngo *nkisi* as a tidalectical method of protection and healing found on both sides of the Atlantic that may also point the way to individual and collective re-membrance and concomitant healing on both sides of the Atlantic and beyond.

In Chapter 3 I again take up the *bociǫ* to explore how these transformed but still empowered objects vis-à-vis Fon and Bakôngo epistemologies also made their way—however transformed—across the water to Haiti. I propose that vestiges of the *bociǫ* that come through in the recycled artwork by artists who are members of an art collective called Atis Rezistans on the Grand Rue in downtown Port-au-Prince, Haiti, is evidence of a "habit of attention" oriented toward a Kôngo episteme.[118] I also propose that the gods who manifest visually in the recycled art by several members of the collective evoke those from Dahomey who made their way into the diaspora. Finally, the chapter explores the interworkings of the dead, the living, and the unborn; the invisible and visible worlds; the past, the present, and the future facilitated by the tidalectical relationship that persists between Africa and its diaspora. Woven into my discussion is an exploration of how Haitian, Dahomean, and Bakôngo cosmological heritages are manifest through the artwork being produced by the artists.

Chapter 4 explores the workings of the Marasa in the context of the earthquake that struck Haiti in 2010 and its aftermath. It argues that, from a metaphysical standpoint, the twinned relationship between the living and the dead has been severely disrupted, and it is up to the living in collaboration with the dead to return order to the land, as the oral stories from the chapter suggests. Again, like the distant historical violence that Haiti has suffered, this contemporary violence that is not "natural" has implications for the nation presently and in the future.

Finally, in the epilogue, I pull all of the chapters together by reaffirming my advocacy for a reading of Haiti's history, memory, and cultural production through the lens of its spiritual tradition in general and the Marasa specifically.

All of these chapters are tied together by Story, loosely defined to encompass both visual and oral arts as a way of arguing for the centrality of these forms of cultural production to understand the impact that history has on those who live it. The cultural imagination has been critical to the work of passing down the history of Africa and its diaspora from one generation to the next and offers an important lens though which to view the picture of both the interiority and the exteriority of the past.[119] The forms of cultural production—fueled by a deep consciousness of the connectedness of visible and invisible worlds, the human world and the natural world, and the cyclical nature of time that I explore herein—provide insight into the contemporary Haitian majority's relationship to their distant and more recent past and how they impact and fuel their present and future realities and possibilities as inextricably related to those *lòt bo dlo*, on the other side of the water.

1

The Changing Same

Bokọ́fíọ́ across the Sea

> God never dies and thus, I never die.
> —Patrick Bellegarde-Smith

Literary scholar Omise'eke Natasha Tinsley has argued that the work of surfacing "submerged histories" demands that researchers be open to exploring outside narrow conceptions of the factual to find them.[1] Such work also involves "muddying divisions between documented and intuited, material and metaphoric, past and present so that 'who is remembered—and how—is continually being transformed through a web of interpretive systems . . . collapsing, ultimately, the demarcation of the prescriptive past, present and future of linear time.'"[2] In many ways Tinsley's pronouncement points us to the meaning behind oral literature scholar Harold Scheub's position that story is a way of getting at truths about the past.[3] Both Tinsley and Scheub's "alternative" approaches to history are instructive to scholars who are interested in uncovering "submerged" or hidden histories about the transatlantic slave trade and slavery, marked as they are by erasures and silences. Indeed, as the process of erasure and silencing took place over several centuries using such diverse tools as slave ship ledgers, plantation owner journals, paintings, novels, and historical texts to name a few, so too must the process of recuperating lost voices take time and deploy a variety of different approaches.[4] Story, broadly defined to include oral, written, and visual "texts," is critical to recovering voices that have been traditionally silenced in the historiography precisely because of its ability to simultaneously conceal and reveal. Metaphors and symbols, aesthetically trenchant, offer insight into sociopolitical and historical realities. As such, stories offer insight into the interiority of the impact of the historical events on the lives of people who experienced them. As Toni Morrison avers in "The Site of Memory" (1995) stories, especially those from marginalized populations, are a way to throw the veil off of events "too terrible to relate."[5] The transatlantic slave trade, an event that has yet to be fully reconciled in Africa as well as the diaspora, qualifies as one that is "too terrible to relate" directly for many of the descendants of those who were affected by it on both sides of the Atlantic divide.

In the first part of this initial chapter I turn to the African oral tradition of storytelling and explore a narrative that anthropologist Melville J. Herskovits collected and published in the second of his two-volume ethnographic study titled *Dahomey: An Ancient West African Kingdom* (1938). Using the history of the transatlantic slave trade as a backdrop for my exploration of the story through what I see as workings of Spirit, I discuss the story as a metaphorical rendering of the processes and consequences of the trade on both those who were exiled and those who remained and, perhaps, even those who returned. For me, the story provides valuable insight into this critical history that remains largely obscured, ignored, and silenced. While the story is ostensibly about a Fon man who presumably dies and is brought back to life, I propose that, when read through Vodun, the story, as *istwa*, offers insight into the history of the transatlantic slave trade and people's fraught relationship to it. Given the timing and conditions under which Herskovits collected the story, it is a very real possibility that the story functions as a veiled delineation of the capture and exile of enslaved people and their impact on the social and spiritual structure of the community where Herskovits recorded the story.

The chapter is guided by the state and condition of liminality; betwixt and between. It is conceived under the aegis of Legba and the Marasa, both associated with thresholds and in-between spaces. They are not of one world, but straddle both the old world and the new, the seen and the unseen, ushering their adherents from one realm into the next. As such, while the story that Herskovits retells was told to him in Dahomey, I argue that the narrative is very much about the exile of the African captive to the New World and with it, the experience of the middle-passage voyage—a time of death, both literally and spiritually for those on board the slave ship, but also of rebirth. Finally, I propose that the story also recalls the back-and-forth movement of the ocean in its ending in return but which may be read in a couple of different ways.

There are issues that arise with this kind of project. For example, we must consider the political conditions under which Herskovits was collecting his data. We must also take into consideration that he was conducting his research in 1931, a time when Dahomey was under French colonial rule—a fact that might have impacted the kind of information that he had access to. We should also remember that, for all the time that he spent in Dahomey conducting research, he was nonetheless an outsider, a privileged white man in colonial Africa. Furthermore, although he spoke French, it is doubtful that he was fluent in Fongbe, the language that the story was probably told in. Thus, the story would have been interpreted and translated for him to be then transcribed, presenting several layers of mediation between the original story and what was finally published in his text. The narrative is mediated not only by Herskovits' foreignness but also by his inaccessibility to the storyteller's indigenous means of expression, for example, subtle differences in words depending on tone or context, significant genuflections, or movements that might have accompanied the story and none of which the reader has access to. Additionally, we should take into account the possible motivations and desires of those who shared their stories as "informants" with Herskovits. Herskovits does not say whether he asked to be told specific stories about specific subjects, or if he offered remuneration to the storyteller. These variables almost certainly influenced the kinds of stories that he would have been told. Nonetheless, if we consider not only that the story may be one that is "too terrible to relate," such as we see in interviews conducted by Anne Bailey around the slave trade in Ghana, but may be acted out in ritual, as we see in Rosalind Shaw's work and, I would add, story, as Elizabeth Isichei has shown, then we can appreciate the usefulness of the story as an example of *istwa*.[6]

The story's framing through death and rebirth is an appropriate context in which to relate the *istwa* if we consider that the African diaspora died to one way of being in the world and were reborn to another. We might also consider that Spirit speaks *through* the storyteller to bring this particular *istwa* to the surface. In other words, from a metaphysical standpoint, regardless of—and, paradoxically, *because of*—the mediating circumstances that I mention here, we have access to a story that may be useful in the uncovering of a hidden history, one that reveals the impact that the slave trade had on the physical beings who witnessed and those who underwent the forced exile as well as their spiritual interlocutors in that process.

My discussion is grounded in the belief that in order to understand history and its impact and impressions on our presents and futures, we must be attentive to the multitude of voices that are traditionally silenced in the historical narrative. One of those voices can be found in the story that I discuss here in the tension between the history and memory about the diaspora's separation from Africa expressed in the ambiguity of the story vis-à-vis the captured protagonist, Bokǫfíǫ́, and in its deployment of the gods/*lwa*, who act as metaphysical negotiators and who are central to understanding the story's multiple layers of meaning.

In the second half of the chapter I explore how, while in Dahomey the traditional power object called *bociǫ* offers insight into the transatlantic slave trade, across the water in a country where many of those who left Dahomey's shores landed—that is, Saint-Domingue—a class of people called *bòkò* (sorcerer), who use their powers to both heal and harm, also offers insight into the slave era. As such, I read the Haitian *bòkò* as a site of memory in the diaspora that, like the Dahomean oral narrative that I discuss in the first part of the chapter, reflects and comments on the African experience of capture and enslavement.

The story that Herskovits retells may be read both in form and content as evidence of a memory of and testament to the traumatic history of those who were exiled by those who remained in Africa. It is also evidence of black expressive cultures' practices of remembrance and the ways that it is associated with the distinctive and disjunctive temporality of the subordinated that is constructed and marked out publicly. In this case, the expression is in storytelling. As film critic, Françoise Pfaff avers,

> Until recently, the verbal richness of black Africa was found outside of books. It was kept alive in people's minds and expressed in specific circumstances such as festivals or evening storytelling sessions by professional or extemporaneous performers. In Africa, oral literature is still very much a part of deep-rooted collective custom, adapted to a communal, largely illiterate, and agriculturally based society. Through its myths, legends, epics, tales, or historical poems,

it has celebrated the prowess of kings and warriors, perpetuated its past, and preserved its ancestral wisdom while strengthening the sociocultural and historical identity of the group. The story is probably the most common and the most appreciated literary genre of black Africa's oral tradition.[7]

Indeed, Pfaff wrote these words in 1995, and much has changed since then. Although stories such as the one I discuss here are no longer extant (except in Herskovits' book, published in 1938), we can look to them for insight into the temporality and historicity of the slave trade through their invocation and evocation of Fon gods. I contend that in the story of Bokọfíó, even when the gods or *voduns* are not mentioned by name, they make their presence known through the unfolding of the narrative.

Through the prism of the storytelling tradition with its audience participatory practice, I read the existence of the *bòkò* from across the water as evidence of engagement by the "audience-participants" (meaning those who inherited the history, interpreting, and transforming it as a kind of participatory audience in a "Long Conversation") in a kind of call and response from Dahomey / Benin Republic to Saint-Domingue/Haiti that is facilitated by the ocean's waves (tidalectics). The parallels that I am drawing here between Bokọfíó, *bociọ*, and *bòkò* are based on linguistic similarities between the three, similarities that, as I discuss later, are also seen in their relationship to the fraught history between Dahomey and Saint-Domingue and its contemporary manifestations. The story that Herskovits retells goes as follows:

One day, as this man, Bokọfíó, lay ill on his mat, he heard a whistling in his ear and soon found himself in a large clearing where two men came forward, one carrying a long rope, the other whip in hand. The first one said, "Walk in front of us. We are going to leave this place," and tied the rope around his neck. Holding the other end of it, he pulled poor Bokọfíó as he would a dog. The other walked behind him and lashed him to make him walk faster. As the three made their way up the path they were climbing a high mountain. They did not stop when they reached the top, but descended the other slope when they came to a river. They did not pause at the river, however, but continued on their way, walking on the water as though it were land. Though they met with some difficulty in getting up the farther bank of the stream because it was slippery, they at last found themselves in a land of great banana plantations. After some time, as the three walked rapidly, they came upon a clearing and some low thatched houses, in front of which were bamboo leaves. It held no shrines, apparently as Bokǫfíó did not even see an *aizan*. He was also unable to see whether or not this village had any inhabitants, though he did notice that smoke issued from one of the houses. Those who had him in charge passed quickly through the village; and when he tried to cry out one of his captors put a hand over his mouth.

A little later they again came upon open country. Here there was nothing but earth; no trees, no water, no grass, just bare earth. Some distance ahead, Bokǫfíó saw some men seated one after another in a long row, and the road which they were following led to these seated figures. Arrived at the place where the row of stools began, his captors turned abruptly and went along a by-path, which led to the slope of a second great mountain. While making his descent down the other side of the mountain, Bokǫfíó saw another river before him. Again, however, they walked on the water as though it were land. On the other side they were met by two great, threatening dogs who barred their way, but the two who had Bokǫfíó in charge cried out a "strong" name, the power of which caused the animals to step aside.

Now a third mountain even steeper than the other two confronted them, a mountain whose summit receded from them as they climbed it, and the path grew steeper and steeper. At each step, Bokǫfíó was met by guards, who asked him his name but refused to tell him their own. All this time his two captors continually urged him to go faster and faster. When at last they reached the summit, they came to an enclosure, watched over by a guard who was seated at a door constructed of plaited banana leaves. The guard told them to wait, and as they waited, Bokǫfíó heard the soft sound of many voices, and knew there were a great number of people about. He was not allowed, however, to look within the enclosure. Presently, a guard came through the door, accompanied by a man dressed in raffia cloth, who held a stone in one hand. On the stone were no marks that Bokǫfíó could see, but the man who held it appeared to be reading something from it. After a time, a second man came out of the enclosure and this one held many banana leaves in his hand, which he examined like a notebook, each leaf acting as a page. This second man whispered to the first, who then answered in a language that Bokọfíó could not understand. The second one, however, spoke Fon—"the language of Abomey itself"—and asked Bokọfíó why he came. Poor Bokọfíó said that these two men brought him by force. The man who spoke Fon then turned to the captors, and demanded to know who had sent them to bring their captive. When they made no answer, the man who spoke Fon called out, "*Adjotǒ!*" The man in the raffia cloth took up a stone and hurled it at the two who had brought Bokọfíó and they took to their heels, leaving their captive free. The man who had first come from the enclosure looked at his stone again and after scrutinizing it carefully he ordered Bokọfíó to raise his head. As Bokọfíó raised it, this man spurted water from his mouth and the stream covered Bokọfíó's face. At this the guard took a great club and drove him away. Bokọfíó ran so fast that he had no idea how he surmounted all the obstacles he had to pass as he retraced his way home. At last he found himself at home on his mat.

Now it so happened that his son had been away when his "death" had occurred and his corpse had been kept in his hut for four days, awaiting the first ceremony of burial. Therefore, when he revived, while he knew he laid on his mat, he could not see, and he felt his mouth tied. He began to toss about and as he removed the bandage that covered his eyes, those watching him ran away. When they returned with help they found him sitting upright. The first words they heard him speak were a request for water. Then those who had courage undid his bonds and gave him water. He wanted no food, but lay down again and at once fell into a deep sleep. When he awoke, he was well, and hungry.[8]

Herskovits offers no commentary except to note, as would be expected, that a diviner was consulted to determine the identity of the various characters who participated in the experience. As a result, it was determined that the figure in raffia who had saved Bokọfíó from the two captors was Legba, Master of the Crossroads, while the two who enslaved him were Dan, the creation god.

I read the story of Bokɔ́fɔ́ as a "Crossing Text," one that fissures "History" through discursive intervention and that insists upon the indispensability of "histories" that testify to the Afro-Atlantic experience.[9] As this story demonstrates, these "fissured histories" are not only told from the diasporic divide of the Atlantic—that is, those who were dispersed to various locations in the Atlantic world—but also from the site of origin/departure. Such "histories" told by those subjected to the violence of Eurocentric imperial and racist behaviors and the linear, progressive, chronological discourses that support them formally disrupt linear, prescriptive constructions. They thus point scholars in the direction of reading histories about the transatlantic slave trade and slavery in ways that subvert hegemonic authority, allowing us to identify and locate unvoiced realities and glean a more comprehensive picture of hi/story, one that accounts for both seen and unseen worlds as well as nature's inextricable role in the unfolding of the human–spirit experience.

The story of Bokɔ́fɔ́ is attentive to tidalectics as a back-and-forth movement that the transatlantic trade engendered. As such, the protagonist's journey into the diaspora and back again is a reflection of and commentary on the African exile and diasporic return, even if only in spirit. While some of those who were enslaved did return to Africa—for example, those who had been enslaved in Brazil—the vast majority of those enslaved never saw their homelands again.[10] The story from Herskovits offers insight into the physical and metaphysical trauma resultant from the forced removal of millions of people from their homeland that, in turn, had repercussions for both those who were taken and those who were left behind. Thus, I add to Stuart Hall's proposition that the African diasporic experience is characterized by rupture and continuity that this is also true of the African societies that were touched by the slave trade.[11] Furthermore, I argue that both the African and African diasporic experience are also characterized by presence and absence or presence *in* absence, a kind of haunting by that which has been thrown away (*jete*).[12] This is evidenced by the testimonies that abound from the continent about those who were left behind not knowing the fates of those who were taken, and by "fictional" stories such as the one I explore here.[13] They are both evidence of the sense of haunting that persists on both sides of the Atlantic precisely because of the lack of closure that the slave trade engendered.

Although on the surface the story's form is linear, my attention to the memory that is embedded in the telling reveals the back-and-forth orientation of the narrative, which looks to both Africa and its diaspora and their respective hauntings.

Historical Underpinnings

In 1992 UNESCO (the United Nations Educational, Scientific, and Cultural Organization) launched its Slave Route Project based on the organization's belief that ignorance or concealment of major historical events constitutes an obstacle to mutual understanding, reconciliation, and cooperation among peoples. The project was meant to break the silence surrounding the slave trade and slavery. Organized in collaboration with local governments, several monuments and commemorative ceremonies were held at some of the former strongholds of the slave trade such as Benin Republic, Ghana, and the Ivory Coast. In Ouidah, Benin Republic, it culminated in Ouidah '92: The First International Festival of Vodun Arts and Culture, an art festival to remember and memorialize the history of the transatlantic slave trade internationally.[14] As part of the project, dozens of African and African diasporic artists were commissioned to create artwork, including statues and murals to commemorate the slave trade. Several of the statues line a stretch of land that extends from the center of Ouidah to Djebaji Beach, where captives are believed to have been held in a holding pen called Zomaï, which means "place where light does not go," before being loaded into pirogues and then out to slave ships destined for the middle passage.

One particular statue located in an open field that is believed to have once been Zomaï epitomizes African captives' experience of liminality—the period of "betwixt and between," no longer part of a community in Africa and not yet part of the African diaspora. The statue depicts a crouching man with a bit in his mouth, his entire body close to the pedestal, which represents the ground (Fig. 1). According to a guide during one of my tours of the slave route, this position was a form of punishment for captives who resisted the traders. Another guide told me that people were put in this position in order to prepare them for the cramped conditions of the slave ship, the spiderlike position that they would have to assume during the three-month or more journey and made manifest in the oral tradition as Ananse, the trickster. Whatever the explanation, the statue's location a few feet before one reaches Ouidah's shores and outside of any

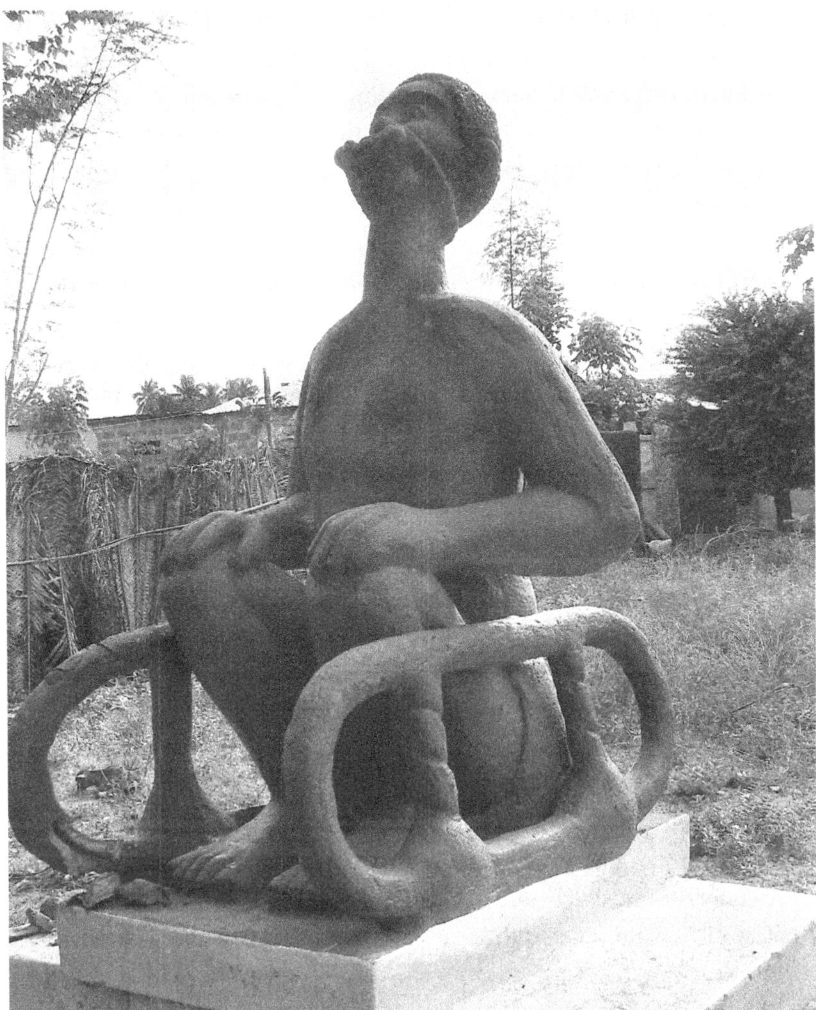

Figure 1. Zomaï statue by Cyprien Tokoudagba. Ouidah, Benin Republic. Photo: Toni Pressley-Sanon, 2005.

defined community reinforces the sense of liminality of the enslaved person's experience.

While the statue at Zomaï captures the sense of liminality visually, the story of Bokọfíó does so orally. It begins at the moment when Bokọfíó is removed or exiled from his community and ends with his return. The bulk of the story recounts his trials while in exile. Its ending is ambiguous and can be read as the man returning to his community or entering into one that is itself born anew, transformed as he is transformed. If we read the story as the man's return to his former community, the historical record supports such a theory. According to S. Y. Boadi-Siaw, following an uprising in 1835 of the black population, both enslaved and free, in Salvador, Bahia, significant numbers of Brazilians who had been enslaved as children began to arrive in West Africa in the first decades of the nineteenth century. The uprisings had prompted the authorities to force many ex-slaves to leave for West Africa. In addition, as local authorities placed severe restrictions on people of African descent, including fines and deportations of those who in any way were "'suspected of trying to provoke slaves into insurrection' . . . many freed Africans left seeking a more congenial life elsewhere."[15] The return did not stop there, however, as more immigrants continued to come throughout the nineteenth century as they acquired freedom and money to pay their passage.[16] Finally,

> the abolition of slavery, which occurred in Brazil in 1888, provided another impetus for ex-slaves to migrate to West Africa. Many of those who had been sent to Brazil as young people nurtured the remembrances of their homes in Africa and longed to return. The total abolition of slavery opened the way for them to attempt to fulfill this longing. Many thus found money and boarded ships coming to the West African coast in the period immediately after 1888 and even later. They risked the uncertainties of the voyage and reception to come to Lagos, Whydah, Badagry, and other port cities of West Africa. The most recent estimates put the number that left Brazil at approximately three thousand for the whole of the nineteenth century.[17]

Significant numbers of the Brazilian returnees reportedly found their way to Whydah (Ouidah). We may ask ourselves if the storyteller possibly had knowledge of some of these returnees, the conditions under which they were taken, and their experiences once in the diaspora. Given that some Brazilians who had been taken into the slave trade as children and returned later than 1888, and given that Herskovits was conducting research in Dahomey 1931, it is quite possible that the storyteller was himself a returnee, or he knew of one or several, or he had heard stories. As such, the story reflects a historical reality that is contextualized vis-à-vis Vodun.

There are also stories of individuals that support an outcome of return. One such story is that told by historian Edna Bay of the hero status that some of those who returned to their communities after being exiled took on. For example, there is the case of King Tegbesu, who was said to have been sent to Oyo as a hostage. When he returned to Dahomey, the fact that he survived and returned was used to justify his accession to power. Bay concludes that "survival and return . . . seem to have a particular importance in Dahomean thinking—almost as if exile as a captive in a foreign land was perceived as a period of trial or testing."[18] Those who returned were seen as special for having survived such an ordeal and thus were thought to possess special spiritual powers. Taking into account the fact that, as Boadi-Siaw explains, returnees greatly influenced the West African communities they (re)integrated into and Bay's discussion of the hero status of those who were exiled and who returned to their former communities, it would stand to reason that Bokọfíó would have an elevated status in his community after he returns from the land of the dead—that is, exile.

At the same time, the story may be read as depicting the African diasporic experience whereby those enslaved and exiled underwent a number of trials as part of new communities in the diaspora that were (re)born out of the middle-passage voyage. The liminal period that spanned the trek to the shore, the period of waiting in barracoons, and the middle-passage voyage where captives transitioned from one state of being into another is captured in the story that is replete with images that evoke the enslaved person's journey. The images are found in the river on which Bokọfíó's captors can walk, landscapes across which he is marched, the three mountains that become steeper, and his captors, both of whom can read. In his new community where he is taken for dead until he proves otherwise, he asks for water, a cleansing element that washes his past from him. Afterward, when he awakens he is refreshed, made new and ready to be fully (re)integrated into the society.

The African diasporic experience is also conveyed in the way that Bokọfíó's process of enslavement is described. The whip of the slave driver is present from the beginning and the treatment of the enslaved as something other than human is threaded throughout the story. For example, the narrator states that Bokọfíó's captor pulled him as he would a dog while the other lashed him to make him walk faster. This reference in the oral tradition is important because people who lived near the coast of Dahomey claimed that they did not know the fates of those who were taken away, a claim that Dr. Akosua Perbi refutes in Henry Louis Gates Jr.'s

Wonders of the African World.[19] Moreover, although people who lived inland in Abomey, the seat of power at the height of the slave trade, may not have known that there was an overseas trade, Bay argues that "the ruling elite, at the very least, knew full well that people being sold to Europeans at the coast were carried off across a vast body of water" thus, the need for their own *bociọ*, power objects from the Dahomean cultural tradition.[20] Even those who lived inland, who did not know about the overseas voyage, probably saw people being marched to the coast. The story of Bokọfíó is evidence of people's knowledge of at least some form of human trade as it depicts the treatment of captives with precision. The imagery that is used corresponds to that used by someone who had clear knowledge of the treatment of captives. Thus, even if because of time (the slave trade had, of course, ended one hundred years before) or location, Bokọfíó and the storyteller did not witness the trade themselves, it is likely that they would have known about it, with stories being passed down over several generations.

The water imagery suggests the great distance that some enslaved people traveled in order to reach the coast. It also recalls the middle-passage crossing whereby the captives, who may have never even seen the ocean, let alone sailed on it before their encounter with it as captives, perceived the ships traversing the water "as though it were land." Furthermore, the village that Bokọfíó and his captors pass through in which his captors stifle his cries for help may refer to people he encountered along the way who resisted the trade. Such local opposition to the trade is exemplified in the historical figure of King Béhanzin, who attempted to stop the trade and colonization by the French. For his efforts, he and his entire entourage were exiled to Martinique and Algeria, where he died. The fact that the man in raffia cloth calls the other men "*adjotǒ*," meaning "thief" in Fongbe, and in the process, reveals their identity to his rescuers, reinforces this possibility. The reference to local resistance and attempts to abolish the slave trade is repeated when Bokọfíó and his captors come to the men sitting on stools and turn abruptly so as to avoid them. Not only is this slight alteration of a repeated gesture a common narrative device to signal progression in the oral tradition but it may also offer insight into localized tactics of people who were sent into the interior to retrieve captives changing routes to avoid detection once opposition to the slave trade spread.

Between History and Spirit

On a metaphysical level, the path that Bokǫfíó takes is to the land of the dead, which hinges on myth and depends on the cooperation of the gods. This metaphysical world bleeds into the physical world as it is part of the Vodun and Vodou belief system that the visible world informs the invisible world and vice versa, and the dead and the living walk side by side.

Later in his study, Herskovits writes that the Fon believe that the soul of the dead takes a long path and then comes to a river known as the Azile. This river is guarded by a watchman who demands money to ferry the departing soul and his burdens across. Afterward the departed comes to a second river called Gudu. The boatman demands tobacco before he will permit the dead soul to reach the other side. After a steep mountain is climbed and a toll of clothing is paid, the departed must cross a final river called Selu. The departed is only allowed to cross if the living prevails upon the boatman.[21] This final step with the deceased having the ability to cross over into the land of the dead is only possible if he or she is remembered and given a proper burial by his or her family members. If the proper rites are performed, the deceased is welcomed into his or her new community of family members who have already passed into the world of the dead. Conversely, if the final step is not completed, the deceased's ghost would remain in a liminal state, wandering between worlds. Restless, he or she would eventually become an evil spirit, wreaking vengeance on his or her neglectful children.[22] This description of death resembles a rites-of-passage ritual whereby the person's social death or exile is followed by a series of trials before he or she is incorporated into his or her community reborn. As John Mbiti describes it, the rites-of-passage ritual "is a symbolic experience of the process of dying, living in the spirit world and being reborn (resurrected). The rebirth, that is the act of rejoining their families, emphasizes and dramatizes that the young people are now new, they have new personalities, they have lost their childhood, and in some societies they even receive completely new names."[23]

When Bokǫfíó is on the threshold of another land and is about to be sold to the man who "reads banana leaves like pages," he is saved from an eternity of servitude by a man who speaks his own language. This gesture may again be read through the rites-of-passage motif with the initiate being welcomed back to his community as signified by the shared language. It may also be read in relation to the transatlantic slave trade, illustrating that Legba did not abandon his faithful adepts when they boarded the ships bound for the New World. He was also on the other side of the "river" facilitating their transition, rebirth, and incorporation into their new environments. Although it may seem on one hand that, as the gatekeeper, Legba saved the man from enslavement, he may also be read as having facilitated either Bokọfíó's reintroduction as a transformed presence into his former community or his introduction into a diasporic community.

While Legba guards the crossroads between the land of the living and that of the dead, Dan, the god of creation, facilitates the rebirth of the captured in his or her new community. The latter god seems to be, in this case, forcing a rebirth since Bokọfíó's time to die has not yet arrived. This is signified by the arrival of Gede, god of the cemetery, whose dominion is death and rebirth and who makes an appearance in the form of the stone that the man dressed in raffia cloth (Legba) appears to read. The ability for Gede to manifest as an object in nature is apparently ancient as, according to Herskovits, "history tells us of men and women who became angry, and disappeared into trees and rocks. The great Gẹde rock is regarded as a *vodun*, but that is because long ago the soul of Gẹde entered it after a quarrel."[24] Thus, although Gede is not explicitly mentioned in the story, he makes his presence known through the rock. Also, because he holds dominion over death and rebirth—the subject of the story—in much the same way that Leah Gordon is able to infer that he was there on the battlefield offering succor to the wounded, we can read his presence here in the realm that Bokọfíó inhabits, between life and death, a liminal space.

It is possible that, in the story, Legba consults the god of the cemetery to verify that Bokọfíó is indeed supposed to be in the land of the dead. Gede's answer is presumably negative because, after Legba chases the captives away with another stone, he consults the original stone again before blessing Bokọfíó with water from his mouth and then driving him back to the land of the living. This belief in gods inhabiting stones, caves, trees, waterfalls, and springs can also be found in Haiti, in the form of "*wòch lwa*," which are identified by their forms and their ability to pass certain tests. They "must be able to 'whistle,' to perspire when blown upon and 'talk.'"[25] The goddess Ezili is also said to inhabit the waterfall of the village for which it is named (So Do), and Loko, the *lwa* whose name derives from the iroko tree of West Africa, is said to inhabit trees.[26]

Dan from Dahomey to Haiti

Among the Fon, Dan is represented as a snake who assisted in the creation of the universe and supports it with 3,500 coils above and 3,500 below the universe. He is coiled in on himself with half of his body above the earth and the other half below because he acts as a cushioning for the earth (Fig. 2). He is also depicted as "coiling himself around the inchoate earth, gathering it together and keeping it firm."[27] But Dan is more than a snake. "It is a living quality expressed in all things that are flexible, sinuous and moist; all things that fold and refold and coil, and do not move on feet, though sometimes those things that are Dan go through the air. The rainbow has these qualities . . . and so has the umbilical cord, and some say the nerves too."[28] Dan's duality can be witnessed in its appearance as a rainbow, with the male being the red portion, and the blue, the female.[29] The red and the blue also recall the colors of Dantò and Ogou across the water, who worked together to support their descendants in their fight for

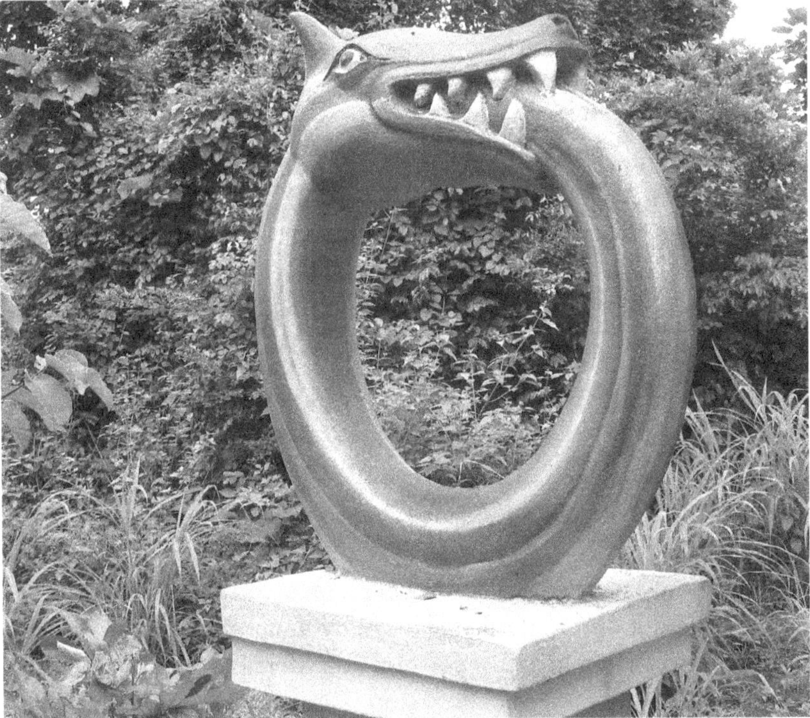

Figure 2. Dan statue by unidentified artist in Kpassezoumé (Sacred Forest). Ouidah, Benin Republic. Photo: Toni Pressley-Sanon, 2006.

freedom. Thus, we may also read Dan as present in the dual form of the *lwa* in the diaspora.

In the same text, Herskovits relates a myth that explains the importance of the serpent in Dahomean culture.[30] In it, the *vodun* Aido Hwedo, the serpent, is introduced. According to Herskovits, there are two Aido Hwedo; one of them lives in the sea while the other dwells in the sky and transports the thunderbolts of the gods to the earth. This Aido Hwedo is, in fact, the rainbow serpent or Dan, and Dan represents riches. According to some, the two are regarded as twins. Although Aido Hwedo is powerful and to be feared, his power derives from his role as the servant of the royal master among the thunder deities. He is considered an "influential retainer."[31] For my purposes, what is important about the myth is the insight that it provides into the *vodun*, Dan, and its relationship to Aido Hwedo as the essence of equilibrium:

> At the beginning of the world, before Mawú had borne children, and before Sogbó existed, Aido Hwedo, the serpent, had been created by whoever created the world. Unlike other *vodų* [*sic*] who revealed themselves to sibs that they might be worshipped by men, Aido Hwedo is the god of no family group, and is the child of none of the other gods. When the Creator began making the world as it exists today, he was carried everywhere in the mouth of Aido Hwedo, the serpent, who was his servant. Wherever they spent their nights mountains would appear from the excrement of Aido Hwedo. That is why when a man digs into a mountain slope, he finds riches.[32]

Following the logic of the myth, while Bokọfíó's captors are Dan, the mountains that he must climb are also Dan as they are born from his creativity. Thus, he is of the earth and the sky. In fact, the name Aido Hwedo means "You were created before the earth and before the sky" or "You are both in the earth and in the sky."[33] His dual nature is housed in one body, signifying perfect balance; his very existence representing the Marasa Twa.

Dan is also associated with water because, according to the myth, the Creator allowed him to submerge his body under the water in order to stay cool. According to anthropologist Paul Mercier, "Beneath the earth *Ayido Hwedo* is submerged in the waters. He may be recognized in standing pools which recall the memory of the primordial waters: he is seen cleaving the waters like a flash of light."[34] In his travels over the earth, Dan traced out the courses of the streams, which before that time were just stagnant waters; he dug out channels in which the waters were to move.[35] Furthermore, as anthropologist Bernard Maupoil says, "If it is said that Dan dwells in the ocean this is because he represents for man the greatest conceivable power in ceaseless motion."[36] Thus, if seen as an origins myth, one that explains how things came to be as they are, then the streams and rivers that Bokǫ́fíó crosses were those just created from the stagnant water that would empty into the ocean and take him into the diaspora. As such, in addition to Legba, Dan also facilitated the captives' movement from Africa into the diaspora. As Dan is the beginning, it also stands to reason that Bokǫ́fíó asks for water when he is reborn because it is the building block of life.

Finally, we may read Dan as personified by the two kidnappers who force Bokǫ́fíó to traverse both water and mountain ranges, associated as he is with both. While the mountains represent wealth, one wonders if those that Bokǫ́fíó traverses mean wealth for him or for those to whom he would be sold as a slave. Though only rivers are mentioned in the story, as we have seen from descriptions of Dan's characteristics, he is associated with oceans as well. Thus, he could very well have facilitated the captives' voyage across the sea to accrue wealth for their captors.

The ambiguity of stories such as the one that is at the center of the chapter are echoed in the historical record. An example of such ambiguity can be found in two articles by Paul Hazoumé, one of which explores the Dahomey-Ouidah War of 1727, driven as it was by competition over access to European trade. Likewise, Hazoumé's account of Ouidah's origins includes the story of the first arrival of "'whites,' who were met on the beach by a local man called Kpate, who then took them to see King Kpase at his capital Savi."[37] In neither of the stories does Hazoumé emphasize what the Europeans were trading for: human beings. At one point the sale of people is mentioned, but only to highlight the high cost that King Agadja (1718–40) was willing to pay for a gun (one person for a gun). As Robin Law observes about the stories, "the relative invisibility of the human victims of the slave trade in these accounts . . . seems to reflect, less any moral scruples about the trade, than the perspective of the African sellers of slaves, which emphasized the benefits obtained from it."[38] There is no indication in Hazoumé's account of how many people were sold, where they arrived from, under what conditions they were captured, or where they were destined for. Such excisions from historical narratives, similar to those that I argue may be found in the oral tradition but that come through in the use of metaphor, make the work of reading these texts through a different lens—ones that again, contribute to the work of surfacing "submerged histories"—prescient.

We know that people like those mentioned in Hazoumé's accounts were shipped to Saint-Domingue. The evidence is in Haiti, where Danbala Wedo also preceded the world. He is so venerated that his songs are generally only praise songs, exulting him as the great serpent and referring to his affinity with water. Dan—like his corollary, Danbala Wedo, in Haiti—is believed to come out of the underworld to drink after a rain.[39] When he arrives at ceremonies, he comes as a snake, plunging first into the basin of water that is prepared for him and then writhing upon the ground or mounting a tree, a primordial source of all wisdom.[40] Like Dan, origin and essence of life, Danbala is itself unchanged by life and so is at once the ancient past and the assurance of the future.[41] Dan and its New World counterpart, Danbala, embody both the Marasa and tidalectics as they straddle two worlds—the world above and the world below, the past and the future.

Aizan

The *aizan*, mentioned as an absence in the story, means "mat of the earth." Among the Fon, Aizan is one of the most important *voduns*, and its shrine, *aizan*, is one of three that are historically and contemporarily normally found at the entrances to homes, villages, markets, districts, and temples.[42] Aizan's adherents make offerings, and in return Aizan bestows prosperity to them.[43] The way that the *aizan* is depicted in the story comments on presence-in-absence in the lack of shrines in the land that Bokofíó and his captors cross into, where there is "not even an *aizan*." The absence of the *aizan* seems to signal the foreignness of Bokofíó's surroundings. However, as with Gede, I would suggest that Bokofíó's not seeing any shrines to the *voduns* does not mean that they are not there. Rather, during this period of liminality, the gods are manifest in his life and in his death, accompanying him on his journey in forms that he may not immediately recognize, such as he learns when the diviner is consulted and tells him that his enslavers were Dan, and he was saved from slavery by Legba.

Aizan has not only crossed the Atlantic metaphorically in the story but also in the *lwa* Aizan and in its enactment in ritual. Along with Loko, chief of Legba's escorts, the Haitian Aizan is in line with Legba, "as if on a place concentric with him."[44] The two together, Loko and Aizan, are known as the first priest and the first priestess, and they are preeminent among the ancestral *lwa*.[45] Maya Deren describes Aizan as being the last echo of the androgynous divinity which, in her association with the ancient androgynous founders of the race, Silibo-Gweto and Nana-Bouclou, is said to have preceded even Mawu-Lisa, the original twin birth in Dahomean belief from whom the divinities originated.[46] Aizan's duality thus puts the *lwa* squarely in the realm of the Marasa.

Aizan is the patron of the ritual stages of initiation into Vodou, which culminates in the Kanzo ceremony of spiritual birth. According to Deren, "It is her palm leaf which purifies and protects when shredded into a fringe; it is worn as a sort of mask by the initiate on the occasion of his or her first emergence into the world. Thus, she is the loa of the psychic womb of the race and she is guardian of the place of spiritual birth, the hounfor."[47] As we see Aizan did in Dahomey, she, as wife of Loko, and closely associated with Legba, Guardian of the Crossroads, provides protection to her adherents in Haiti, watching over them as they are birthed into a new way of experiencing the world, as Karen McCarthy Brown counsels that initiation does.[48]

In *African Civilisations in the New World* (1971) the sociologist and anthropologist Roger Bastide describes the initiation ritual thus: "First comes a rite of separation from one's old life, which includes such features as the *chiré aizan*, in which a cabbage-palm's leaves are torn up (this process in Dahomey, symbolizes the separation of sacred and profane). . . . When the initiates leave the peristyle to retire to the djévo (a special chamber) everyone weeps as they are now 'dead.'"[49] Following several days of seclusion, while other rituals are performed, the initiates are then baptized by the *pè-savan* or *prèt savan*, the functionary who reads or recites Catholic prayers in a Vodun ceremony (a practice taken from the Yorùbá tradition of giving an initiate a new name). The initiates, those who have passed through certain stages of initiation and are qualified to assist in various ritual activities, are reborn to their communities as *hounsi-kanzo*.[50] They are thus knowledgeable of the ways of Vodou, a knowledge that is kept alive through "motor memory" or "bodily labor."[51]

What Histories Reveal

It is my contention that, although it is not historically traceable and is filled with gods and elements of the supernatural, the story of Bokọ́fíọ́ reflects and comments on the historical reality, shedding light on the physical, emotional, and spiritual toll that the events of the past took on those who were subjected to it and that has been passed down to their descendants. In the oral tradition, it is a given that stories will change depending on who is telling the story, who is listening, and the conditions under which the story is being told as well as the motivations of the storyteller. The same may be said of historical narratives, which, as Hayden White has argued, are constructed narratives around what the historian chooses to record or omit based on his or her goals. White writes, "The same event can serve as a different kind of element of many different historical stories, depending on the role it is assigned in a specific motific characterization of the set to which it belongs."[52] Part of the work of "emplotment" of the historical narrative that White discusses also involves deciding what elements of the story will be included, which will be omitted, and how they will be arranged, all of which will be shaped by the largely European "historical imagination."[53] White further argues for a recognition of the subjective nature of historical narratives when he states

> And so the historian must interpret his data by including certain facts from his account as irrelevant to his narrative purpose. On the other hand, in his efforts to reconstruct "what happened" in any given period of history, the historian inevitably must include in his narrative an account of an event or complex of events for which the facts that would permit a plausible explanation of its occurrence are lacking. And this means that the historian must "interpret" his materials by filling in the gaps in his information on inferential speculative grounds. A historical narrative is thus necessarily a mixture of adequately and inadequately explained events, a congeries of established and inferred facts, at once a representation that is an interpretation that passes for an explanation of the whole process mirrored in the narrative.[54]

Key to this process of writing the historical narrative is the historian's imperative to decide what is relevant and what is irrelevant, what to include and what to exclude.

There are historical realities that do not fit into the rational, linear, empirically evidencible realm of "historiography," and so it is left out. As such, the questions that Stephan Palmié asks regarding the plausibility of a guardian spirit of a man named Tomás that a diviner and priest of Cuban *regla ocho* identifies as walking with him are relevant here. Palmié questioned whether the person that Tomás may have once been is beyond historiographic recovery because the nature of the evidence we deem admissible simply erases his historical being and subjectivity.[55] Similarly, I ask if the story of Bokọfíó and its potential insights are beyond what History finds admissible.[56] Might not stories such as Bokọfíó's haunt us precisely because all the writing of history has not just obliterated the historical reality of the lives of the enslaved but has also artificially distanced or displaced them from ours?[57] "The dead do not like to be forgotten," counsels M. Jacqui Alexander.[58] Moreover, "Spirit energy both travels in Time and differently through linear time, so that there is no distance between space and time that it is unable to navigate."[59] As such, while these voices of the dead may be silenced or obscured in the historical narrative, the dead are able to use other creative means to announce their presence. As such, I contend that the parallels between the oral tradition and the historical narrative shed light on the historical reality even as the historiography obscures it. One of the ways the story of Bokọfíó serves as a site of memory and lends itself to fruitful speculation about the historical experience of capture and transportation is linguistically in the naming of the protagonist, which draws connections between Bokọfíó and cultural practices among the Fon and their descendants in Saint-Domingue as well as in contemporary Haiti. This connection speaks to the history of the slave trade and slavery as well as the continued disfranchisement of Africans in the diaspora. While the connection is not conclusive, it is highly suggestive of linguistic memory, reflection, and commentary.

Liminal Naming

There are two elements that make up the name Bokọfíó: "*boko*," which in Fongbe means supreme priest, someone who reads the Fa, the system of divination. There is also "*fíó*," which is a Mina or Aja word, meaning ruler of a village. According to Mercier, culturally and linguistically the Fon belong to the Aja group, whose chronology was established around the eighteenth century when the Dahomean conquest of the coastal areas brought them in contact with European traders in Ouidah. The economy of the kingdom was dependent on the slave trade, which was in turn fed by repeated wars, again, a reality that Hazoumé's articles obscure.[60] When the slave trade was at its height, the Fon raided neighboring polities to sell their people into the transatlantic slave trade. Among those raided were the Mina to the north. We can read the combination of names that make up "Bokofíó" as evidence of the captives' in-betweenness, embodying both the Fon and the Mina and neither. The story likewise reinforces liminality in its depiction of Bokofíó's status as not free but not fully enslaved, not dead and not alive. He is between multiple renderings of nonbeing with several significations, which I discuss below in relation to bòkò.

Bociǫ, Boko, **and** *Bòkò*

According to art historian Suzanne Preston Blier, Dahomean *bociǫ* sculptural power objects and *bo* (amulets) are examples of memory that reflect the sense of disempowerment and anxiety that plagued peasants or commoners during the slave era. Not only do they reflect the disempowerment and anxiety that the majority of the population suffered historically and continue to suffer, they also "work" to address and counteract the conditions that cause the anxiety. As an "empowered object," a *bociǫ* or *bo* "works" for its owner to empower him or her under disempowering conditions. They gave those who were potentially subjected to the slave traders' chains a means to defy their seemingly all-encompassing power. The means by which those who were caught in the traders' nets enacted their power, however, transmuted in order to facilitate the victims' physical and spiritual survival under conditions that promoted death. In other words, the *bociǫ* figure and *bo* embodied power for those who held them under the political and "social disorder" that threatened their lives.[61]

Bay interrogates the connection that Blier makes between *bociǫ, bo,* and the slave trade. Citing Herskovits, who devoted a whole chapter to *bo* but made no link between it and the slave trade, Bay concludes that there is no evidence that they were created in response to the slave trade or even that their usage increased during that period of time.[62] In addition, while Blier shows that *bociǫ* and *bo* were used by "commoners" who were potential victims of the slave trade, Bay argues that some of the most powerful *bociǫ* and *bo* were actually "used by the very people who planned and directed predatory raids for captives, and who profited most handsomely from the overseas trade—the ruling elite of Dahomey."[63] For Bay, this evidence supports the belief that the slave trade "created widespread social disruptions that affected cultures as a whole," not just certain segments of the population, as Blier's concentration on the *bo*'s usage by "commoners" suggests.[64]

According to Blier, the form that *bociǫ* takes reflects the "garbage heap" of conditions that make their production necessary.[65] It is an embodiment of the *marasa* concept in its "ambiguous and anomalous simultaneity of body interior and exterior" that "projects a quality of intrigue and foreboding, making visible a psychological landscape of striking complexity."[66] In addition, since it is a ritual object, it is always in transition, constantly being added to and changed with new layers of blood, palm oil, and feathers of sacrificed animals that feed the *vodun*, thus serving as a "visceral reminder" of its ritual history. It therefore also reflects Mikhail Bakhtin's description of the "grotesque body," one that is "in the act of becoming . . . never finished, never completed."[67]

The connection can be made between the ritual object that is never completed with the culture from which it originates, as several scholars have argued was one of layering and adoption.[68] Examples of this layering can be found in Vodun. As Maupoil argued, in Dahomey there was a tradition of bringing foreign *voduns* into the state deity pantheon with their identity, rituals, and ritual significance being subsumed in the state religion. Besides the foreign deities who were brought into local Vodun through warfare in which the kingdom of Abomey assumed control over the conquered enemies' gods and in turn used them to their own benefit, "foreign religious powers were introduced into the Vodun pantheon through the marriage of kings to foreign women and the kingdom's vodun."[69] Bay suggests that these "cultural influences from outside were without exception grafted onto a worldview that is associated with Vodun."[70] Art historian Dana Rush pushes Bay's idea a bit further, suggesting that "these outside influences were not just grafted onto a particular Vodun worldview, but rather were the sustenance of the worldview itself, and the motivation for accumulative art and expression."[71] This accumulation and adaptation is a continuously transformative process, which is embodied in the *bociǫ*.

The incorporation, adaptation, and transformation of historical realities and their symbolism may also be found in contemporary Vodun practices. Although Rush does not date the practice, she briefly discusses as part of her section entitled "Slavery Cognizance" in her article "In Remembrance of Slavery: Tchamba Vodun Arts" the fact that the idea of enslavement "plays out in an explicit ephemeral assemblage type object called *vosiso*," or *vo*, "offered as sacrifices to spirits for healing and problem-solving."[72] These *vo* and the ritual associated with them seem to be evidence of a transformed meaning of shackles, an object associated with transatlantic slavery but that have a different meaning in rituals among the Tchamba complex, a strong spirit grouping along coastal Benin, Togo, and into eastern coastal Ghana. Rush discusses how one type of *vo* is shaped like shackles that were used to hold slaves. Contemporarily,

> this type of *vo* is used when a person has troubles with his or her own life. Under the guidance of a diviner, an individual gathers prescribed items, ranging from shells and feathers to money and foodstuffs, which are assembled and bound as a representation of the person's life. Once shackled into place, the individual's life will be stabilized, held still, and controlled. In concept, this is similar to how shackles were used to hold slaves, but in this case, the person involved is controlling his or her own life rather than being dominated by another.[73]

This transformed usage of shackles may be read as evidence of continued exchanges of meaning between Africa and its diaspora that is facilitated by tidalectics and overseen by Legba, Master of Change, and the Marasa who direct the melding of complementary and contradictory energies that coalesce into the power to turn a disempowering history marked by loss of control and instability into a present and future of empowerment, control and stability.

To return to the *bociọ*, across the ocean, African diasporic identity is also marked by transformation and the process of becoming. As such, we can argue for the connection between the layering that is evidence of the *bociọ*'s ritual history and the African diasporic history of addition and transformation when enslaved people made their way into exile in the New World. While the memory of the threat of enslavement in their homelands stayed with them in their new settings, captives were also faced with the realization of the threat that the *bociọ* was enlisted to stave off: European enslavement. In "The Social History of Haitian Vodou" (1995) Michel-Rolph Trouillot and Sidney Mintz explain that life in the New World entailed an intensely drastic resocialization process that "demanded the learning of wholly different behavioral patterns by its subjects and victims."[74] The acculturation or "seasoning process" covered "the simplest acts—of eating, of elimination, as well as of dressing and toilette, not to mention courting, establishing kinship ties, or managing life crises such as birth and death."[75] These all had to be "relearned to fit the new (and mostly very oppressive) circumstances, in the absence of one-society governing principles based on cultural content. The right way to fall in love, to give birth, to bless, to bury had, in this situation, to be fashioned through social acts."[76] This "relearning" or, I would contend, "learning" new ways of being in addition to retaining what was remembered, entailed a kind of intellectual, social, and spiritual layering that may not be as easily discernible as the patina that forms on the *bociǫ* but nonetheless leaves its mark on the being who has undergone the process.

Indeed, the transformation from a member of an ethnic group in one land to a member of the African diaspora in another marked a profoundly jarring moment of negotiation that continues in the present moment. The experience of enslavement and making of a life for one's self and one's family (ever changing, expanding, or shrinking because of the nature of slavery) was a constant struggle to reconcile and negotiate past knowledge and new conditions and institutions within which the enslaved person had to learn to fit under threat of death. Therefore, the African diaspora stands as a kind of human articulation of the *bociǫ*. Those people who came with the knowledge of *bociǫ* and its meanings and who eventually integrated with the larger New World–community brought their sensibility and knowledge to bear on the culture that evolved. Evidence of this remembered and transformed knowledge is seen in the figure of the Haitian *bòkò*, born in the cauldron of slavery and still necessary as disempowering sociopolitical and economic systems persist.

Bociǫ, Boko, Bòkò, and the *Zonbi*

Whereas a Dahomean *boko* is one who is knowledgeable in *bo* or *bokonon*, master of *bo* knowledge among the Fon, across the water, the linguistically related word, *bòkò*, refers to "a Haitian expert in supernatural matters . . . an entrepreneur, . . . [who] has a reputation as a man who will work with both hands, that is, for healing *and* revenge," referred to in traditional anthropology as a sorcerer.[77] While the name for the power object among the Fon means an empowered cadaver, the being that the *bòkò* creates in Haiti—a *zonbi*—is a disempowered cadaver. Although their uses are oppositional, with one being used to empower while the other disempowers, the existence of both reveals relations of power in their deployment.

As I discuss in the next chapter, in its most basic sense, a *zonbi* is a corpse that a *bòkò* has extracted from his or her tomb and raised to work. As several scholars have argued, stories and images of *zonbi* are essentially about power and powerlessness as well as the distorted relationship between the overly powered and those who are in various ways enslaved.[78] Similarly, the *bociọ* signifies the "different statuses of object, those of commoners versus royalty, popular versus elite, slaves versus owners."[79] Thus, there are clear connections between the power object in Benin (*bociọ*) and the object of the *bòkò* in Haiti (*zonbi*). Where in Benin it references the incongruity and disorder of everyday life and, as Blier argues, "challenges the status quo," in Haiti the *zonbi* seems to succumb to the forces that disempower him or her.[80] He or she lingers between life and death, working for whatever unseasoned crumbs are tossed his or her way.

The story of Bokọfíó prompted Herskovits to raise the issue of *zonbification*. Perhaps the gods were trying to turn Bokọfíó into a *zonbi*, a possibility that is suggested also by his liminal name. The slave trader who removes the enslaved from his or her kin in order to sell him or her "into servitude in some far-away land" is likened to a sorcerer who raises the dead and turns him or her into a mindless worker.[81] Like the slave trader who removed the enslaved person from his or her community, the *bòkò* in Haiti raises the dead from his or her place of rest to make him or her work. But although the *zonbi* is often read as a powerless being, it can also be read as powerful potential that will one day awaken, rise up, and disrupt the status quo. There is always the possibility that the *zonbi* will overthrow his or her master. All it takes is a grain of salt—in historical terms, a spark of revolutionary consciousness.

Stories from Dahomey, once a major hub of the transatlantic slave trade, such as the one that I have explored here provide insight into the general conditions and effects of the slave trade and slavery as well as the unique conditions and effects of the trade on the societies from which people were taken as well as those to which they were taken. In addition, such stories from *either* side of the Atlantic from a tidalectial orientation with attention to spirits' workings—especially Legba and the Marasa—can challenge a Western scholarly tendency to read history and story linearly while honoring and incorporating the worldsense from whence these stories originate. In such a way, the oral tradition can shed light on symbolic meanings and on how people process their historical reality, reflect, and comment on it, perhaps warning future generations against making the same mistakes and continuing the cycle of alienation, disfranchisement, and exploitation that continues to circumscribe African and African diasporic life. Finally, they offer insight into the changing sociopolitical conditions and people's reactions and feelings toward them both in the past and in the present.

2

Of *Bociọ, Bo, Cakatú, Zonbi, Nkisi,* and *Pakèt Kongo*

Both order and disorder are at the heart of creation.

—Rachel Beauvoir-Dominique

Botanist and historian of the Haitian Revolution Michel Etienne Descourtilz wrote of seeing a rebel band of Congos wearing small packets that contained heads of toads and snakes as well as other amulets tied to their arms and legs during the battles. The amulets were believed to make the insurgents invulnerable to the bullets of the colonists.[1] A Creole refugee from Saint-Domingue who only identified himself by the initial "P" wrote of catching one insurgent who, by his regalia, the author took to be one the "principal chiefs."[2] The insurgent tried twice to shoot P but was unsuccessful. Upon searching his person, P and the accompanying French soldiers found in one of the insurgent's pockets pamphlets printed in France, "filled with commonplaces about the *Rights of Man* and the *Sacred Revolution*" as well as "in his vest pocket a large packet of tinder and phosphate of lime" and on his chest, a small "sack full of hair, herbs, bits of bone, which they call a fetish."[3] P offers that with it "they expect to be sheltered from all danger" and concludes that it was because of this amulet that the man "had the intrepidity which the philosophers call Stoicism."[4]

This chapter reads material culture as extant evidence of tidalectics' workings on both sides of the Atlantic Ocean. First, I read the "fetish" identified in Saint-Domingue in the above accounts in relation to an ancient power object from Dahomey / Benin Republic—the *bociọ* statue and its nonfigural complement, *bo*, an amulet or talisman. I also discuss how the *cakatú*, a Dahomean cultural icon and form of societal control, may have also made its way across the water and been folded into the Haitian *zonbi,* another cultural icon with origins in Dahomey and the Kôngo. The figure of the *zonbi,* popularized internationally during the first American occupation of Haiti from 1915 to 1934, is often read as an embodiment of alienation and exploitation, dehumanization, and, more recently, the creative potential that emerged from the middle-passage experience. Recently Franck Degoul has undertaken reading the *zonbi* as a form of collective memory, which brings the past into the present, incarnating and embodying the remembered history of colonialism and slavery, but one that has been appropriated by Haitians.[5] I am interested in how the *zonbi* may also be read as evidence of and a response to historical as well as more recent attempts to silence and disempower the poor majority (*pèp la*) who nonetheless continue to resist their subjugation.

In the latter part of the chapter, I explore the multiple meanings of the Kôngo *nkisi* (plur. *minkisi*) and their transformation in the Haitian context to become *pakèt kongo,* bound "gardes against illness and evil."[6] I also propose that the *pakèt kongo* may be both an iteration of the *bo* in its mission to guard against illness and evil and a synthesis of both *bo* and *nkisi.* My discussion then doubles back on itself where at the end of the chapter I return to the *bociɔ̀* figure to argue that both it and the *nkisi* offer insight into the slave trade and slavery even though they both existed pre-transatlantic trade. Ultimately, all of these examples of material culture from both sides of the Atlantic taken together provide a lens through which to understand how they and the beliefs that inspire them empower those who deploy them to determine how they experience the world while they also, in some ways, influence it.

Bociɔ̀ and *Cakatú*

Bociɔ̀ sculptures and their nonfigural complements in the form of amulets, *bo,* are produced primarily in the West African countries of Benin Republic (formerly Dahomey) and Togo in areas populated by the linguistically related Fon, Gun Ayizo, Mahi, Heuda, Ouatchi, Aja, Ouemenu, Evhe, Gen, and affiliated peoples.[7] Many of the people from this region also share a belief in *vodun,* forces of power that govern the world and the lives of those who reside within it as part of the religion, Vodun, by the same name, which means "Spirit."

Aesthetically, *bociǫ* sculptures are not appealing. They are "strong" objects, but they are not things of beauty. They are not ornamental, refined, elegant, or attractive in any standard sense of the words.[8] They are meant to "work" for their owners, to shield them against harm and function in conjunction with *vodun* energies to protect humans and offer avenues of individual empowerment and change.[9] Suzanne Preston Blier proposes that in Dahomey *bociǫ* sculpture and *bo* as empowered objects were meant to literally protect the owner against being swept up in the slave trade. They also served to psychologically help people get beyond the violence and danger that resulted from the constant threat of capture and enslavement.[10]

For Blier, the relevance of these power objects did not end with the transatlantic slave trade. Rather, they remained important strategies for responding to the difficult social conditions under which people found themselves post-transatlantic trade, when the subsequent demand for labor in palm oil factories increased, and then afterward, during the French conquest of Dahomey in 1894. While Blier makes clear that works of this sort were made and used prior to the slave trade, she posits that they assumed special poignancy and meaning during that time because of the sense of vulnerability and powerlessness that the era engendered. Physical representation of the work that the *bociǫ* was meant to perform can be found in, for example, the prominent use of raffia cord, which is characteristic of solidity and resistance and used to signify the *bociǫ*'s power in turning discord and danger away from their owners. In addition, the *bociǫ*'s being tightly bound in cords evokes the image of a prisoner or slave. It suggests what the Fon call "*kannumon*," meaning "thing belonging in cords," and is in essence a "slave" made to "work" for its master, a condition the *bociǫ* was meant to protect against.[11]

Across the water contemporarily, performance artist Salnave Raphael, a.k.a. Nabot Power, tells Leah Gordon that when he was a child, during Kanaval (carnival), one of his favorite groups was the *Lanceurs de Corde* (Lanse Kòd, or Rope Throwers). He explains to Gordon that his group, Lanse Kòd, in their dress and performance, make a statement about slavery and being freed from slavery:

This is a celebration of our independence in 1804. The cords we carry are the cords that were used to bind us. We are always menacing and we never smile. The blackness of our skin is made with pot black crushed charcoal, *kleren* (cane spirit) and cane syrup mixed with a little water in a bucket. Although we know that slaves never wore horns, this is about the revolt of the slaves, and we wear the horns to give us more power and to look even more frightening.

When we take to the streets we stop at the first crossroads, and at the blow of my whistle we all start doing push-ups. This is to show that even though the slaves suffered they were still very strong. Some of the slaves are so strong that they must wear chains to hold back their massive strength.[12]

Gordon remarks in her introduction to *Kanaval* that "Haitian culture is a potent vessel of . . . history, continually transmitting, telling, retelling and reinterpreting Haitian history."[13] But beyond Haitian history, Raphael's explanation of his group's dress and performance intersects with the distant history of slavery in Dahomey and its representation and resistance through Vodun, and in Saint-Domingue and Vodou's strategies of representation and resistance as well as the contemporary reality for the Haitian majority and Vodou's continued interventions. Raphael's explanation recalls not only the treatment of enslaved workers in Saint-Domingue in his group's wearing of cords and sometimes chains but also in their wearing of horns, striving to appear as menacing as possible and in the layering of substances on their physical bodies. During their performance, they may be read as enacting and embodying the *bociọ* and, as such, contemporarily performing the role that the *bociọ* was meant to play in Dahomey during the transatlantic slave trade—that is, as an embodied amulet or *garde* against their enslavement. This enslavement, while no longer accompanied by ropes and chains, is nonetheless maintained through the poor majority's disfranchisement and exploitation by the elite class in collaboration with the Haitian government and the international community. This disfranchisement and exploitation is now in the form of low-wage labor in foreign-owned factories, military occupation, and the undermining of the agricultural sector, to name a few. Given this current state of disfranchisement of the Haitian majority, Raphael's group's summoning of not only their ancestral enslavement but also the taking of their freedom—the throwing off of their chains and their displays of their physical prowess—also recalls the threat that their revolutionary ancestors posed to the institution of slavery. In the way that these carnival performers have both historical and contemporary lessons to teach,

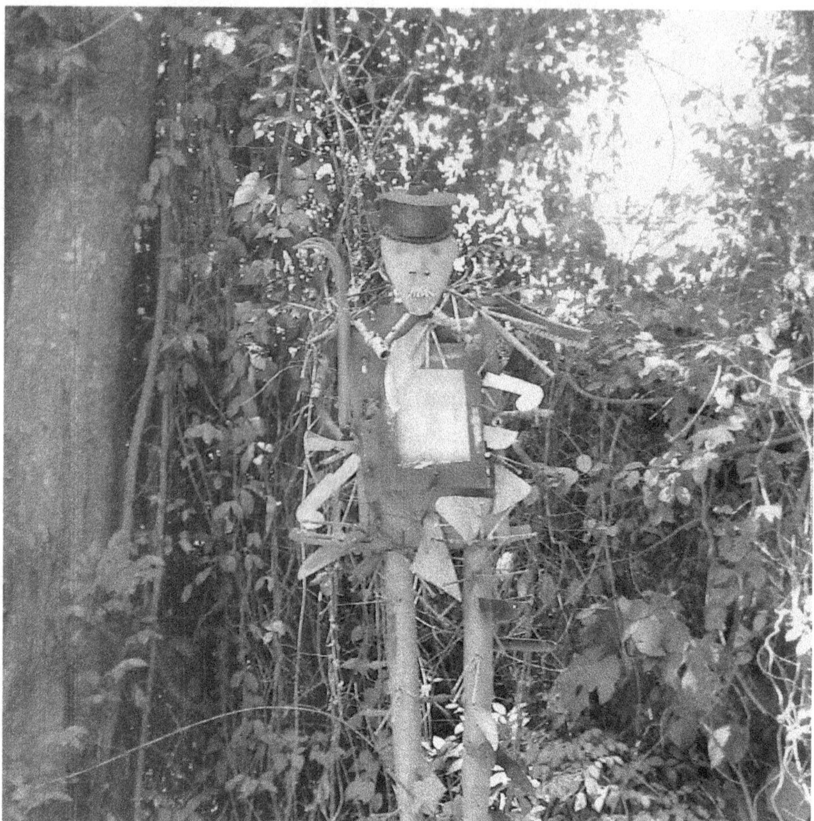

Figure 3. Statue of *cakatú*, a personification of the Vodun force, used to kill an enemy. Sculpted by Théodore Dakpogan and Calixte Dakpogan. Kpassezoumé, Ouidah, Benin Republic. Photo: Toni Pressley-Sanon, 2005.

they resemble the Haitian performance of Rara, which is a certain kind of performative orality. This performative orality includes public verbal wordsmithing (naming themselves Lanse Kòd), displaying masculinity (appearing menacing, performing push-ups at the crossroads, being too strong for ropes to hold and thus needing chains), and taking an oppositional stance (revolt).[14] Contemporarily, this performative orality remains prescient as slavery's legacy persists in the ways that I discuss above.[15]

In general, in Vodou, binding is avoided. Rather, Vodou's use as a force of healing depends on "a free-flowing life."[16] As Karen McCarthy Brown counsels, "In order to get things flowing among persons and between persons and spirits, gates have to be opened, pathways cleared, chains broken, blockages removed and knots untied."[17] However, while the healing aspects of Vodou prevail, there is also space for *bòkò*, those who work with the left hand, such as in secret societies where chains and knots are pervasive images. In such altar rooms, slave chains bind crosses or the crosses are planted in the floor and are caught in multiple-knotted ropes that extend from floor to ceiling, signifying a double binding.[18]

This binding of others may also be seen in the *cakatú* (Fig. 3), another cultural icon that made its way from Dahomey to the New World during the slave era. The *cakatú* of Dahomey, as Dana Rush defines it, is the infliction of a type of power or force.[19] According to Rémi Seglonou, a guide in Kpassezoumé, the Sacred Forest in Ouidah, "*cakatú* were used as a *vodun* power in the distant past to punish those who went against the laws of the tribe."[20] As Mr. Seglonou explained, "If the person obeyed they were set free. It was used, first of all, as an instrument of punishment. However, wicked people discovered the power and used it to hurt people. That is what is now widely spread and known about Vodun."[21]

Rush avers that *cakatú* is a force that can be transmitted in a number of ways and results in debilitating pain both inside and outside the body; it is meant to be followed by death.[22] "Victims are said to feel as though their entire bodies are being pierced by shards of glass, nails, and metal fragments."[23] Rush relates a case that she heard about in which a man went to a Western hospital with pain. When the surgeon opened him up, he found glass, razor blades, and nails inside the man's body.[24] Her story highlights questions about how the articulations of the punishment (whether real or symbolic) reflect how the mind, body, and spirit are enlisted in the work of ensuring societal harmony and balance.

In "The Mindful Body" (1987), medical anthropologists Nancy Scheper-Hughes and Margaret M. Lock discuss the individual's relationship to the community and the way that a potential threat to societal balance is handled collectively. They argue that not only do the relationships between individual and societal bodies concern more than metaphors and collective representations of the natural and the cultural (as in the figure of the *cakatú*, for example), but the "relationships are also about power and control."[25] Paraphrasing anthropologist Mary Douglas, they assert, "When a community experiences itself as threatened it will respond by expanding the number of social controls regulating the group's boundaries."[26] Furthermore—and this is what is most interesting for my reading of *cakatú*—the authors contend that "points where outside threats may infiltrate and pollute the inside become the focus of particular regulation and surveillance. The three bodies—individual, social, and the body politic—may be closed off, protected by a nervous vigilance about exits and entrances."[27] If we look at the *cakatú* figure, we can see how it mimetically represents the protective apparatus that is put in place to shield the body politic from individuals who threaten its collective health. The shards that penetrate the body of the *cakatú* may be read as representative of both the individual threat and the collective body that is being threatened. The piercing of the body in that sense, then, may act as a protective talisman against "sharp" attacks against collective harmony that the one who has transgressed represents. The *cakatú* thus works both ways: attacking the transgressor while also actively shielding the threatened community in its articulation. It is used to remove the wild and savage from the social fabric of the community by inflicting a social death on the offending party that is very often followed by physical death.

In Haiti, zombification may be seen as serving a similar purpose. It is carried out by members of the Chanpwèl Society, a secret society that is considered "an extreme form of the Petro rite, and . . . sometimes referred to as *Petro Sauvage*—the wild Petro."[28] According to Wade Davis, the Chanpwèl Society appears to have a benevolent function in that it supports its members both materially and spiritually. However, "If you get into trouble with it, it can be very hard on you."[29] Echoing the explanation given to me by Mr. Seglonou, Davis was told that someone who was found to be guilty of transgressing against a member of the community may be judged and punished for his or her "antisocial offence."[30] These offenses include seeking excessive material advancement at the expense of friends and family, displaying lack of respect for one's fellows, denigrating the Chanpwèl Society, stealing another's woman, slandering that affects the well-being of others, harming members of one's family, and unjustly keeping others from working the land.[31] These are all actions that would cause profound disharmony within a community and so must be dealt with. Where, in Dahomey, the offender might have been punished to the point of death, in Haiti, perhaps indicative of a recognition of difficult circumstances that would lead to such antisocial behavior as well as the need for human labor, the practice of killing the offender seems to have been abandoned. Rather, according to one Bizango emperor, "What is important is to pass him under a tribunal of hardship until he is disgusted and worn out and thinks of what he did."[32]

Death

Social and physical death were closely aligned realities during the slave era, when there were a number of ways that someone could be considered offensive to the social fabric of the community and consequently exiled or killed. One way was to threaten the power of the ruling elite, which may have resulted in physical death or political exile.[33] Death was meant to be the fate of a prince, for example, who contested the throne against King Tegbesu of Dahomey, who came to power in 1740. For his transgression, the prince was reportedly sewn into a hammock, carried to the coast in Ouidah, and thrown into the sea.[34] Others, considered too spiritually powerful to kill, were stripped of visible political influence but allowed to live in the community. Still others were sold into the European trade, effectively neutralized but leaving the seller free of guilt about causing the offending party's physical death. This was apparently a relatively common practice as, during his field research in Dahomey, Melville J. Herskovits heard of several people who were sold into the trade precisely for political reasons, some of which intersected or coincided with the supernatural strength exhibited by the exiled. Of one family, Herskovits was told that almost all of its members were in the diaspora because they "knew too much magic" and "made too much trouble." Another family who had "strong men" but who "troubled" the king "were caught and sold."[35] The condition of the exiled that I want to stress here is twofold: one is the consumption of the body by force and the other is the status of the victim as outside the protection of his or her former community and thus exposed to a consumptive demise. The *cakatú* of Dahomey as well as the *zonbi* of Haiti embody these two different aspects of consumption.

Claudine Michel describes a similar sensibility to that described by Scheper-Hughes and Lock in Haitian culture. Quoting philosopher John Mbiti's paradigm, "We are, therefore I am," Michel explains that there is a societary essence of the Haitian community: "Human connection is the assumption in the Haitian worldview: there is a suppression of unique life history in favor of a collective personhood from which energy is derived."[36] Members of a community are part of the human web and are not only accountable for their individual acts but are also responsible for people around them according to an understanding that each person's actions and deeds influence the balance of the outer world.[37] While Michel's explanation highlights the accountability aspect of the individual's relationship to his or her community, it may also be seen as the other side of the coin that Scheper-Hughes and Lock describe. It is this belief in an interconnected fate and accountability from whence the need to sanction the individual who threatens the collective harmony springs.

To push this linkage between material culture and societal dis-ease further, I would argue that the representational reflections of and responses to the threat that the slave trade and slavery posed found in the *bociǫ* and *bo* as well as the means of social control found in the *cakatú* are embodied in the *zonbi* from the Haitian cultural imagination. Not only does the *zonbi* address the distant past, it also provides insight into how the historical processes of subjugation that haunts Haitian memory is played out contemporarily. It is both a sign *of* history, preserving the memory of a socioeconomic practice from the past, and a sign *in* history, evolving into a key element in religiocultural practices in the present.

Zonbi

Hans Ackerman and Jeanine Gauthier make a strong case for the source for the etymology of the term "zombi," as it is spelled in French, as West or Central African where, according to them, "similar words abound."[38] For example, the word, *"fúmbi"* meaning "spirit," has been recorded in Cuba, but according to the authors probably originated from the Yorùbá or Congo, the two principal African languages spoken in Cuba. *Mvumbi* (cataleptic individual or invisible part of man), *nsumbi* (devil), *nvumbi* (body without a soul), *nzambi* (spirit of a dead person), and *zumbi* (fetish) all originate from the Congo region, while *zan bibi* or *zan bii*, meaning night bogey, is from the Ghana/Togo/Benin area. As Doris Garraway espouses, "the idea that through sorcery souls may be captured and humans reduced to slavery exists throughout West and Central Africa, the latter notion occurring frequently in the context of real or imagined labor exploitation suggestive of European influence, slavery, or colonialism."[39] Moreover, echoing Mr. Seglonou's explanation for the *cakatú*, several scholars of Vodou have proposed that zombification was punishment for social misbehavior meted out by the Bizango secret society.[40] This etymological explanation, along with the history of slavery and European exploitation as well as the concept of punishment for transgression according to both Dahomean and Haitian belief, provides a tripartite picture that, reflecting processes on the ground, gave rise to the *zonbi*. Alienated from his or her community because of some transgression, the exiled person was sent to the New World. This exiled or socially dead person took those social and political systems with him or her into the middle passage and the New World experience. I propose that, along the way, they folded the iconography of the *cakatú* as well as that of *zan bibi* or *zan bii*, the night bogeyman, into that brought by the Bakôngo, also enslaved. Enslaved people syncretized and synthesized their preexisting iconography that they brought with them across the water, molding it in a way that spoke to and reflected the multiple layers of their experience. While not pierced as the *cakatú*, the *zonbi* is sanctioned publicly and is made to suffer until physical death ends his or her suffering.

If we consider the experience of the *cakatú* as well as the *zonbi* in the context of slavery, the physical manifestations of their suffering resonate. They are both bound or tied up, and they are made to suffer. While the element of physical piercings (i.e., shards of glass and needles) that are part of the *cakatú* may be missing in the *zonbi*, history has taught us that enslaved people were regularly subjected to physical abuse that, in many cases, resulted in their physical death. The *cakatú* captures this aspect of the enslaved person's experience that encompasses, yet surpasses, that of binding or tying. As such, it combines and transfigures these two individual iconographies and, while deploying the nomenclature that most readily can be associated with it (one can easily find images of bound enslaved people being marched to the coast of Africa), reflects and comments on deeper dimensions of the complex experience of the enslaved.

The consumption of one's life force constitutes zombification. That is, the victim is made into a "living-dead."[41] *Zonbi* can be either *zonbi kadav*, corpses that a *bòkò* (sorcerer) has extracted from their tombs and raised to be made to work, or they may be *zonbi astral*, spirits without a body. I will limit my discussion to *zonbi kadav*.[42] Such *zonbi* are not quite alive as the spark of life that sorcerers wake in a corpse does not wholly give the dead person back his or her place in the land of the living. He or she instead remains in the misty zone that divides life from death, in a liminal zone, betwixt and between. *Zonbi* eat, move, hear what is said to them, even speak, but they are socially dead because they are simply beasts of burden that their master exploits without mercy, making them work on plantations, weighing them down with labor, whipping them freely, and feeding them meager tasteless food.[43] Their labor is consumed until physical death releases them from their liminal state.

Laënnec Hurbon writes in *Le Barbare imaginaire* (1988) that a person with an enemy may commission a *bòkò* to place a certain powder in the path of the person who is to be turned into a *zonbi*. When the person walks on it, he or she dies almost immediately. After the person is interred, the *bòkò* must perform certain rites, which include calling the name of the *zonbi* three times. When the *zonbi* rises, he or she is no longer dead but may be considered in a sleep-state or brainwashed. Zora Neale Hurston recounts her own investigation into the *zonbi* in Haiti in her work *Tell My Horse* (1937). In her reading, *zonbi* are "aware of everything happening but do not have available the means to act."[44] A true living dead, they have listless eyes, a stiff walk, and a nasal voice, all of which mark them as being of the "other world."[45]

Alfred Métraux wrote that *zonbi* have no recollection of their past lives and possess no will of their own. From a theoretical position that accommodates people's current incarnation as well as those of several generations past, I suggest that, in fact, the memory of slavery migrates across several generations, both physically and spiritually. As such, the recollection of "past lives" to which Métraux refers is not simply the most immediate or recent incarnation. It spans several generations as the spirits of those who were captured, transported via the transatlantic route, and then disembarked enslaved in Saint-Domingue live and continue to be regenerated in the bodies of their descendants. Métraux's proposition thus raises an important issue as it relates to the Vodou song, which serves as a guiding principle of this text—that of throwing away and forgetting, remembering and gathering together. If, as several scholars suggest, the *zonbi* acts as a metaphor for the enslaved person's condition, then this issue of forgetting versus remembering is a contested one. According to Hurbon, based on the stories of zombification that he recounts in his text, *"les zombis racontent tout ce qu'ils avaient vécu. Car ils n'étaient pas morts pour de vrai"* (zonbi remember everything they'd experienced. Because they were not really dead).[46] Thus, as a result of the trauma around slavery, there may have been a kind of forgetting that was called for on both sides of the tidalectical divide. However, the complete erasure of African diasporic memory was never complete and, as such, was/is able to be summoned when, in Saint-Domingue and later in Haiti, at various times, revolutionary consciousness was/is sparked (metaphorical grains of salt).

Hurston relates the process of zombification from a ritualistic perspective, giving a detailed description of how a *zonbi* is made.[47] I read the description that she gives as *istwa*, one of several that constitute this project in relation to another that I heard during my own field research across the water in Ouidah. According to Hurston:

> The victim is surrounded by the Bocor's associates and the march to the hounfort (Voodoo temples and its surrounding) begins. He is hustled along in the middle of the crowd. Thus he is screened from prying eyes to a great degree and in his half-waking state he is unable to reorient himself. But the victim is not carried directly to the hounfort. First, he is carried past the house where he lived. This is always done. Must be. If the victim were not taken past his former house, later on he would recognize it and return. But once he is taken past, it is gone from his consciousness forever. It is as if it never existed for him. He is then taken to the hounfort and given a drop of liquid, the formula for which is most secret. After that the victim is a Zombie. He will work ferociously and tirelessly without consciousness of his surroundings and conditions and without memory of his former state.[48]

This description of the process can be read against the recent oral tradition from Ouidah about the process of enslavement there.[49] According to the story that I heard several times in Ouidah, as captives approached the last leg of their trek to the shore where pirogues would take them to the slave ships, they were forced to circumambulate a tree called the Tree of Forgetting (nine times for men, seven times for women), and then a few feet further along the Slave Route they would be made to circumambulate a second tree called the Tree of Return three times to facilitate the captives' return to their native land in death. The ritual of forgetting and hope for return that King Agadja is reputed to have devised resembles Hurston's description of the process of turning people into *zonbi*. The tree represented the land that connected them to their kinspeople, their culture, and their history.[50] Following the logic of the story, the captives' circumambulation of the Tree of Forgetting was a tool of the slave traders to produce subservient workers who would have no desire to revolt or resist their enslavement. Evidence of the slave traders' intentions is inscribed below the statue of Mami Wata that stands where the Tree of Forgetting is supposed to have stood. It reads:

Ouidah 92
L'Arbre de l'Oubli

> En ce lieu se trouvait l'arbre de l'oubli
> Les esclaves mâles devaient
> Tourner autour de lui neuf fois
> Les femmes sept fois
> Ces tours étant accomplis les esclaves
> Étaient censés devenir amnésiques
> Ils oubliaient complétement leur passé.
> Leur origines et leur identité culturelle
> Pour devenir des êtres sans aucune volonté
> De réagir ou de se rebeller
> Ce monument commémoratif a été inauguré le 7 février 1993
> Par son excellence,
> Le président Nicéphore Dieudonné Soglo
> A l'occasion du premier festival mondial des arts et des cultures
>   Vodun

Ouidah 92
The Tree of Forgetting

> In this place we find the Tree of Forgetting
> Male slaves had to turn around it nine times
> Women seven times
> These turns were supposed to induce amnesia in the slaves
> They completely forgot their pasts
> Their origins and their cultural identity
> In order to become devoid of will or agency
> To react or rebel
> This monument was inaugurated on February 7, 1993
> By his Excellency, President Nicéphore Dieudonné Soglo
> At the first world festival of Vodun arts and culture).[51]

According to the story that is told contemporarily, the ritual was meant to make captives forget their past, turning them into tabula rasa to be shaped by their enslavers. The story—recently invented, according to historian Robin Law—may be seen as evidence that *istwa* is never stagnant but constantly evolving, emerging from and responding to its sociopolitical context. It is also an example of how Vodun has a long history of assimilating and absorbing different cultural influences into itself.

Since the early 1990s, when UNESCO began its project to commemorate the slave trade, there has been local involvement in the process in the realm of art making as evidenced by the sculptures and murals that are dispersed throughout Ouidah. This oral story—part of the larger Story that memorializes the relationship between Africa and the diaspora engendered by the transatlantic slave trade—is part and parcel of this emerging *istwa* that is responding to this renewed interest in that distant history. Like Herskovits' story about Bokọfíó, circumscribed as it was by the political conditions, source, and researcher but that offers valuable insight into the distant history of the slave trade as well as that of the colonial era when Herskovits was conducting his research, the story of the Tree of Forgetting and the Tree of Return offers insight into not only the distant history of the trade but also people's relationship to that history contemporarily, given the context in which it is told and to whom.

In a Haitian setting, passing in front of the house where one lived before death, as Hurston explains, like circling the tree, is supposed to induce amnesia about one's past, thus ensuring that one will never again recognize one's origins. With no recollection of familial ties, the enslaved are "free" to be made into "slaves," unable to remember a time before.[52] Likewise, once the ritual of forgetting is completed, the *zonbi* is doomed to liminality. The captives who underwent the ritual circling of the Tree of Forgetting and then made the passage to the New World as "slaves" were supposed to be like the *zonbi,* who were then meant to "work ferociously and tirelessly . . . without memory of [their] former state."[53] The slave traders can thus be compared to the *bòkò* who gives the drop of the secret formula to his captive.

Salt

With the tasting of salt, *zonbi* become conscious of their terrible servitude.[54] As Métraux explains, "Realization arouses in them a vast rage and an ungovernable desire for vengeance. They hurl themselves at their master, kill him, destroy his property and then go in search of their tombs."[55] The story that Hurbon tells about the *zonbi* of *Rosanfe* seems to bear this out. According to the story, a woman who had too many *zonbi* to take care of decided to liberate them by feeding them salt. Once awakened, not only did they abuse her verbally, they also beat her. She subsequently loaded them into her car and "freed them."[56] Those who had been gone a long time had trouble remembering family members.

According to Métraux, rather than seek reintegration into human society, *zonbi* embrace death, a move that seems counterintuitive if one considers it in relation to the rites-of-passage motif whereby those who have endured the liminal state are welcomed back into their community. In the case of *zonbi*, the community would seem to be in the land of the living. However, one thing to consider is that a community of ancestors awaits the newly freed souls. Rather than return to the community of the living (and a life of suffering) after they have conquered the challenges of liminality, *zonbi* join the community of ancestors as a transformed soul. This forward trajectory, rather than one of return, is comparable to the move of African people who became African diasporic as a result of the slave trade. They, like the *zonbi*, were members of communities, suffered exile and trials, and formed or were integrated into other communities in the barracoons, on the slave ships, and across the ocean in the New World. Since the slave trade at its height was a pervasive system that transformed all members of the societies that were affected by it, from the elite to the poor, there was no going back to a time or place that slavery had not touched. This meant that those who returned to their homelands were in danger of being swept into the trade for a second time, or they at least found nothing of their past lives.[57] The only way was forward. Read in this context, the *zonbi*'s "choice" to go forward can be read as reflecting that distant history. At the same time, if we consider tidalectics, that back-and-forth movement that spirals out and the fact that energy cannot be created or destroyed, then it becomes clear that the *zonbi* is not simply going forward but rather, like the peasant woman who performs "that humble repetitive action(n)" from Brathwaite's prose/poem, is always on the journey.

Embodied Liminality

Sociologist Orlando Patterson argues in *Slavery and Social Death* that slavery signaled an end to kinship ties, thus signifying a social death. Drawing on the work of Claude Meillassoux, Patterson explains that, from a structural standpoint, "slavery must be seen as a process involving several transitional phases."[58] First, the "slave is violently uprooted from his milieu. He is desocialized and depersonalized. This process of social negation constitutes the first, essentially external, phase of enslavement. The next phase involves the introduction of the slave into the community of his master, but it involves the paradox of introducing him as a non-being."[59] Indeed, this description echoes the process of zombification whereby the *zonbi*, after being "killed," is violently removed from his or her community; beaten by the *bòkò*, according to Hurbon; and integrated into his or her master's community as a nonbeing, as simply a source of exploited labor.[60]

The enslavement process in turn summons elements of the rites-of-passage ritual, which John Mbiti explains is a symbolic experience of the process of dying and living in the spirit world before being reborn and, as anthropologist Victor Turner explains about the rites-of-passage ritual among the Ndembu, the initiate neophyte is structurally dead during the liminal period.[61] He or she "may be buried, forced to lie motionless in the posture and direction of a customary burial, may be stained black or may be forced to live for a while in the company of masked and monstrous mummers representing, *inter alia*, the dead, or worse still, the un-dead."[62] Turner also relates that, in the rites-of-passage ritual, the neophyte is "allowed to go filthy and identified with the earth, the generalized manner in which every specific matter is rendered down," and referred to by the generic term, "neophyte" or "initiad."[63] In this state, the initiate represents potential. They are neither living nor dead in one aspect, but both living and dead in another.[64] The same can be said of the *zonbi*, which is both and neither living and dead but in-between. Thus, while ostensibly the *zonbi* embodies disfranchisement, it also embodies potential that could be released either chaotically or creatively.

Liminality, a critical component of the rites-of-passage ritual also characterizes zombification with one critical difference, at least on the surface. While in the rites-of-passage ritual, the movement beyond liminality results in the initiate being reintegrated into her community as a new person, in the case of the Haitian *zonbi*, the movement beyond liminality happens when a *zonbi* becomes aware of her denigrated state and then rises up against her master. A grain of salt facilitates this new awareness. However, it is unclear if a *zonbi* can be reintegrated into her society, as there are differing accounts around *zonbi* memory, as I discuss earlier.[65] In any case, as Hurbon remarks, both the real and imaginary aspects of the *zonbi* resonate on both an individual and a collective level.[66]

The rites-of-passage movement beyond liminality can also be read alongside and against historical processes as the cultural process of awakened self- and collective-awareness as people in Africa and the African diaspora remember, confront, and reconcile the slave-trading past and its legacy through avenues such as UNESCO's Slave Route Project, which are meant to facilitate healing. However, like the Haitian *zonbi*, the reintegration of the African diaspora into an African "community" is, as yet, uncertain. Although terms like "brother" and "sister" are used in interviews and on cultural tours in sites such as Ouidah in which members of the diaspora are present, there is a deep psychic and spiritual rupture that haunts and estranges Africa and its diaspora and that mediates and disrupts unmitigated claims of kinship. Without the full recognition of human history that has shaped our contemporary reality and Spirit's workings on that history and our contemporary reality articulated in the remembering and gathering that the Vodou song from the epigraph calls for, then the possibility of the full reintegration or re-membering of Africa to its diaspora and the healing that it would facilitate both in the physical and spiritual realm will remain out of reach.

Zonbi's Legacy

Several scholars have written about zombification as a reflection of and comment on the history of colonization and enslavement as well as the Haitian poor's current subjugation under neoliberal policies as a reinvigoration of zombification that their ancestors experienced under slavery. For example, in "Necropolitics," philosopher and political scientist Achille Mbembe discusses slavery as zombification, although he does not use the term. As he says, "First, in the context of the plantation, the humanity of the slave appears to be the perfect figure of a shadow. Indeed, the slave condition results from a triple loss: loss of home, loss of rights over his or her body, and loss of political status. This triple loss is identical with absolute domination, natal alienation, and social death (expulsion from humanity altogether)."[67] He concludes that "slave life, in many ways, is a form of life-in-death."[68] The enslaved person's life, his existence appearing as a "perfect figure of a shadow," is like a "thing" possessed by another person.[69] Similarly, Karen McCarthy Brown has claimed that in Haiti the *zonbi* is a memory of the loss of control over the self suffered during slavery.[70] Furthermore, echoing Haitian writers and scholars who discuss Haiti's lack of sociopolitical and economic development, René Depestre, the ethnologist and writer, has argued that "it is not by chance that there exists in Haiti the myth of the *zonbi*, that is, of the living dead, the man whose mind and soul have been stolen and who has been left only with the ability to work. . . . The history of colonization is the process of man's zombification."[71] While Depestre views the *zonbi* as a Haitian myth, he sees it as a way to understand slavery and colonialism via a Marxist paradigm. His comment speaks to the physical state of enslavement as well as the psychic and spiritual hold that slavery and colonialism continues to have on members of the diaspora.

Like Métraux, Mbembe, Depestre, and Brown see a *zonbi*'s life in terms that echo the harsh existence of an enslaved person in Saint-Domingue. As such, turning someone into a *zonbi* is the worst thing that someone can do to someone else. Robbing the victim of free will and severing her kinship ties is seen as a reinstatement of slavery. But exploited labor as zombification is not a thing of the past. The fate of the living dead as mindless, soulless workers persists contemporarily as Haiti continues on a path of political, economic, and ecological impoverishment and violence perpetuated both from inside and from outside the country. This can be seen, for example, in, first, President René Préval and, then, Michel Martelly's refrain, "Haiti is open for business," pitching the country to the international community as the perfect environment for cheap factory labor and beach resort vacations.[72]

According to literary scholar Maximilien Laroche, zombification functions in the Haitian imagination "as the most powerful emblem of apathy, anonymity, and loss and the concept of zombification effectively places the Marxist theory of alienation—victimization at the hands of an exploitative external agent—in a specifically Haitian context."[73] After all, as Laroche asks, "What is victimization if not a zombification?"[74] The concept serves as a metaphor to illustrate the various forms of institutional oppression that the Haitian majority have suffered throughout their colonial and postcolonial history as well as contemporarily under neocolonialism. It speaks to both the individual and collective experience of Haiti as "the creature's victimhood, mutism, social disenfranchisement, and infinite capacity for suffering, make it a fitting metaphor for the postcolonial Haitian in particular and the alienated individual in general," according to literary scholar Kaiama L. Glover.[75] Therefore, the story about the process of zombification in Haiti that bears a striking resemblance to the story of the enslavement process in Ouidah and to the way that labor is exchanged contemporarily points to slavery's haunting legacy in its descendants and the precautions that they take to avoid such a fate, which Hurston has written about. In her experience, "Some will keep watch for thirty-six hours after the burial. Some have the bodies cut open insuring real death. Some put a knife in the right hand of the corpse and flex the arm in such a way that it will deal a blow with the knife to whomever disturbs it for the first day or so. The most popular defense is to poison the body."[76] Stories about such rituals, like the *cakatú*, do memory work that is useful to the project of gathering together that which has been scattered both in the distant and not-so-distant past.

The Dezombification of Jean Zombi

Although Glover states that the *zonbi* does not come from a specific myth with an "originary victim-protagonist," Joan Dayan discusses a legendary figure from the revolutionary era that would seem to provide a historical and mythical explanation for the *zonbi*'s origins. According to the myth, in 1804, during Dessalines' massacre of whites, Jean Zombi, a mulatto from Port-au-Prince, earned a reputation for his brutality. Known to be one of the fiercest slaughterers, he was described as having a "vile face," "red hair," and "wild eyes."[77] As the story goes, "He would leave his house, wild with fury, stop a white, then strip him naked."[78] Zombi then led the object of his fury "to the government palace and thrust a dagger in his chest," a gesture that horrified the spectators, including Dessalines.

In the context of postrevolutionary Haiti, Zombi represents several things.[79] For one, he epitomizes liminality and the potential that the *zonbi* represents in his adaptability to various interpretations of Saint-Domingue/Haitian conditions. As Dayan argues, he "crystallizes the crossing not only of spirit and man in Vodun practices [he was a living being who is now a *lwa* of Vodun, part of the Petwo nation[80]], but also the intertwining of black and yellow, African and Creole in the struggle for independence."[81] Zombi also represents the product of the often violent and depraved union of slave masters or overseers with enslaved black women. As such, he embodied the rage and violence to which such unions gave birth. In the newly independent nation, he embodied the ambiguities of systems redefined by changing hopes, fears, and remembering, as he was there when the fledgling republic was taking shape. His behavior may be seen as what Roger Bastide calls "the disappearance, *in toto*, of Fon mythology and its replacement by" a new mythology that identifies the history of the *lwa* with the conduct of its devotees.[82] "As a result we get biographies of the god's horses, complete with miraculous adventures [that] serve as a substitute for the ancestral myths, which have dropped out of the collective memory altogether."[83]

Seemingly in line with the myth that Dayan relates, Maya Deren has argued that the Petwo nation came out of the African diasporic experience.[84] She says, "It is the rage against the evil fate which the African suffered, the brutality of his displacement and his enslavement. It is the violence that rose out of that rage to protest it. It is the crack of the slave-ship sounding constantly, a never-to-be-forgotten ghost."[85] Furthermore, commenting on Depestre's poem entitled "Cap'tain Zombi" from his "The Epiphanies of the Voodoo Gods," Dayan notes that Zombi's inclusion seems to be a contradiction, "For the zombie is not a loa in the Voodoo pantheon, but one of the most macabre figures in Haitian folk belief."[86] Although it would seem that the biography of a Petwo god's horse named Jean Zombi expresses the rage about which Deren speaks, it would also seem that this is impossible given Dayan's declaration. Zombi, rather, is the awakened conscience of the enslaved laborer. He represents the destructively creative potential (another contradiction) that lies dormant in the *zonbi.*

Doris Garraway complicates this picture of the historical origins of the *zonbi* in her discussion of the 1697 novel *Le Zombi du Grand-Pérou, ou la comtesse de Cocagne* by Pierre Corneille Blessebois. In her discussion of the female character, the Comtesse de Cocagne, who believes that she has been granted the ability to "do the zombi" (*faire le zombi*) by someone she believes to be a sorcerer in Guadeloupe, Garraway remarks that what is striking about the novel is not only that it may well contain the earliest appearance of the word *zombi* in any European language but also the comtesse's imitation of the zombi as brutal and destructive.[87] Illuminating the Creole nature of the *zonbi* that is implied in the brutal character of Jean Zombi, Garraway states that there are at least three distinct occult systems present in the colonial system that could have interacted to produce the figure of the zombi: European, Aja-Fon, Kongo, as well as Carib—a confluence that emerged from what Dayan characterizes as Caribbean slavery's "peculiar brand of sensuous domination" and violence.[88]

In *The Spirits and the Law*, historian Kate Ramsey discusses William Seabrook's treatment of *zonbi* in his book as a comment on the not-so-distant history of U.S.-owned companies' exploitation of Haitian laborers.[89] Recounting a story that he heard from his informant, a landowning farmer and tax collector named Constant Polynice, Seabrook claims that in 1918 a team of *zonbi* worked for months in the newly opened Haytian American Sugar Company (HASCO), an American-owned sugar company with factories, railways, and plantations located on the Cul-de-Sac and Léogâne plains. When the company offered a bonus on the wages of new workers, a man named Ti Joseph of Colombier approached HASCO with a "band of ragged creatures who shuffled along behind him, staring dumbly, like people walking in a daze."[90] Apparently the men were actually *zonbi* under his control. He and his wife, Croyance, were enriched financially for a number of months until the wife unwittingly gave the workers a piece of candy with salt in it.[91] While Seabrook expresses surprise that this wholesome "chunk of Hoboken" should be associated with sorcery, Ramsey points out that HASCO was a highly likely object of sorcery for a few reasons: 1918 was the year that HASCO opened and produced its first harvest, the year protests began over the *kòve* (corvée) system of forced labor reintroduced by the occupying U.S. marines. In June of that year, a new U.S.-sponsored constitution, which allowed foreigners to own land, went into effect with U.S. Marine enforcement. This story of the HASCO *zonbi* may be read in several ways, one of which is that Polynice, whom Seabrook describes as sly and often amusing, is a mythologized rendering of the reality that Haitians saw unfolding around them whereby peasants were disfranchised by the destruction of the *demwatye* (sharecropping) system and the subsequent complete exploitation of their labor for others' benefit.[92]

The *demwatye* system, which existed prior to the Marine occupation and the arrival of HASCO, while problematic, had its merits with the landowner having access to free farm labor for crops such as sugar cane to be sold in exchange for the sharecropper being able to harvest three-quarters of the food crop that he interplanted. Not only did the sharecroppers control the distribution of staple crops, which yielded income, but they also had food throughout the year. In *Migration and Vodou*, Karen Richman tells the story of one such landowner, Joseph Lacome, "a cosmopolitan coffee-sugar magnate" who, through manipulation of the contradictions between the meanings of land ownership in the official legal code and in the customary system of law, managed to acquire vast amounts of land in Léogâne. Through his "lawful racketeering of the judicial system," Lacome managed to acquire a good portion of small landowners' land, making them landless and turning them into sharecroppers. According to Richman, "The oral tradition gives the impression of unlimited land to work and a Joseph Lacome so desperate to recruit farm labor that he personally visited the peasant homesteads offering money to residents to meet their planting requirements for sharecropping his lands."[93] While the *demwatye* system seemed to have worked for those invested in it, in 1916 the West Indies Management and Consultation Company, hired by HASCO, labeled the arrangement "uneconomic" and "inefficient" and brought it to an abrupt end. Following the recommendations of the management company, HASCO leased almost all of Lacome's lands in order to cultivate the monocrop, sugar cane. Lacome in turn dismissed all of the sharecroppers, leaving HASCO to subsequently rehire them as irrigation canal diggers, tree cutters, and sugar cane cutters. Although these workers were paid well in the beginning, soon corrupt Haitian lower-level management began cheating the workers out of their wages, using the money they stole to build their own private sugar mills. Laurent Dubois rightly remarks that Haitian farmers recognized this period as a profound threat to their sustained and cherished autonomy," and, as Richman avers, "for the increasingly desperate wage workers, accumulation of property . . . by a corrupt, every man for himself Haitian lover-level management was a cruelly tangible symbol of exploitation."[94] It is this exploitation that comes through in the story of Polynice and his wife, representative of the Haitian low-level management workers who were also the faces of "the occupation administration's labor policies in favor of capitalized companies . . . like HASCO."[95]

The threat to the peasants' self-sufficiency came both from within as well as outside as elite landowners like Joseph Lacome leased their lands to the American company, which in turn modernized production and allowed them to pay their labor force one-fifth of the wages they were paid for the same labor in Cuba.[96] As such, Polynice's story may also have served as a warning to not only Seabrook but also his American readership that, once the Haitian people got tired of being exploited, they would revolt, which is exactly what happened during the Caco rebellion, which lasted off and on from 1915 to 1919.[97]

Thus, while the *zonbi* has been commonly read as a being devoid of life and, consequently, of potential, I would argue, as Glover does, that the *zonbi* also represents dormant potential. If we think about zombification metaphorically, as the dissolution of personhood or a liminal period, then the state of zombification—a state of transition—can be seen as possessing transformative potential.[98] Glover notes, "While the zombie's subjugation is profound it is not necessarily definitive."[99] I would add, nor is it complete. Glover continues: "Rather, the zombie is a creature within whom coexists an utter powerlessness and an enduring chance for rebirth. *It incarnates a condition of perpetual becoming*."[100] This condition of perpetual becoming that the *zonbi* incarnates can also be attributed to the Haitian majority contemporarily who continue to resist their subjugation.

This embodied potential comes through in Mbembe's remark that, in spite of the terror and the symbolic sealing off of the enslaved person, that person maintains alternative perspectives of time, work, and self. Although the enslaved person is treated as if he or she were a mere tool and instrument of production, he or she "nevertheless is able to draw almost any object, instrument, language, or gesture into a performance and then stylize it. Breaking with uprootedness and the pure world of things of which he or she is but a fragment, the slave is able to demonstrate the protean capabilities of the human bond through music and the very body that was supposedly possessed by another."[101] While Mbembe calls this potential a paradoxical element of the plantation world, it is logical—in fact, inevitable—if we "think of identity as a 'production' which is never complete, always in process, and always constituted within, not outside, representation," as Hall suggests.[102] In discussing the black Caribbean identity in particular, this paradox seems inevitable as Hall argues that black Caribbean identities are "'framed' by two axes or vectors, simultaneously operative: the vector of similarity and continuity; the vector of difference and rupture. Caribbean identities always have to be thought of in terms of the dialogic relationship between these two axes. The one gives us some grounding in, some continuity with, the past. The second reminds us that what we share is precisely the experience of a profound discontinuity."[103] Like the *zonbi*, the black Caribbean subject is always of and outside of, in and between, as she negotiates these axes, continuity and rupture, that equally constitute her being. The *zonbi* nonetheless, has the potential to perform her way out of her zombification. This can be accomplished through the "humble repetitive action(n)" of ritual that both Brathwaite and Brown remind us bring the body, mind, and spirit into communion to facilitate transformation.[104] It also erupts from time to time in violent revolution, as is the way of the *zonbi* once she tastes "salt." The world has witnessed this violent uprising at various times in Haitian history, as I have discussed. Jean Zombi, the mythical deliverer of violent justice, embodies the two axes clashing in one body; the swirl of uncontainable energy that such a confluence engenders and is overseen by Legba—creativity within the chaos.

Both alive and dead, neither alive nor dead, the *zonbi* always retains the possibility, albeit slim, of reclaiming his essence and in this sense serves at once as a reflection of the Haitian poor's extreme misery and their inextinguishable fire, a destructive but also generative energy. While we can argue that much of Haitian reality is expressed in this tension—"the latent presence of an element of hope in every situation of despair"[105]—I would also posit that Jean Zombi embodies the violent uprising that the zombified creatures represent once they get the taste of salt that is reputed to liberate them from their alienated state and makes them conscious of their "terrible servitude."[106] This realization rouses in them a vast rage and an ungovernable desire for vengeance.

The killing and destroying of the master who would work the *zonbi* until final death's sweet release that Métraux posits follows her awakening has manifested itself on numerous occasions in Haitian history, one of the most revolutionary of which is the start of the rebellion that would end in the island nation's liberation. Another occasion was the scorched-earth campaign that the revolutionaries practiced in order to drive the French from their land in 1803. Still another notable moment of *déchoukaj* was in 1986 during the mass uprising to rid the country of the Duvaliers and those whom they viewed as their agents of repression: the Tonton Macoutes and the now-defunct military that, as an outgrowth of the Haitian Garde, was an effective tool in the repression of the Haitian population.[107]

What the Story of Jean Zombi Reveals

The story of Zombi "arrived" at a liminal moment in Haiti's history, the transitional time between its status as a French colony and an independent black nation in a world ruled by whites. It is an example of the violent potential of the awakened *zonbi* as the war, the scorched-earth campaign, and 1986 *déchoukaj* are also examples. The new nation was outside of the global order—exiled—but struggling to get back in. Zombi thus personifies the violent collective reaction to such an unjust fate—to strike out at the people who had excluded him. His actions would not have been possible under slavery. His license to first humiliate and then kill a white man with impunity thus marks a short-lived revolutionary period in power relations between the former colonizer and the formerly colonized.

Zombi also embodies the founding of a nation that was steeped in the memory of the horrors that its new citizens had suffered as enslaved workers. At the same time, its leaders lived with the new threat of possible invasion by France and the hope that the nation would be accepted and respected as a valuable member of the world economy. Since then Haiti has repeatedly fallen short of realizing its dream of freedom as the United States invaded the country, first in 1915 and then again between September 1994 and March 1995 in a mission called Operation Uphold Democracy. The operation was replaced by the UN Mission to Haiti under the command of U.S. president Bill Clinton, followed by Operation New Horizons in March 1996. Although the tenure of the UN Mission to Haiti ended, UN forces with the U.S. forces in command remained in Haiti until 2000. Since 2004 the United States has been part of a multinational military force called MINUSTAH, the United Nations Stabilization Mission in Haiti, whose directive has been to maintain order following the second ouster of Jean-Bertrand Aristide in February of that year, the year of the independent nation's bicentennial anniversary.[108] All of these interventions were carried out with the United States showing nothing but scorn for Haitian cultural systems, conflating any dysfunctional system with their misunderstanding of Haitian spiritual beliefs.[109] Nonetheless, the power of that revolutionary moment—a liminal period—remains alive as many Haitians cite their origins in revolution as a source of pride even though the majority continue to toil as severely exploited workers for the tiny elite class, in internationally owned companies in their own homeland, and in other Caribbean, North American and South American countries.[110] They refuse to be subjected to conditions of zombification just as their distant ancestors had refused, choosing instead to periodically place a bit of salt on their tongues in order to manifest their awakened state more fully.

Minkisi and *Pakèt Kongo*

In this final section of the chapter, I turn to the Kôngo to discuss the power object known in several western Bantu languages as *nkisi* (plur. *minkisi*) and read it tidalectically in its manifestation in Haiti as the *pakèt kongo*. Like the *bociọ* from Dahomey, *minkisi* can be read as offering insight into the transatlantic slave trade and slavery, although they predate them. This ability to do so points to the richness embedded in the material culture that makes it transcendent, able to comment and reflect on various moments in time and space as well as cross oceans and transform as those who deploy them transform.

Minkisi are primarily containers or any object that can contain spiritually charged substances. Some are used in divination by *nganga* (healers, diviners, mediators) for a number of purposes, including healing or to ensure success in hunting, trade, or sex. While they can be simple containers like gourds, shells, bundles, or graves, *minkisi* can also take the form of anthropomorphic or zoomorphic wooden statues. The form that is of interest for my purposes is the *nkisi nkondi*, believed to work as hunters that pursue witches, thieves, adulterers, and wrongdoers by night. Most such *minkisi* are "activated by driving nails, blades and other pieces of iron into them to provoke them to deliver similar injuries to the guilty," a system that we find, again, with the *cakatú* among the Fon (Fig. 3).[111]

Robert Farris Thompson recognizes *nkisi* as a "strategic object in black Atlantic art, said to effect healing and other phenomena."[112] According to Nsemi Isaki, who is from the Congo, *nkisi* is

the name of the thing we use to help when that person is sick and from which we obtain health; the name refers to leaves and medicines combined together. . . . It is also called *nkisi* because there is one to protect the human soul and guard it against illness for whoever is sick and wishes to be healed. Thus an *nkisi* is also something which hunts down illness and chases it away from the body.

An *nkisi* is also a chosen companion, in whom all people find confidence. It is a hiding place for people's souls, to keep and compose in order to preserve life.[113]

Minkisi can be visually compared to the *bociǫ* as they also feature ingredients such as cords, teeth, special earth, and water. They also "work" for those for whom they are made and can be found as far east as Tanzania. Reflecting a similar usage as *bociǫ* and *bo* in slave era Dahomey, the description card in the exhibit of *minkisi* at the Smithsonian National Museum of African Art describes the purpose of *minkisi* among groups affected by the trade in East Africa: "Tying or closing off is an aesthetic strategy employed by healers in the related Zingua and Shambala communities of Tanzania to prevent the spread of negative powers. This practice is likely related to the history of slavery in East Africa where enslaved men and women were forced from their land bound . . ."[114] Also, like the *bociǫ*, evolving as the sociopolitical context changed, with the increased ravages of disease, famine, and slave raiding in late-nineteenth-century Congo, the functional specificity of *minkisi* to battle both concrete and unseen dangers increased, a change that reflected, as Stephan Palmié suggests, that objects like the *minkisi* (and I would add *bociǫ*) "concretize conceptions about relations between human and cosmic spheres."[115] As such, these objects are signs in and of history, providing clues into the multiple ways that people have responded to and have reflected and commented on their worldly experience vis-à-vis the "spiritist doctrines" to which they subscribe.[116]

Again, *minkisi* resemble the *bociǫ* or *bo* in the kinds of materials that compose them and their means of activation. They also evoke the image of the *zonbi* in their dependence on the harnessing of a soul. *Minkisi* combine what Palmié calls "heterogeneous objects" or medicines (*bilongo*) and a soul to give it life and power. These combined objects "are assigned specific symbolic valence in relation to each other and together acquire a 'systemic' character."[117] According to Thompson

Spirit-embodying materials include cemetery earth—considered one with the spirit of a buried person—or equivalents such as white clay (*impemba*), taken from riverbeds, or powdered camwood, the reddish color which traditionally signals transition and mediation to Bakongo.

Spirit-embodying materials are usually wrapped or concealed in a charm, but such objects as mirrors or pieces of porcelain attached to the exterior of the *nkisi* may also signify power—the flash and arrest of the spirit.

The vital spark or soul within the spirit-embodying medicine may be, according to the Bakongo, an ancestor come back from the dead to serve the owner of the charm, or a victim of witchcraft, captured in the charm by the owner and forced to do his bidding for the good of the community (if the owner is generous and responsible) or for selfish ends (if he is not).[118]

The *bilongo* are activated substances that include minerals from the land of the dead, items chosen for their names, and metaphorical ingredients. "The most important minerals include kaolin, white clay associated with the world of the dead, and red ocher, whose red color refers symbolically to blood and the danger even as it signifies mediation of the powers of the dead to the living for both affliction and cure."[119] Certain leaves and seeds will be included for their names as puns on the attributes of the *nkisi,* and metaphorical materials include the heads of poisonous snakes, the claws of birds of prey, and nets, all of which suggest the power to attack, to produce sickness, or to cause death.[120]

Minkisi also share many attributes in common with *bociọ,* such as the necessity of an accumulation of cords, blades, nails, mirrors, hides, and other materials in order for them to be powerful. Without it, the figures are meaningless.[121] Like the *bociọ*'s patina, the *nkisi*'s form is a record of its use.[122] Finally, like the *bociọ, minkisi* are empowered objects that use the soul of another being to do the bidding of their owner. In other words, similar to *bociọ* and *zonbi, minkisi* work for their owners. Like the *bòkò* who works with both hands, the *nganga,* the expert who empowers the *nkisi,* may use the *nkisi* to support the health of the community or undermine it. The singular figure has a dual purpose, which may be deployed either way, depending on whose hands into which it falls. In this sense, the figure is not good or bad. It just is. In what art historian Zdenka Volavkova calls an "antithetical way," the *nkisi*'s function was and is ambiguous and may be both a "benefactor and malefactor."[123] Its beneficence or malevolence comes from its usage.

We can make the connection between material culture in Dahomey and the Kôngo in its deployment in the diaspora as the *nkisi*'s counterpart found across the water in the *pakèt kongo* in Haiti. *Pakèt kongo* are spirit-activated healing bundles that consist of curative herbs wrapped in cloth crisscrossed with satin ribbons held in place with straight pins and topped with feathers.[124] They are also used as protective amulets to bring wealth, health, and happiness to their owners. Thompson rightly calls the *pakèt kongo* of Haiti an ingenious reformulation of *nkisi* charms.[125] However, instead of cord, they are wrapped in broad silk ribbon secured with pins, and instead of ancestral cloth, silk. Like the *nkisi mangaaka* ("the executioner"), which uses nails, the pins that secure the silk ribbons of the *pakèt kongo* emphasizes the capture of forces that guard the households that own such charms.

Pakèt kongo also have other things in common with *minkisi*. For example, both have protective or medicinal materials concealed and wrapped in bags, cloths, or other containers located in the belly of an anthropomorphic figure. Some *pakèt kongo* are provided with mirrors like their Kôngo counterparts.[126] They are also animated similarly, with the *nkisi* being activated with explosions of gunpowder and the *pakèt kongo* being passed over open flames to activate the entrapped spirit. The connection may also be seen on the western side of the continent in the way that *bocio* are also "heated up" with pepper and alcohol used in its activation.[127] Finally, Métraux was informed during his ethnographic research that *pakèt kongo* were used to treat people who were ill, although the treatments that the ill received were ambiguous.[128] Métraux precedes his use of the term, "treatment" with the statement that he had never heard the functions of *pakèt kongo* "clearly described."[129] This evasiveness of the *oungan* with whom he consults or ambivalence around the uses of *pakèt kongo*, like *minkisi*, may speak to its duality. While the object itself might be neutral, its usage in treatments to heal or to harm, whether for collective or individual health, bring it into the realm of Marasa Twa. It is neither good nor bad but embodies the potential of both in one object, the third element.

Volavkova speaks of different forms of a particular kind of *nkisi* called *nkosi*, with the female one being a sack and the male one being an anthropomorphic figure. The gendered *nkosi* may have been transmitted but transformed in Haiti, where the *pakèt kongo* can also be identified as female or male representing what Thompson calls "visual creolization of traditional *nkisi* forms."[130] While in the Kôngo, the male and female *minkisi* take on different forms, with the male one being anthropomorphic and the female being a sack, the *minkisi* in the diaspora are both "sacks."[131] They resemble the human form, with those that have a vertical stem being male and those that are short and squat with "arms" akimbo being female.[132] *Bisimbi,* Kôngo spirits of the dead, are believed in part to preside over the making of *pakèt kongo* and, according to Donald Cosentino, are consecrated to spirits Simbi Makaya and Ren Kongo, proclaiming their Kôngo identity.[133] They are also considered "guards" capable of exciting and heating up the deities on their owner's behalf.

Haiti's Spirited Political Origins

To return to the beginning, Rachel Beauvoir-Dominique and Eddie Lubin who, in 1999, conducted oral historical interviews about the Bwa Kayiman ceremony at various sites throughout Haiti, highlight the layered religious significance of the dates of August 14 and 15. They

> point out that 14 August is the eve of the annual celebration of Ezili Kawoulo, a spirit who is "before all the appanage of secret societies and is popularly believed to have spiritually embodied the woman who partnered with Boukman at the ceremony "all the night of the 14th, which is to say until the 15th." That night, 14 August, was also the eve of one of the most important religious holidays in Saint-Domingue's calendar—the feast day of Notre-Dame de l'Assomption, patron saint of the colony, after the cathedral in Cap-Français was named in 1718. The feast day was significant to many enslaved and free people of color in the colony, and among enslaved Kongolese Catholics the cult of the Virgin was particularly strong. . . . 15 August is also the occasion for honoring Kongo *lwa* at the historic *lakou* Nan Soukri, in the area of Gonaïves.[134]

In marking the spiritual significance of the dates on which the ceremony that inaugurated the Haitian Revolution was held, Kate Ramsey observes that the oral historians remind us of the inextricable relationship between the political history of Haiti and its spiritual heritage.[135]

We can see this inextricable connection in other times and places in Haiti's inaugural history. Like Ogou, who rode Dessalines and spoke through him when the latter made his famous pronouncement on the day that he declared Haiti's independence, the *lwa* made themselves known in the supplicants that Descourtilz identified on the battlefield. These possessions are not recorded as such in history books because they were not recognized as such. However, if we consider the description that is given of insurgents during the revolution—read through the lens of the spiritual systems that, at the time of the revolution, inhabited the island and its enslaved population—then the workings of Ogou become recognizable. For example, there are stories of "slaves advancing on Le Cap" and troops under the order of Saint-Domingue's governor, Philibert François Rouxel de Blanchelande, firing "three times but without the least effect" against the insurgents, who were wearing "a kind of light mattress stuffed with cotton as a vest to prevent the bullets from penetrating" and who "thus, stood the fire without shewing any signs of fear."[136] Other insurgents reportedly suffocated "the cannon of the enemy with their arms and bodies, and so routed them."[137] As Descourtilz writes, although at first many insurgents did not know how to use the cannons they captured, loading them improperly, they soon learned. One group took control of a battery along the coast, and when a French ship fired on the battery to destroy them, they braved a barrage of 250 cannon shots. They then used the cannon balls that had landed around them to fire back at the ship, which was seriously damaged before its crew managed to sail it away.[138] Cannons, bullets, and firearms are all the domain of Ogou, the god of iron, who supported the insurgents' mastery over these tools of war as they fought for their freedom. Perhaps seeking fortification in the amulets, the insurgents invoked the power of the invisible world in deploying the materials that were included in their African counterparts—bones, earth from cemeteries, clay, hair, and other organic and inorganic matter—to empower the objects. As empowered objects, the amulets, like their African counterparts and complements, *bo*, can be interpreted cosmologically as *pwen* (points), "mediating protective grace between the living and the dead."[139] In other words, as living beings, insurgents used the amulets as *pwen* on which to focus their liberatory aspirations.

We can return again to the beginning of the chapter, which opens with Descourtilz and P's observations about the amulets that they identified insurgents wearing. As *sèvitè* are believed to become the gods who ride them, then it is perfectly reasonable to interpret the enslaved people who Descourtilz described as empowered gods, excited and "heated" up *lwa*. The insurgent who P describes in his memoire as once caught and condemned to death, "furiously [reviling] his captors through laughter, song, and joke, [jeering] at them in mockery" before "[giving] the signal for his own execution with neither fear nor complaint" was not a madman. With the insurgent's physical death imminent, perhaps, as he does at the end of Vodou ceremonies, Gede arrived to have a little fun, reveling in his spiritual victory even if the war in the worldly realm had not yet been won. Echoing Brown's assertion that "no matter which of the Vodou spirits is guest of honor at a ceremony, Gede usually comes at the end to provide light-hearted fun," Katherine Smith avers in "Gede Rising: Haiti in the Age of *Vagabondaj*" that "Gede's possession performance could be . . . described as *vagabondaj,* or disorderly conduct."[140] Thus, while it was Ogou and Ezili Dantò who were "the guests of honor" on the battlefield, it was Gede who made his appearance at the end of this particular ceremony/confrontation through this lone warrior, dancing in his head and, recalling the words of Leah Gordon, "laughing back at the enemy."[141] Gede was there ready to perform his duty, to *balanse* the struggle between the would-be colonizer and the already liberated worker, proclaiming his freedom. Led by Spirit, we understand that what these writers were witnessing were physical *and* spiritual warriors who combined their relationship with their ancestors, the *lwa,* their knowledge of the protective and aggressive (when necessary) power objects from Dahomey and the Kôngo in the diaspora, to construct *garde-corps, bo,* or amulets in Saint-Domingue, all in the service of resisting their zombification. While the amulets summoned the power of the ancestors and the *lwa* as protection from harm in the metaphysical realm, in the worldly realm the insurgents also carried pamphlets on the *Rights of Man* (itself perhaps a kind of amulet as many enslaved workers did not know how to read), and tinder and phosphate of lime with which to wage war against their oppressors.

This confluence of spiritual knowledge that made its way into the diaspora in the form of protections, such as the *bociọ* and *bo* as well as those with polyvalent uses such as *minkisi,* were creolized, a patina of the African diasporic experience added to them so that original uses shifted and transformed while recalling their original roles. As such, materials that stood for one thing in Africa transformed as the conditions of supplicants changed in the diaspora. Healers began "working with both hands" as the hell of slavery forged new systems of relation and a need for new ways to deal with them. Just as the deities shifted, transformed, and transmogrified to become the *lwa* in the diaspora, these material *pwen* reenact "a complex history which not only reflects the bodily assaults of slavery," but the ability of the dispossessed to change and adapt the tools that they have at hand as a means of speaking *and* fighting back against persistent disempowering systems that seek to zombify them.[142]

3

Boc̣iọ, Nkisi, Legba, Ogun, and Ghede
across the Water

Ugliness is a disease.

—LeGrace Benson

The *bocị̣ọ* and *nkisi*, two power objects, may have found their way across the water to Grand Rue in downtown Port-au-Prince.[1] In this chapter I continue with my exploration of these transformed but still empowered objects vis-à-vis epistemologies that I argue also made their way—but transformed—across the water. I propose that traces of the *bocị̣ọ* and *nkisi* that come through in the work of Atis Rezistans, a collective of Grand Rue artists, are evidence of a "habit of attention" as LeGrace Benson defines it: "persisting modes of attending to the world . . . preserved from Lan Ginée and manifest in much of the painting and sculpture of Kreyòl-speaking Haitians."[2] I also argue that the gods who manifest visually in the recycled art by several members of Atis Rezistans evoke those from Dahomey who made their way into the diaspora to Saint-Domingue/Haiti. Finally, I propose that the artists' approach to their work is reflective of a memory of origins from a Bakôngo cosmological orientation that does not see the cemetery as "a final resting place" but as a "door (*mwelo*) between two worlds."[3]

Haitian art straddles two worlds, owing a debt to the ancient African Atlantic aesthetic of appropriation and assemblage. Nonetheless, we must also recognize, as the artists insist, that their work is contemporary rather than simply "folkloric African continuities," products of the diasporic experience.[4] It is these complementary tidalectical spirits—West, Central West African, and diasporic—that this chapter argues are at work in the art from Grand Rue. As is true throughout this text, the chapter explores the interworkings of the dead, the living, and the unborn; invisible and visible worlds; the past, the present, and the future that is facilitated by the tidalectical relationship that persists between Africa and its diaspora.[5]

Benson instructs that, in Haiti, nothing is ever totally discarded. She remarks, "Stacks of hubcaps or universal joints: lengths of bamboo, ragged planks torn in a hurricane; dark computer screens and silent radios; lightless lamps and toneless telephones; shoes, hats, shirts and dresses: all lie ready at hand for some truck repair, the framing for a house, clothing to be worn again. Someone will spot the thing from among the resistant rags and shards. Whatever defies disintegration becomes another state of being."[6] The artists of Grand Rue have taken this ability to salvage to a new level, giving new life to something that is perceived as dead.

Sculptor André Eugene, along with fellow artists Jean Hérard Celeur and Guyodo, founded *Atis Rezistans* in early 2000.[7] Leah Gordon has remarked about the group that they are "the new heirs of a radical and challenging arts practice that has reached down through both modernist and post-modernist arts practice" with work that is "transformative on many different allegorical levels while transforming the "wreckage of art," and bringing "disunity to harmony."[8] Her assessment is echoed by Eugene who, during an interview, related to me that the atelier got started after someone dumped old cars in a nearby soccer field. The rotting carcasses of cars were not only another blight on the already litter-strewn neighborhood but they also deprived people who lived there of the space that they needed to engage in one of their favorite past times: playing soccer. He got the idea to use the old metal to make art—both a taking-away and a gathering-together—to create something new, thus accomplishing two things in one bold move.

The art collective that Eugene helped found, Atis Rezistans, has had several international shows; has been featured in numerous journals, magazines, and catalogs; and has hosted to date four Ghetto Biennale conferences, all of which have garnered strong international attendance and recognition. The artists are prolific, and almost every inch of Eugene's atelier is taken up with art pieces by members of the collective as well as those by Timoun Rezistans, the youth arm of the collective, and by various people from the community.

Bocịo across the Water

Suzanne Preston Blier posits that, as a "garbage heap of matter," the *bocịo* sculpture is not an object of "sublime beauty."[9] However, it has the ability to powerfully jar sensibilities and confront silent spaces. Furthermore, she remarks that certain African-derived cultures living in the Americas create similar works.[10] I propose that the works by members of Atis Rezistans who have been making art from discarded car parts and other refuse can also be compared to "garbage heaps of matter." However, I would contend that they are, in fact, works of sublime beauty that also jar the viewer's sensibilities. In addition, they comment on and reflect contemporary crises of spirit that Haiti—as part of the African diaspora—faces.

Many of the works use the bones of the dead, which adds to their visual and visceral power. The incorporation of those who have died into the creative works by the living also speaks to the *marasa*-ness of the artist and their artwork in the way that the old and young are connected. In other words, conceptualized from within Vodou, the children make their ancestors live again in the way that they incorporate them into their art. As Eugene is fond of saying about the skulls in his art, "When this man was alive he could not travel; now he travels all over the world." This twinning vis-à-vis facilitation of revitalization in turn denotes a tidalectical relationship between the children and their ancestors, both those on the same land and those across the water.

Twinning across the Water

Twinning on the same land and across the water can be seen in the *bocịo* and *bo* figures of Dahomey that are joined with the *nkisi* of the Kôngo to become something new, transformed, and innovative while also looking back to sites of origin in Haiti. In "Vodun: West African Roots of Vodou" Blier describes the wealth of materials that cover the *bocịo* and *bo*. These materials include

> cords, iron, skeletal matter, locks, pegs, beads, cloth, gourds, leaves, earth, fur, and feathers, which individually and in combination activate the sculpture and convey key concerns addressed within. Most such objects also emphasize attributes of binding, knotting, or piercing as a means of promoting their larger empowerment

and protection roles. In figural works, the body often serves as a symbolic frame, with particular anatomical parts being bound in cord or pierced with pegs in conjunction with specific problems or desires of the user. Anger for example, is conveyed through wrapping a cord around or placing a peg in the stomach, fears of death are suggested by a peg in the neck, loss of memory by a peg in the forehead, binding or pegging the arms alludes to the diminishment of one's strength.[11]

The *nkisi mangaaka* ("the executioner") shares characteristics with the *bociǫ*. Like all *minkisi, minkisi mangaaka* are empowered objects with medicines added to them. The medicines whose names and other associations suggest the powers to be attributed to the *nkisi* are sealed with resin in the pack behind the mirror on the belly of the figure, and in the beard. The mirror is a divination device to identify witches. It also features nails, which are driven into the object after the client identifies each one with a task and then licks to activate its power (Figs. 4 and 5).[12]

The first piece by Eugene, *Dr. Zozo* (Fig. 6), uses materials that may be attributable to *bociǫ, bo,* or *minkisi,* including skeletal matter (in this case, a skull, where people's spiritual power is believed to rest). Like their African counterparts, they use iron in the form of coils while also invoking the power of technology in the form of a computer monitor. In addition, cloth and rubber bind the large erect phallus that is attached to the cadaver in the wooden coffin that sits in front of the doctor whose stethoscope is attached to the phallus. The phallus is topped off with a bright red head, the color of the god of war, Ogou. His sexual prowess also invokes Gede, as here "dead men achieve erections."[13] Even though the man is dead and ostensibly buried, his phallus remains erect, ready to do battle, to create new life.

Eugene manifests in the diaspora what Bruno Gilli has commented on in regard to African Vodun, that "*vodu* . . . is inexplicable in itself [but] helps to explain the realities around it."[14] His sculptures reflect a kind of "ritual recollection" from both West and Central West Africa in the phallus being covered in nails, reminiscent of the pegs that coincide with the user's problems or desires in sculptures from Dahomey.[15] They also reflect a habit of attention that recalls the *nkisi* of the Kôngo in the use of nails as activated materials that will do the bidding of the owner, in this case,

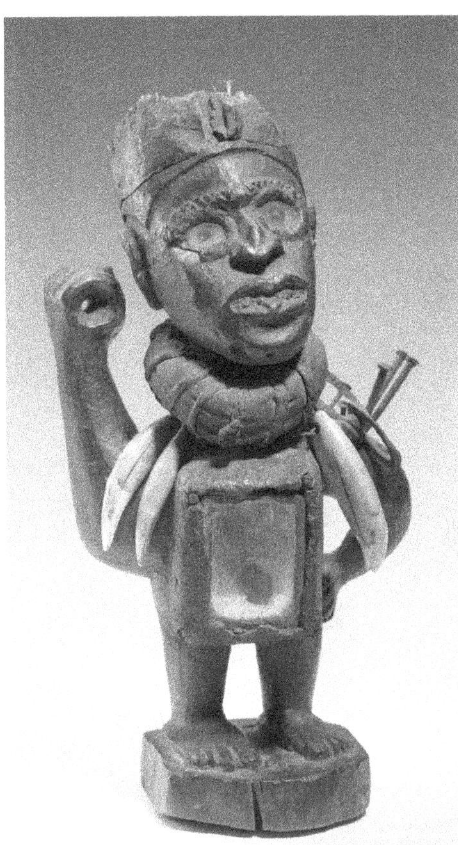

Figure 4. Male figure (*nkisi nkondi*). Democratic Republic of the Congo. Late nineteenth–early twentieth century. Wood, mirror, iron, plant fiber, cloth, leopard teeth, pigment, nails, resin. Bequest of Eliot Elisofon. Photo: Franko Khoury; courtesy of National Museum of African Art, Smithsonian Museum.

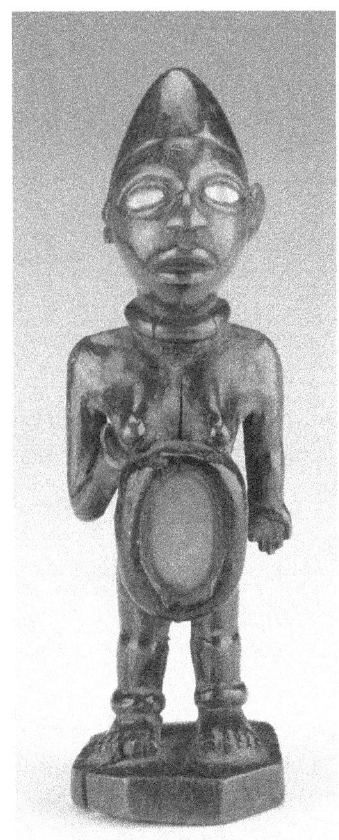

Figure 5. Female figure (*nkisi*). Democratic Republic of the Congo. Late nineteenth–early twentieth century. Wood, resin, pigment, mirror, glass. Gift of Allan Frumkin. Photo: Franko Khoury; courtesy of National Museum of African Art, Smithsonian Museum.

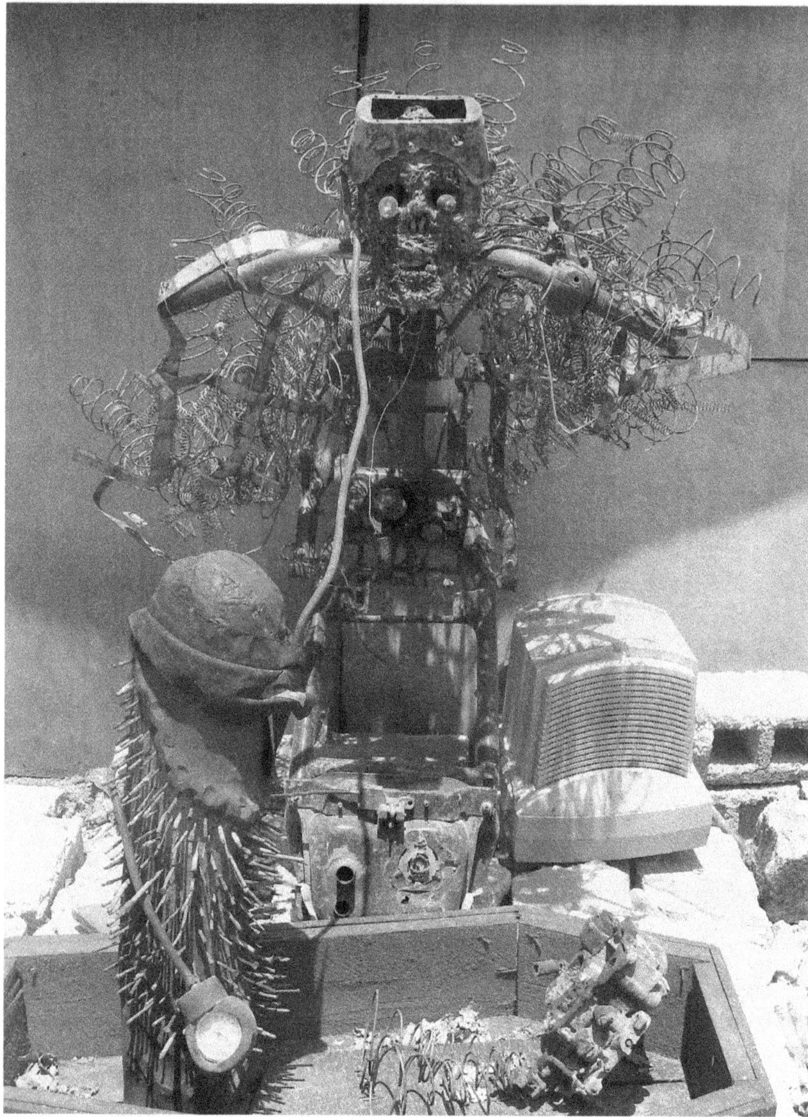

Figure 6. *Dr. Zozo* by André Eugene, 2002, Atelier Atis Rezistans, Grand Rue, Port-au-Prince, Haiti. Photo: Toni Pressley-Sanon, 2009; permission granted by André Eugene.

perhaps to aid in issues around sex and procreation. In explaining the prominence of genitalia in his sculptures, Eugene remarks, "I put dicks and pussies in all my art because I love life. When you put them together they bring you life."[16] During my interview with him I used the French terms, "*pénis*" and "*vagin*" to ask the question about the objects. However,

Eugene's correction, using the Kreyòl terms *"zozo"* and *"koko,"* reflects an ideological positioning that places his conceptualization of his work squarely in Haiti. At the same time, his comment reflects Bakôngo memory, which Robert Farris Thompson notes extends back more than seven hundred years. As Thompson comments about the Bakôngo, "Their art is full of information, precepts, and admonitions communicating abiding concerns with moral continuity and renaissance, healing, [and] justice."[17] It "encodes messages of continuity, beauty, love and law"—and, I would add in the case of Haiti, life.[18] Eugene's orientation toward these principles is manifest through representation from a Vodou episteme: the large phallus; a symbol of Legba, Master of the Crossroads in Africa; and the Gede, a family of spirits in the diaspora that presides over death but also healing and rebirth.

Legba and Gede across the Water

In Eugene's atelier, it seems that both Legba and Gede reign supreme, and it is with them that I begin my discussion of gods and cultural forms that have crossed the ocean. Two of the sculptures that I discuss initially are from Benin Republic, and the last is from Haiti. When looking at the sculptures (Figs. 6, 7, 8), the viewer immediately notes that all three have an erect phallus in common. Whether it is a new fashioning of incongruous objects of refuse, a sculpted mound of earth, or a sculpted statue, they all feature this symbol of fecundity.

In the earthen form of Legba from Ouidah found in Figure 7, there is ritual power behind his material representation. Before the mound is made, a hole is dug in the ground into which is placed a terracotta pot containing materials relating at once to *vodun* power and the human needs that the *vodun* helps to fulfill. The materials enclosed usually include water (from a sacred spring in most cases), food, medicinal leaves, bits of cloth, and beads. The pot and its assembled materials are then empowered through offerings and buried in the hole. The elements buried in the ground, the fertility dance, and the phallus all come together to create a powerful energy that embodies creative power and potential.[19]

There are similarities between the earthen representation of Legba in Dahomey and the *nkisi* of the Kôngo. For example, *minkisi* are constructed with cemetery earth, powdered camwood, white clay taken from riverbeds, and leaves, each of which has a spiritual significance. They are

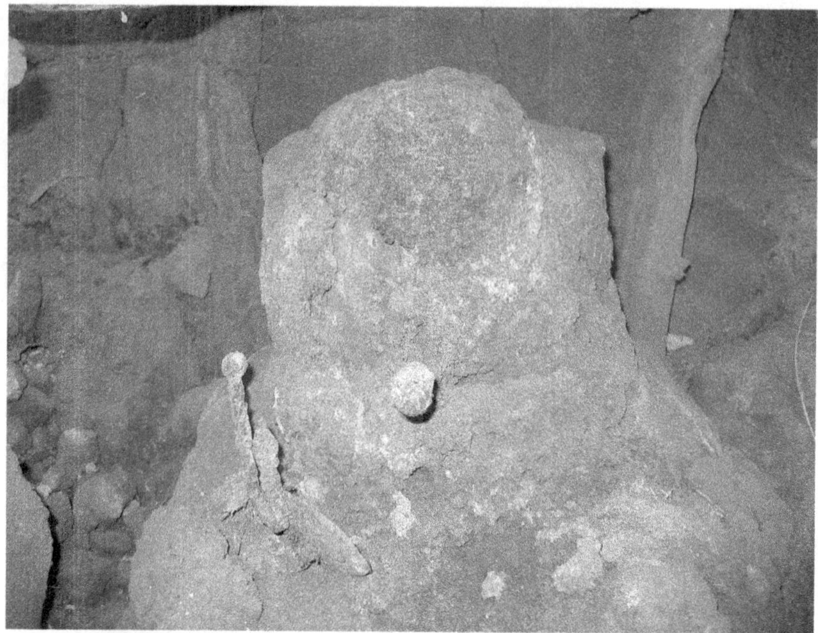

Figure 7. Traditional Legba shrine, on the road in front of a residence in Ouidah, Benin Republic. Photo: Toni Pressley-Sanon, 2006.

also activated by ritual, and the mirror in their lower belly region as well as the nails or blades that are driven through the figure represent the sustenance of life in their usage as a means of identifying witches or beings who threaten the health of the community. They tie people to the land and possess healing properties.

The anthropomorphic representation of this object of healing, like the statue of Legba in Kpassezoumé in Ouidah commissioned for Ouidah '92, opens up avenues of connection between sacred practices among the people from whence the objects originate and those of the African diaspora, particularly Haiti. In other words, they both perform as translators, openers of gates that separate the living from the dead, ancestors from their descendants. They provide a bridge across the Atlantic expanse that divides Africa and its diaspora.

In Figure 8, the sculpture from Kpassezoumé, Legba provides historical and spiritual clues to the deity's significance as he sports horns signifying his misreading by Christian missionaries who, upon encountering him, labeled him the devil.[20] The Fa, a system of divination personified as Gbadu, another deity, adorns his chest, presenting itself to be read by the

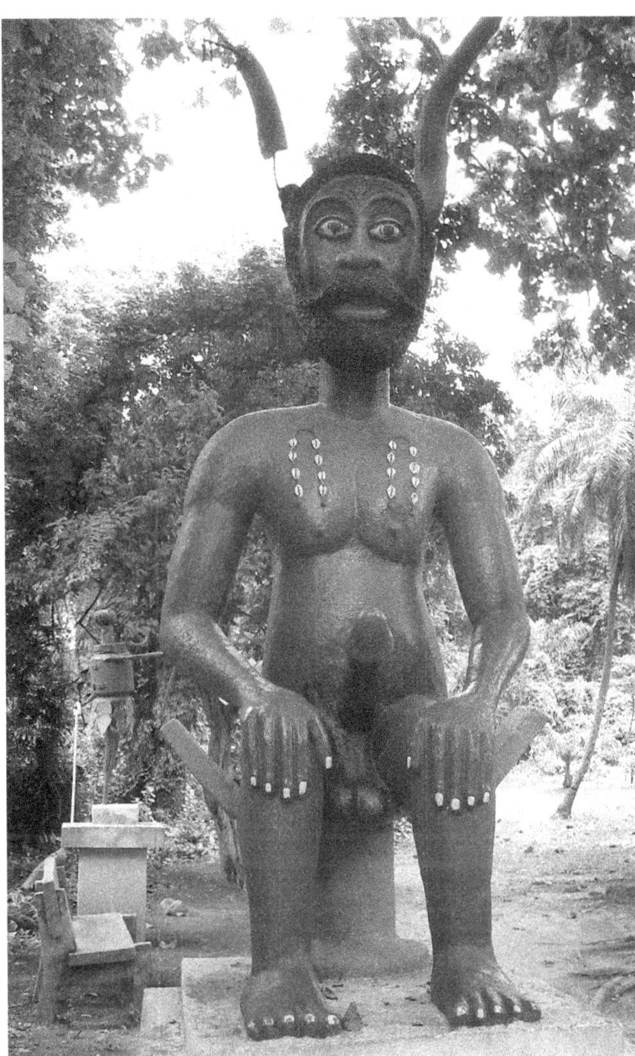

Figure 8. Statue of Legba, Guardian of Kpassezoumé by Abomey artist Cyprien Tokoudagba, Ouidah, Benin Republic. Photo: Toni Pressley-Sanon, 2006.

bokono (priest).[21] The look in his eyes, wide under an astonished brow, hints at spirit possession even as he *is* spirit. As Thompson avers, one of the unifying elements of "African possession faces" is "a frequent bursting quality of the eyes as they fill with inner wisdom (*ojú inún*, in Yoruba terms). When this happens the face takes on a timeless gaze. That bursting quality of the eyes is one of the marvels of the art of African antiquity."[22] This same astonished look can be found in the eyes of many *minkisi* whose eyes are opened wide. Similarly, across the water in Haiti, the sculpture by Eugene with light bulbs that extend beyond the skull also speak of eyes

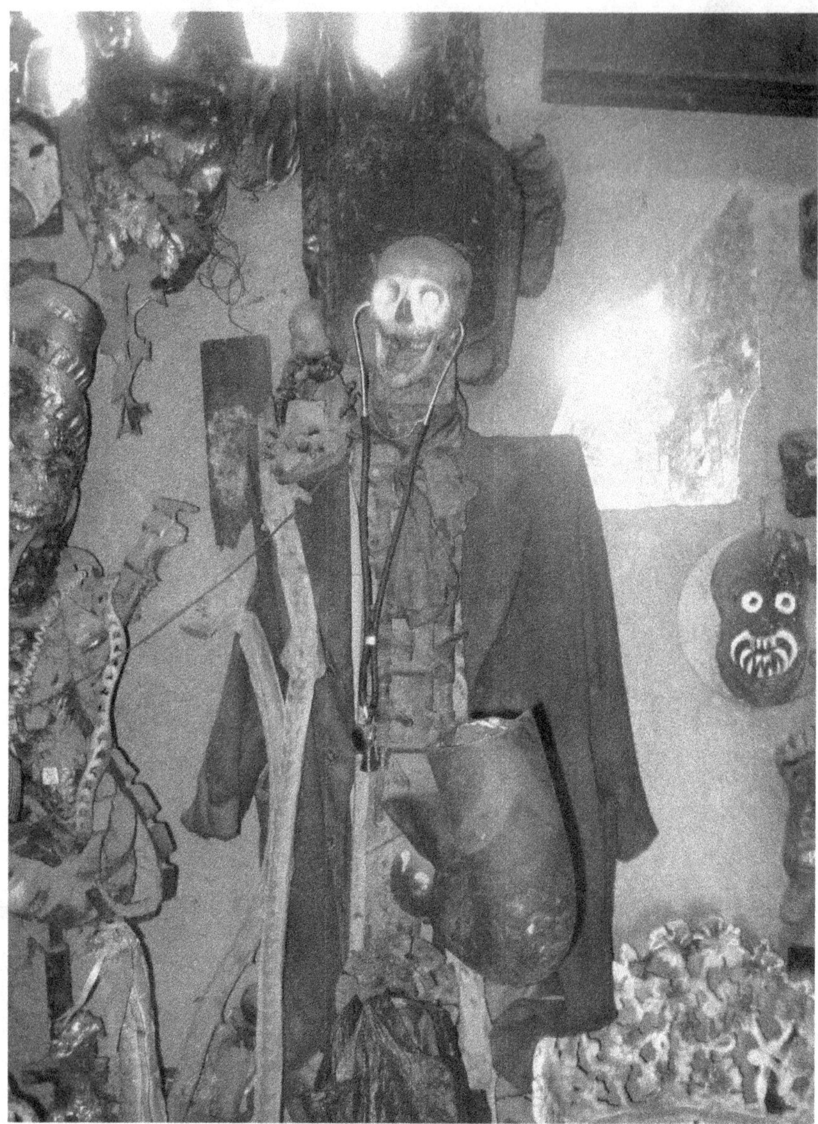

Figure 9. *Chef Seksyon* by André Eugene, 2001, Atelier Atis Rezistans, Grand Rue, Port-au-Prince, Haiti. Photo: Toni Pressley-Sanon, 2009; permission granted by André Eugene.

that hold a profound inner wisdom resultant from having returned from the land of the dead, the embodiment of spirit (Fig. 9).

Legba of Kpassezoumé is one of the dozens of sculptures that were commissioned for Ouidah '92. The artist's rendering of Legba is more human than his earthen representation. He has the body of a man and sits with his hands resting on his knees. His phallus is disproportionately large and painted bright red as though engorged. Though he has human attributes, as a deity in the Sacred Forest, he is larger than life.[23] The Vodun practitioner or tourist who visits the Sacred Forest must first greet Legba before he or she can continue to interact with the other representations of spirits or forces scattered throughout the forest. His placement at the front of the forest emphasizes his importance in the Vodun pantheon.

In Haiti, Legba may also be seen as guarding the entrance to Eugene's atelier (Fig. 10). The sculpture combines detritus and trash from the local environment and abroad, skulls and other bones, and metals to comment and reflect on Haiti's relationship with its past and its future, with itself, and with the international community. Encompassed in both of these renderings of Legba, like the trickster Ananse, is an expression of metamorphic possibilities, a "powerful and many-faced agent of transformation, who mediates among the gods, between the gods and mankind, among humans, and even among the many forces that bring humans into being."[24] The sculpture can also be read as Gede, Legba's complement and counterpart, as explicated by Patrick Bellegarde-Smith in his assertion that "if Legba brings change and uncertainty, and immense possibilities in the beginning, within the realm of one's free will, the Gede introduce certainty, the certainty of death."[25]

Indeed, Legba's role seems to have shifted in his crossing the ocean. In the original Dahomean version of Legba as the procreative and primal energy of all things, his chief mischief is in the realm of sex. His fecund energy is enacted through his supplicants during rituals as, during dances in Dahomey / Benin Republic, "the performers hold a carved phallus between their legs and perform copulating movements."[26] In Haiti, where they dance the *gwiyad*, "a grinding, wining dance of the Banda, a parody of sexual intercourse" they grasp "walking sticks—some with penises carved at the top"—while letting out "a string of unspeakable words in a nasal whine: '*zozo-koko-eya-eya-eya*' ('cock-pussy-yeah-yeah-yeah')."[27] The Gede have taken on Legba's work. Where the Fon say that Legba "everywhere dances in the manner of a man copulating," in Haiti he is seen as old.[28] His "powers go to the Gede, the articulated skeletons of tibia, femur, zozo (metaphysical genitalia) that commune to create the living body capable of entrancing joy."[29]

Cosentino reads the statue that stands in front of Eugene's atelier as Bawon Samdi, remarking that the statue's most outstanding feature is its "four-foot *zozo* (penis) carved from wood and attached to what might be his pelvis by an industrial spring, which renders the *zozo* not only bionic but pneumatic."[30] Even though Cosentino identifies the statue as Bawon, he suggests that it is more than that, resembling "some new hybrid divinity, one with Gede's mooky sexuality grafted onto Samdi's menacing body."[31] Indeed, the statue is the sum of all these things, reflecting the diasporic body that is constituted by transformation, fecundity and impotence, creativity and destruction, history and rootlessness, death and rebirth.

Unlike Legba of Dahomey, Papa Legba or Legba of the Old Bones, as he is commonly addressed in Haiti, is very old and is depicted as an aged limping *lwa*.[32] The carved phallus as a sign of virility with which Legba is associated in Benin Republic is replaced by a gnarled crutch-cane fitted into his crotch. His handicap is a result of the hardships that he has suffered as a god of the diaspora. As *sèvitè* have undergone the trauma of captivity, exile, and servitude, so too has he. He embodies the ravages of the physical world on a metaphysical level. His physical appearance as aged and in need of a cane to keep himself upright reflects the metaphysical toll that enslavement in its multiple stages has taken on his spirit. He is transformed as all of the gods are transformed, and he remains head of all the other *lwa*, the first to be invoked for all rituals. Not only does he guard the entranceway to temples and houses as well as crossroads where he is known as Mèt-Kalfou (Master of the Crossroads) but he also opens the gate that separates humans from the spirit world.

All of the signs seem to point to survival, but an impotent survival where the Legba of creativity in Africa is transformed into one that can *only* open the door of the spirit world to enable the *sèvitè* to communicate with other *lwa*. Joan Dayan's proposal that "it is as if in coming westward to the New World he lost the potential and power of his own history" echoes Maya Deren, who says that Legba, "who once was life and its destiny," has "become an old tattered man shuffling down the road, with his rude twisted cane as crutch, a small fire in his pipe, a little food

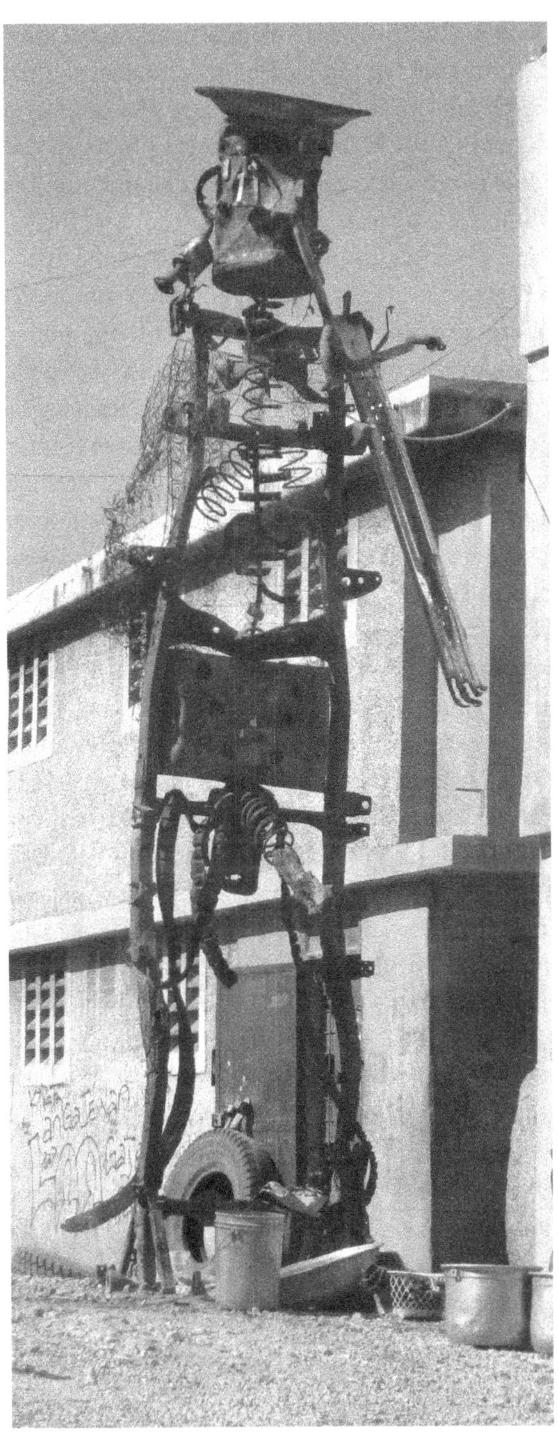

Figure 10. Papa Legba, Bawon Samdi, or Gede by André Eugene, 2006, Atelier Atis Rezistans, Grand Rue, Port-au-Prince, Haiti. Photo: Toni Pressley-Sanon, 2009; permission granted by André Eugene.

in his *macoute*, and sores on his body, as if the maggots had begun their work already."[33] These descriptions may indeed be true, but in the diaspora, Legba and his crutch take on different meanings. His cane, as a transformed phallus—a sign of virility in Benin—no longer points up and outward but downward. It is nonetheless still potent. While in Benin his phallus is erect, perhaps indicating the way to new life, rebirth, and the future, in the diaspora the cane descends, in constant contact with the earth. Each time he takes a step Legba's cane taps the earth, initiating communication and summoning a response from those under the earth, the ancestors who are buried in the ground as well as his fellow *lwa anba dlo* (gods below the water), the mythical Ginen. In this sense, as Leslie Desmangles suggests, his cane as the "odd pole" corresponds to the *poto-mitan* (center post) that not only "establishes contact between the sacred and profane worlds" but is also the pathway through which the *lwa* who follow him in a ceremony may pass.[34] Desmangles' reading of Legba's cane makes sense given that he is "the means and avenue of communication between man and the gods" with his "very symbol [being] the poteau-mitan, the center post of the Vodou temple court."[35] He transmits messages from Africa to the diaspora, from the gods to their supplicants and from the land of the dead to the world of the living. As such, his cane is not a sign of impotence or handicap; it is rather a sign that, though in a different guise, his virility remains intact and he remains equally powerful. His movement across the ocean did not diminish his power. Rather, his ability to adapt and change ensures that he will remain not only relevant but central to the lives of his supplicants in their new environments. His ability to adapt and transform mirrors that of the African diaspora that has used similar tactics as a means of survival.

Death is not the end. The Africans exiled into the diaspora did not end their relationship with their sites of origin. Rather, overseen and facilitated by both Legba and Gede, the captives arrived on the other side of the water transformed and replete with creative potential that is expressed in a myriad number of ways, both historically and contemporarily. Again, this chapter focuses on the creation of visual art on Grand Rue that, through a Vodou episteme, expresses a tidalectical exchange that is ongoing between the physical realm and the spiritual realm.

The Realm of Ogun/Ogou

While the death of the man in the coffin of *Dr. Zozo* (Fig. 6) would normally signify the end of his virility and, consequently, the end of his family line, the nails seem to give the phallus strength. Those protruding from the length of the shaft echo the erection that is straight and unbendable, thus reinforcing the power of the phallus, a creative force in itself. The doctor who stands by checking the vital signs of the phallus is invested in keeping it alive and healthy so that it can continue to be instrumental in procreation. The role of the doctor in the assurance of the health of this phallus reflects the role of the *sèvitè* as it is their job to feed and honor the *lwa* so that they in turn will remain strong and continue to advise, warn, and protect them.[36] Furthermore, the man in the coffin's death does not mean that he is gone since, in the Vodou faith, he may become an ancestor and also intervene on behalf of his descendants.

One finds nails in other important areas of Eugene's art. For example, in his *Benladen* sculpture, nails cover the statue's testicles (Fig. 11). In still another, nails protrude from the lips, forehead, and nose of a sculpted head (Fig. 12). If we read these elements and their positioning in line with Blier's discussion of the use of similar elements in *bociǫ* in Dahomey, then in all three pieces the nails are meant to reflect and comment on the diminishment of power of the figures represented. This would seem a most obvious reading, especially in the case of bin Laden who, after a prolonged war with the United States where he was forced to hide in caves in the desert, was killed by the U.S. military on May 1, 2011. Thus, the nails in the statue's testicles comment on bin Laden's diminished male prowess as a leader of the next generation of fundamentalist Muslims who would continue the Jihad that he started. The immolation of the scrotum signifies a penetration of bin Laden's creative potential, as this is where the sperm that would "impregnate" the movement is held. But just as we can read Legba's crutch another way, so too can we read the nails in bin Laden's scrotum in Eugene's art—that is, as fortifying the immolated body part. Like the *boko/bòkò*, whose meaning has changed in a New World context, so too do the nails take on a different meaning in Haiti through an understanding of Ogou.[37]

In her essay "Systematic Remembering, Systematic Forgetting," Karen McCarthy Brown says that "Ogou has his roots in the Gu or the Ogun of the Dahomean or Yoruba people," where he "was a sky divinity, Lord of the Thunderbolt, of fire and of might."[38] He "was patron of warriors and of the iron-smiths, forgers of war-weapons."[39] Ogun is related to Gede when he manifests as Ogou Badagri, who, like Gede, is related to fertility, wisdom or prophecy, and magic.[40] He is also related to Legba when he manifests as Ogou Baryè (barrier, gateway) and Ogou Panama (straw

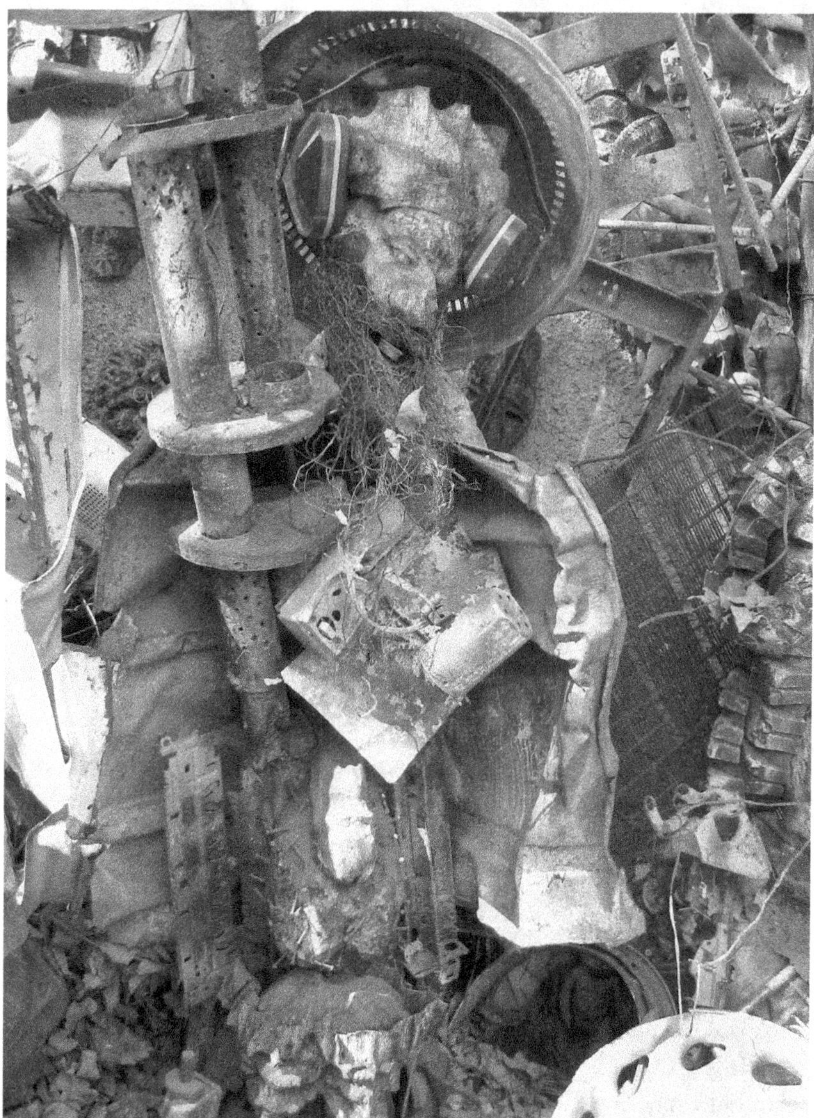

Figure 11. *Benladen* by André Eugene, 2001, Atelier Atis Rezistans, Grand Rue, Port-au-Prince, Haiti. Photo: Toni Pressley-Sanon, 2009; permission granted by André Eugene.

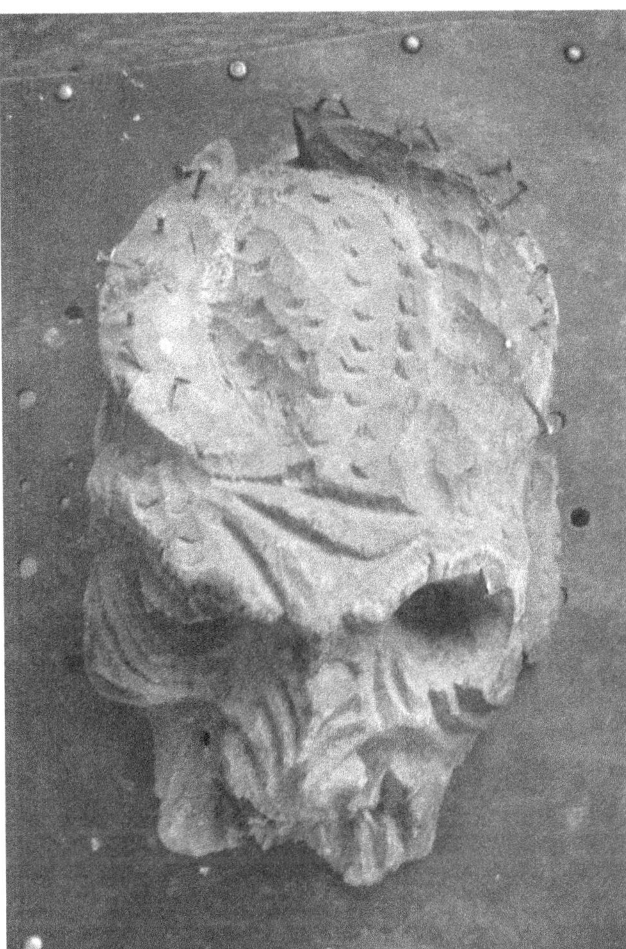

Figure 12. Head with piercing by Louko, date unknown. Author's private collection. Photo: Toni Pressley-Sanon, 2012.

hat), another gate-guardian.[41] As elements of Ogou, the god of iron and war, the nails ready the immolated body part for battle. Thus, the nails immolating bin Laden's testicles may comment on the fact that he had the "balls" to go up against a major world power when he declared war on the American "infidels."

In *Dr. Zozo* we can read the erect penis as gathering all the strength that has drained from the rest of the body that lies in the coffin. That diffused energy that once kept a whole person alive is now concentrated in the phallus, which is again also fortified by Ogou's power. Finally, while in Benin Republic the nails in the lips of the sculpture in Figure 12 may signify the figure's silencing, in the diaspora they may signify its ability to speak with authority or truth. The nails in the forehead may, instead of diminished power as they do in Dahomey, signify activated power as they do in the Kôngo. Thus, the sculpture depicts augmented intellectual strength within Ogou's domain.

All and None

If you ask Eugene who is depicted in the large metal sculpture that stands at the entrance of his *lakou*, surveying all that goes on under his watchful gaze (Fig. 10), he will tell you that it is Papa Gede, a member of the family of gods who rules the cemetery, lords over the underworld, and is known for his sexual potency. Again, both readings of the sculpture—as Legba and Gede—are correct. Legba and Gede are seen as a continuum. As Deren comments, if Legba was the sun, at first young, then growing old, Gede is the master of that abyss into which the sun descends.[42] The epiphany of Gede concentrates on his vitality and eternal life force so that Vodou ceremonies begin with an invocation to Legba to open the gates and often end with Gede's raunchy gyrations.[43] Moreover, as Bellegarde-Smith suggests, whereas Legba is powerful among the Fon, in Haiti his power has been transferred to Gede. Nonetheless, although some of Legba's characteristics are transferred to Gede. he remains a potent figure in his role as guardian of the gates between natural and supernatural worlds.

While in Africa it seems that the roles of the gods were more demarcated, in the diaspora several *lwa* share similar characteristics and are open to different interpretations, as we see in the statue in front of Eugene's atelier being equally recognizable as Legba, as Gede, and as Bawon Samdi.

The Gede's Origins

Blier remarks that most of the Haitian *lwa* have counterparts in Benin and Togo. Most notable of these are Danbala and Ayida Wedo, Ogou, Legba, Loko Agwe, and Gede.[44] Gede, the inspiration for much of Eugene's work, "is widely known to have its origins near the Fon capital of Abomey. His association with cemeteries in Haiti is probably based on the tradition that in the Fon area, the Guede, as autochthonous residents of this area, are held to have ritual control over the land and those buried within it. Because all burials took place under Loko (iroko) trees, the latter are often associated with Guede and the dead as well."[45] While this is Blier's reading of the Guede/Ghede, she does note that religious traditions associated with certain gods in West Africa often offer important insight into their complements in the Americas.[46] Roger Bastide's reading of the Gede supports Blier's findings. He says, "The *guede* are divinities from Dahomey, but have no connection with the Fon; they belong to a people known as *guede-vi*, whom the Fon conquered, and made into the grave-digging caste. Later, to escape their reputed magical powers and wizardry, the Fon sold them off as slaves. In Haiti the *guede* thus became spirits associated with cemeteries and death."[47]

Several scholars, including Melville J. Herskovits, Emmanuel C. Paul, Paul Hazoumé, and Leslie Desmangles, explain the origins of Gede vis-à-vis the Fon oral tradition.[48] Herskovits includes the story that I discuss below in his chapter on ancestor veneration. The story is part of a longer chapter in which he remarks that Dahomean reaction to the news that a large "Negro" population existed in the United States as well as in the West Indies and Guiana who were free and "had preserved many of the customs of their aboriginal African cultural background" was always striking.[49] He was told by one informant about a local family: "You have nearly all the people of this family in your country. They knew too much magic. We sold them because they made too much trouble."[50] Another told him, "This family has strong men. They are good warriors, but bad enemies. When they troubled our king, they were caught and sold. You have their big men in your country."[51] Herskovits surmises that the fact that the souls of those who had been enslaved figured prominently in the ancestral cult is revealed in the story that he relates.[52] The story centers on King Andanzan, who ruled from 1797 to 1818 but who was overthrown in a coup d'état orchestrated by his brother, Ghezo, with the help of the Brazilian slave trader Francisco Félix de Souza. Once he came to power, King Ghezo (1818–58) erased all official history of his brother, thus placing the story that is told about King Andanzan squarely in the realm of *istwa*. Desmangles provides some important background on King Andanzan:

Andanzan, king of Abomey, was an aged monarch whose only ambition was to enrich the state treasury by whatever means possible. He warred incessantly with neighboring peoples and plundered many of their villages, carrying away whatever wealth they possessed; he captured men, women, and children whom he kept in slave camps for a time and later sold to European slave traders. It seems that Andanzan's mother (whose name is not mentioned in the story) became displeased with her son's behavior and attempted to replace him with his younger brother Ghezo.[53]

According to the story that Herskovits tells,

> To deprive Ghezo of the counsel of his mother in the usurpation of his throne, Andanzan, who, it is claimed, was a usurper of the throne, sold her and sixty-three of her retainers, to the Portuguese. They were sent to Brazil where, the tale tells, they found many Dahomeans. From Brazil she and eleven others were sent to "Ame'íka," and while there, founded the "cult of her Dahomean deity." Ghezo, when he took his rightful place [as king of Abomey] dispatched his Portuguese friend, Da Souza to Brazil to find her. After an extensive search, she is said to have returned to Dahomey with six other Dahomeans [to Abomey], at a date which is placed at eighteen years before the monarch's death, or about 1840.[54]

While Herskovits and Paul's versions of the story are very similar, Hazoumé's story ends differently, with Ghezo's mother not being found. In Hazoumé's account, de Souza is believed to have visited Brazil, "the Antilles, possibly Haiti, and Havana."[55]

According to Desmangles, the sixty-three members of Ghezo's mother's retainers were members of the Gédévi clan, and they were the ones who were transported to Brazil and Haiti. As descendants of Ghede, when they arrived they founded their cult to honor their ancestor. Like Herskovits, Desmangles seems to question the historical accuracy of the story. While Herskovits states outright, "How much of this is myth, and how much is fact, it is impossible to determine," Desmangles concludes that if the "story is true, it would account for the connection between Dahomey and the New World, and would explain the presence of Gede in the Vodou pantheon in Haiti and in Candomblé in Brazil."[56] The impossibility of verifying the story may be a result of Ghezo's attempt to erase the history of Andanzan. It may also be a consequence of the nature of oral culture, which is subject to variation depending on who is telling the story, under what circumstances, and to whom. Nonetheless, the story, an example of *istwa*, performs an important function in its delineation of the origins of the Gede. The story explains how the *guede-vi* ended up in what is now

Haiti and brought their connection to the dead with them, passing their knowledge down through the generations, transformed. It may also have been a way for the enslaved to understand and make peace with the constant companion of death on the African slave routes, in the barracoons, during the middle passage, and on the plantation.

Spirit's Workings

If one ventures to Grand Rue where Atis Rezistans is located, one would note immediately the predominant sound of metal hitting metal as mechanics bring barely sputtering cars back to life and metal scrapes against wood as coffin makers busily construct new coffins that will promptly be filled by the very young to the very old. This is all couched within the cacophony of tap taps, buses, and taxis making their way slowly down the congested thoroughfare. Atis Rezistans' work has grown out of this environment. It not only reflects the larger structures that give rise to this environment but also comments on it from a spiritual perspective. Just as the *bociǫ* of Dahomey and the *nkisi* of the Kôngo reflected and commented on a sociopolitical reality of the distant past that gave birth to the population that now inhabits Grand Rue, so too do the artists reflect and comment on their historical and contemporary sociopolitical reality. Spirit allows them to find strength in a reality that would render them impotent in the face of imperialism and neoliberalism. Their use of the phallus in their art reclaims their potency from a spiritual perspective. In my interview with Eugene in his *lakou* we discussed these very issues.

Blier notes that the patina that covers the *bociǫ* is evidence of its ritual history.[57] When I asked Eugene about his practice of layering he said,

> That's why we call it "recycle." Recycling is like a big community. We call that recycling because we recuperate everything completely. In Haiti you find everything. You do whatever you want with it. You put things in disarray or you put things in proper order.
>
> For example we have what you call *pepe* (second-hand clothing).[58] You see someone wearing something. They don't know why they wear it but they wear it.[59] For example, you have people who wear big snow boots. The person sees it in a picture. They don't know why they wear it, but it's pretty so they wear it in the heat. Celeur made a sculpture of that.[60]

For example, you take sunglasses; you're supposed to wear them during the day, but people wear them at night. We talk about everything because we work on issues that are economic, social and political and spiritual. So take Bawon or Gede who wear sunglasses. When someone is welding they have to put on sunglasses too. Recycling expresses the community.[61]

Furthermore, in a phrase that is difficult to translate into English but that illustrates the deep connection between his work and his physical and spiritual community, Eugene says, "*Rekuperasyon genyen plis langaj avek travay kominote a*," which, loosely translated, means "Recycling has many connections to the work of the community."

Eugene's response exemplifies the Bakôngo *dikenga* or cosmogram, a cultural view that describes the individual in relation to the universe, which sets parameters for being in the community as part and parcel of the larger political, spiritual, and economic environment.[62] The *pepe* that Eugene refers to is a major feature of city life in Haiti because people from abroad think that they are doing something to help the poor while being able to write off their donations on their taxes. It is a win-win situation for them; their consciences are eased without being forced to make any major changes to their way of being in the world. They have been able to enjoy the clothing, or cars, and so on until they are no longer useful to them; then in discarding them they can help others *and* get a tax break. But as Charles Kenny notes, "Here's the trouble with dumping stuff we don't want on people in need: What they need is rarely the stuff we don't want. And even when they do need that kind of stuff, there are much better ways for them to get it than for a Western NGO [nongovernmental organization] to gather donations at a suburban warehouse, ship everything off to Africa or South America, and then try to distribute it."[63] In addition, as the narrator in the short documentary *Haiti's Pepe Trade: How Secondhand American Clothes Became a First-Rate Business* shows, *pepe* has undermined the country's local tailor and dressmaking industry even as it has provided employment for small merchants. Moreover, Haiti is being treated as a dumping ground. Businesswoman Ketcia Pierre-Louis remarks, "Haiti has practically become a trashcan where everything that people don't need in other countries comes here."[64] The artists of Grand Rue take these useless items and create something new that enriches their environment instead of allowing it to become litter. As Eugene says regarding how Atis Rezistans started making recycled art, "We took a wrong that was done to us and changed it into something positive." He continues, "The environment is everywhere. Everywhere you live the environment impacts you. For example, if you were brought up in a place that had a lot of *peristil*,[65] or a lot of mechanics, or a lot of sculptors all these things would cross you. They would inspire you."[66]

Several members of Atis Rezistans grew up in the Grand Rue area, a neighborhood populated by mechanics. They also grew up in the Vodou faith in a country of artists. It therefore makes sense that they bring all of these influences to bear in their work. For example, the statue made of wood and chain link and covered in leaves wears sunglasses that never come off (Fig. 13). This figure comments on ecological, economic, political, and spiritual conditions. The sun that beats incessantly in Haiti makes

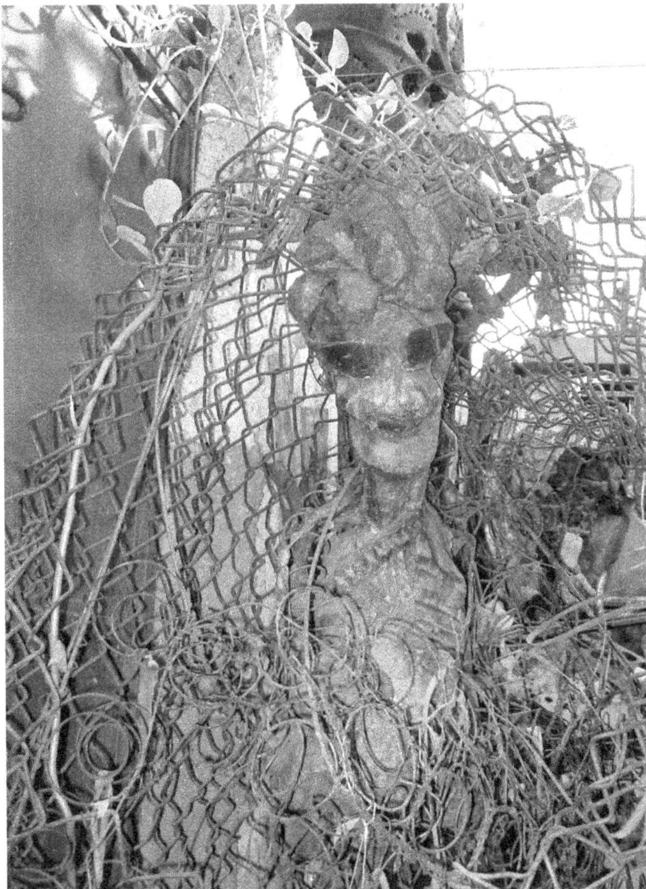

Figure 13. *Granne Machout* by André Eugene, 1998, Atelier Atis Rezistans, Grand Rue, Port-au-Prince, Haiti. Photo: Toni Pressley-Sanon, 2009; permission granted by André Eugene.

it possible to wear sunglasses even at night. The *pepe*, which probably brought the sunglasses to Haiti, comments on the economic and political conditions that maintain the hierarchy between Haiti and the international community. Finally, the sunglasses are a nod to the *lwa* (Bawon Samdi and the Gede) who inspire and speak through the artists.

Commenting on the inspiration for his work, Eugene says, "Everything in the world communicates. There's nothing new under the sun. I may be doing something here and there may be someone in Japan doing the same thing. It's inspiration that communicates all the time. You can compare me with anybody. I have been compared to an *oungan*, with Picasso, with a lot of people, but I've never seen the work of these people. The recycled art that I work on reflects Haiti. It's got its origins here." Eugene also acknowledges Africa's place in his inspiration when he notes, "You know our original base is Africa." But he takes it further, giving substance to a remark that Alfred Métraux made many years ago, that in addition to the African origins of ceremonies and representations associated with Vodou, "*Le vaudou appartient à notre monde moderne . . . ses divinités se meuvent dans un temps industrialisé qui est le nôtre; ne serait-ce qu'à ce titre, il relève de notre civilisation*" [Vodou is part of our modern world . . . its deities emerge from our industrialized time; as such, it is part of our civilization].[67]

Eugene is also reflecting a truth that Stephan Palmié delineates: that the Caribbean has always been modern.

Representing as it does the historic heartland of African America, the Caribbean might well be regarded as one of the first truly modern localities: modern not only in the sense of the "factory in the fields" character of the slave-labor-driven, although highly rationalized, export economy characteristic of the region since at least the mid-seventeenth century (thus anticipating the so-called Industrial Revolution in the metropolis by more than a century); modern also in the sense in which the sheer scale and rationally calculated nature of the appropriation of commoditized human bodies and their destruction in the service of new forms of production and accumulation, prefigured what in their grim reflections on the "dialectics of enlightenment" Horkheimer and Adorno (1972) would call the characteristically modern "identity of domination and reason"; modern finally, in the sense of the displacement, rupture, heterogeneity, instability, flux, and incompleteness that characterizes virtually all social projects enacted in the region's troubled past and contradiction-ridden postcolonial present.[68]

Not only is this "incompleteness" the basis of Brathwaite's conceptualization of tidalectics—"always on this journey"—but it is also in this contradiction-ridden realm where the Vodou concept of *balanse* resides. As such, the Caribbean is a fecund space, a profoundly creative space that is modern for all of the reasons that Palmié gives but also because of its ability to absorb, assimilate, and transform that with which it comes in contact, including the detritus from so-called first world nations, as Atis Rezistans demonstrates. Indeed, Gordon rightly describes the artists' work as modern and postmodern.

Like the *lwa* who, with their African origins, are influenced by their environment, Eugene is inspired by Africa but also by his daily environment and experiences, which are steeped in modernity. Cosentino has observed that the work of Atis Rezistans reflects a cosmopolitanism that in turn reflects the cosmopolitanism of Haitian history since the seventeenth century.[69] The gods that Eugene depicts think and act in the industrialized world of today while also presenting "a dystopian sci-fi view of the future."[70] Eugene deploys the deities who originated in Africa and who have also been impacted by their environments to reflect and comment on his experience as part of a larger community as they relate to the spirit world. This process is not linear but turns in on itself and meets at various intersections of meaning. It reflects a tidalectical positioning that is rooted in West African ontology in which philosopher Paget Henry instructs, "The temporality of divine projects does not follow a linear path. Rather it moves in a cyclical path. . . . Like time, the view of space is also cosmogonic. . . . Time and space are thus cosmogonic categories that help frame the project of creation, but do not in any way, limit or constrain the creator."[71] At the same time, it reflects a Central West African ontology that is illustrated in the cosmogram that depicts the world as a cross with the realm of the living above the cross's horizontal line and the realm of the dead below. At the center, a circle represents water that separates the two worlds. Since the cemetery is not a final resting place in Bakôngo terms but is a door between two worlds that marks the line between the worlds of the living and the dead and is circumscribed by the cosmic journey of the sun, the cosmogram represents the crossroads between and interconnectedness of the realm of the living and that of the ancestors.[72] It also reflects the four moments of the sun: dawn, noon, sunset, and midnight (when the sun is believed to be shining on the kingdom of the dead).[73] Finally, it reflects the eternal movement of the soul as it proceeds from birth, life, death, and rebirth. These energies flow constantly, giving life to and framing the creative process, opening it up. Thus we have Claude Sentius, an *oungan*, artist, and member of Atis Rezistans, declare that when a person dies, he likes to take his head and make him live again: "I take his skull and create a sculpture from it. I make him live again, to be judged."[74] The constant back-and-forth flow of energies between the seen and unseen worlds are made obvious during Sentius' interview with Gordon when he becomes possessed by Gede and, tying a black scarf around his horse's head, the *lwa* announces his presence: "We are Gede spirits. I am Gede. It's a Gede that's speaking to you. I've already died, I just haven't been buried yet. I am Gede. Talk about the dead and I have died already"—and yet, he is with us, speaking, telling his story.[75]

Reflecting and Commenting on One's Environment

Veerle Poupeye contends in *Caribbean Art* (1998) that the degradation of the unique but very fragile Caribbean environment has become a major concern in the Caribbean.[76] The art from the region, which often depicts the landscape and nature, also frequently presents "an aestheticized and even escapist representation of the realities of the region."[77] While this is true for a good deal of Haitian art this is not the case of the art from Atis Rezistans.[78] While art from Atis Rezistans may incorporate wood, it does so in an industrialized environment, one that is surrounded by and sometimes subsumed by metal and signs of technology such as headphones (Fig. 11), electric fans without blades to cool the deceased (Fig. 14), computer monitors turned upside down (Fig. 6), and license plates that become bandanas (Fig. 15).

The *lwa*'s way of being in the world provides a cognitive map for Haitians who take up the challenges of contemporary life.[79] They also provide a creative map delineating "both the possibilities and the potential hazards of doing battle in the modern urban world."[80] In addition, while it may have been true in 1997 that, as Karen McCarthy Brown asserts, the Haitian Ogou had not taken up the challenge of interpreting modern

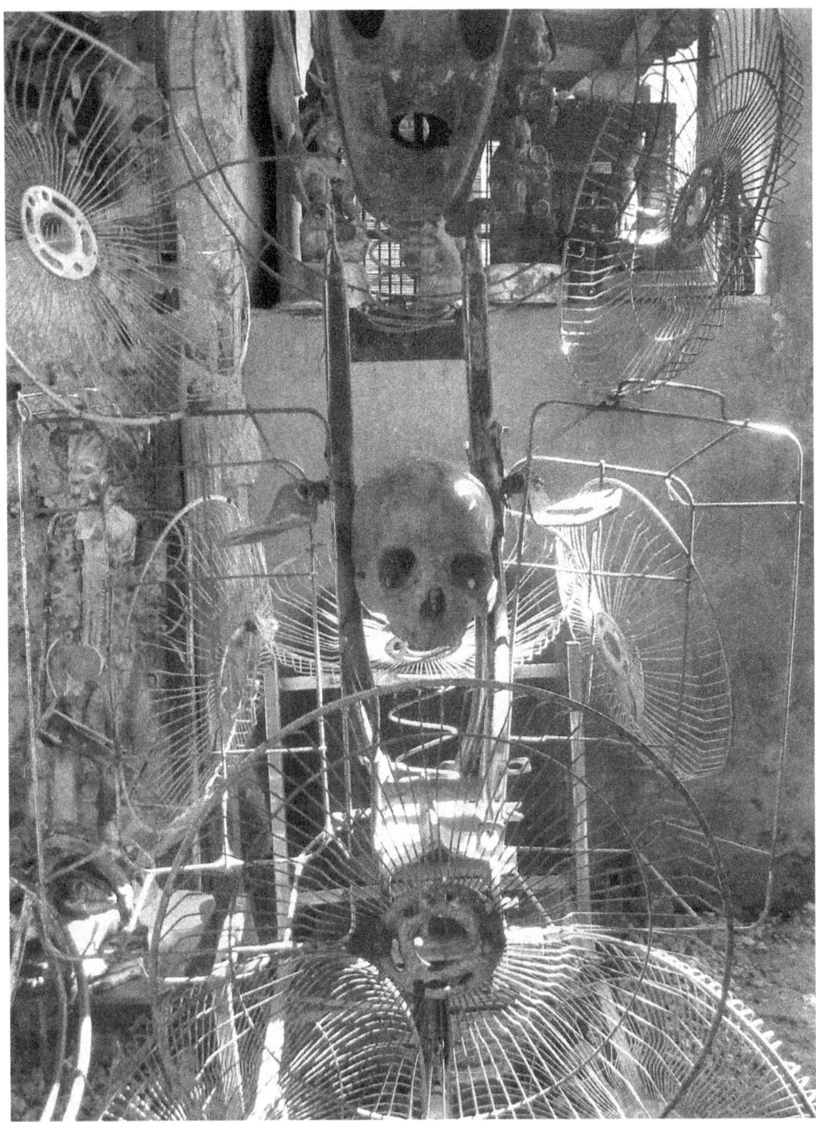

Figure 14. Skull with fans by Papa Da, date unknown, Atelier Atis Rezistans, Grand Rue, Port-au-Prince, Haiti. Photo: Toni Pressley-Sanon, 2009; permission granted by André Eugene.

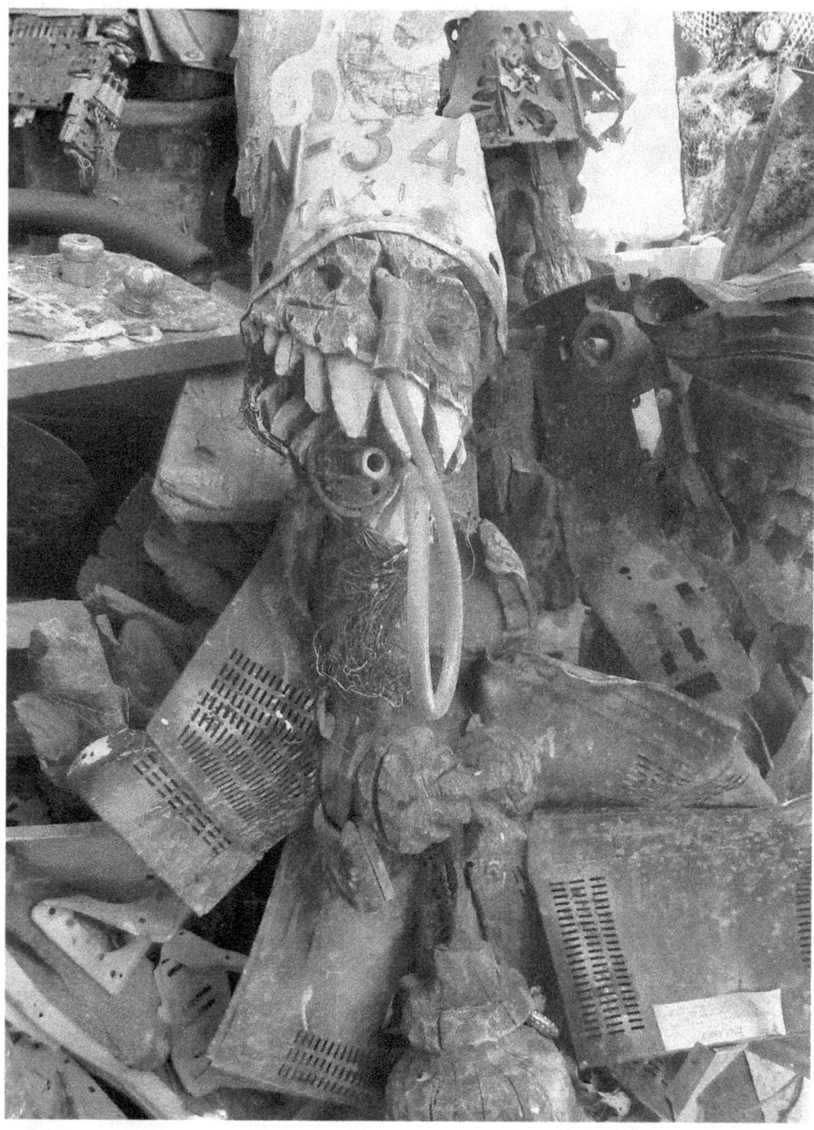

Figure 15. Sculpture with license plate bandana by Louko, 2008, Atelier Atis Rezistans, Grand Rue, Port-au-Prince, Haiti. Photo: Toni Pressley-Sanon, 2009; permission granted by André Eugene.

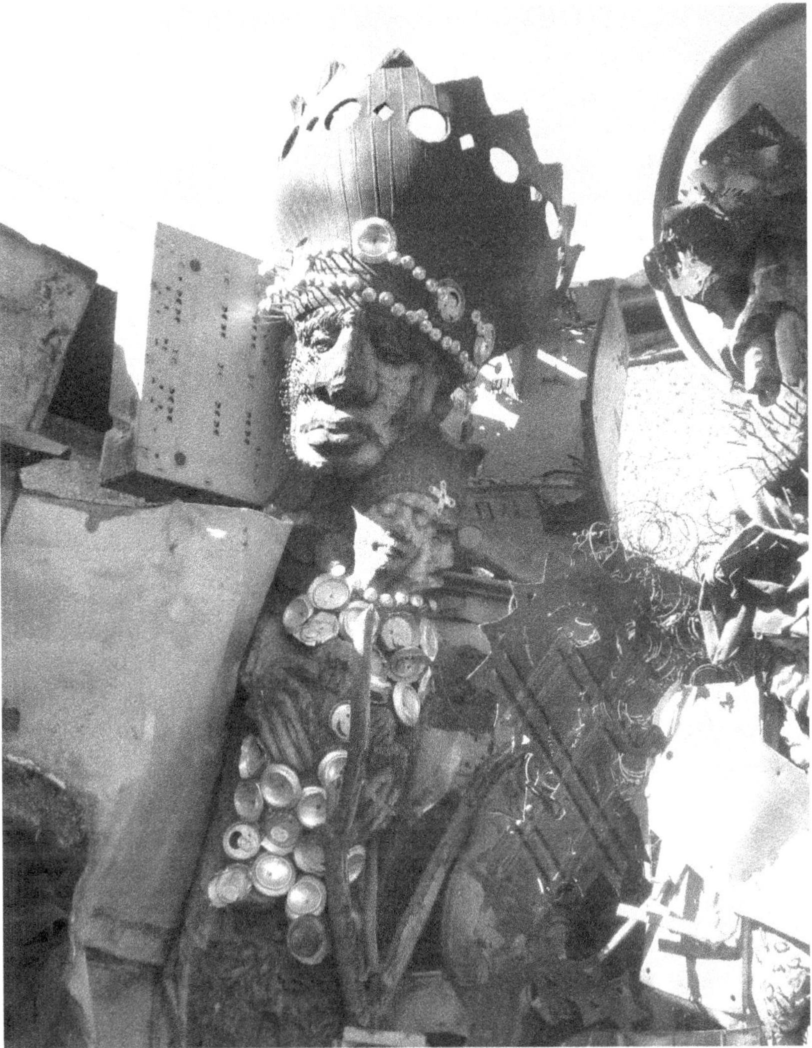

Figure 16. *Ezili Dantò*, *lwa* of love, Atelier Atis Rezistans, Grand Rue, Port-au-Prince, Haiti. Photo: Toni Pressley-Sanon, 2009; permission granted by André Eugene.

technology the way that its Nigerian counterpart had, this is no longer true, as Atis Rezistans demonstrates. According to Brown, to the extent that the role of interpreting modern technology has developed in Haiti—a country that has experienced much less of modern technology than Nigeria—it has accrued a group of spirits called the Gede, who are, in one of their manifestations, auto mechanics.[81] But as the multiple faces of the *lwa* teach us and the artists' deployment of them demonstrates, these attributes are not exclusive; rather, they may be shared by several *lwa*.

The artists are surrounded by and incorporate technology into their creations. The works from the artists represent the work of a generation of artists that has "come of age in an era characterized by disillusionment with social and political ideals of the previous generation."[82] These artists use Vodou iconography in innovative ways that comment on their sociopolitical and economic reality. Therefore, *Ezili Dantò*, mother of the Haitian Revolution and a figure central to the balance of Eugene's *lakou*, holds court in the farthest corner from a vantage point that allows her to survey all that takes place under her watchful eye. She does so surrounded by and made up of motherboards, bejeweled with soda cans, and wearing a crown fashioned from a bicycle tire (Fig. 16). To get a sense of the kind of power that is embodied in her representation in the atelier, a creative revolutionary space, we must return to Ezili's resemblance to Erzulie Fréda Dahomey, to André Pierre's identification of Ezili Dantò as "the woman saint [who] brought the Kongo packet," and to the popular belief that Ezili Kawoulo "spiritually embodied the woman who partnered with Boukman" at Bwa Kayiman. In turn, her association with Notre-Dame de l'Assomption, patron saint of the colony, was significant to not only many enslaved and free people of color in the colony but especially to enslaved Bakôngo Catholics.[83] Her positioning in relation to Legba/Gede is also significant because, while Legba/Gede is out front—"a soldier," in the words of Eugene—guarding the *lakou* and atelier and granting entrance to both the initiated and the uninitiated, it is Ezili with whom one must contend if one decides to pass some time there. The three form their own Marasa Twa in a circle that is protective as well as highly charged historically and creatively.

4

Tidalectical Dishonor

The past is never past and the present is our future.
—Claudine Michel and Patrick Bellegarde-Smith

In the summer of 2008 Haiti was hit by two hurricanes, Fay and Hannah, and two tropical storms, Ike and Gustav. Gonaïves, a port city, as well as nearby Cabaret and St. Marc were devastated by the storms. Hundreds of people died, and thousands were left homeless. Gonaïves was, at one point, under six and a half feet of water. The rain that washed down from the mountains carried mud and everything in its path to flood the Artibonite Valley, forcing many people to seek refuge on their rooftops. Gonaïves' hospitals, understaffed and undersupplied, were flooded and needed help to move their patients. In the end, the deluge caused a profound loss of both human and animal life, land, and revenue.

A little over a year later in December 2009, while participating in the Ghetto Biennale Conference, I was beginning my day as usual at the Hotel Oloffson with several cups of syrupy black, sweet Haitian coffee when I spilled a bit on the buffet table. A disembodied voice over my shoulder intoned, "If you do not give they will take." I turned to find Richard Morse, the hotel manager, smiling mischievously, one eyebrow raised. I tried to remember his words for the rest of my time in Haiti, making sure to share a bit of whatever I drank, whether water, coffee, or Prestige beer, with the ancestors.

Three weeks after the conference ended, at 4:53 p.m. on a Tuesday, an earthquake struck Haiti causing massive devastation. After the earthquake, the streets of Port-au-Prince, Pétionville, Jacmel, and Léogâne quickly filled with the decomposing bodies of those who had perished.

Seeing mothers, fathers, grandmothers, and innocents obscenely splashed across the TV screen evoked memories of similar obscene events in the Haitian people's distant and not-so-distant history. Indeed, the images of mass mortality in 2010 are metaphysically linked to the mass mortality that can be traced back over four hundred years to the Haitian people's historical and mythological site of origin of Dahomey, when the kingdom was a major hub of the transatlantic slave trade.

M. Jacqui Alexander writes in *Pedagogies of Crossing* that "Spirit brings knowledge from past, present, and future to a particular moment called a now."[1] In addition, she avers, "Spirit energy travels in Time and travels differently through linear time, so that there is no distance between space and time that it is unable to navigate. Thus, linear time does not exist because energy simply does not obey the human idiom."[2] Spirit is able to go where it needs to go, whenever it needs, in order to do the work that it must do, which is to engage in "Spirit truth-telling," a term that Alexander uses and that I take to mean "truths" that exceed the "human idiom," and that concern themselves with exigencies that are not limited to a time and place but are transcendent. Reflecting the connection between humans and the Sacred as well as nature, beyond "idiom," André Pierre asserts that "the first magician is God who created people with his own hands from the dust of the earth. No one lives of the flesh. Everyone lives of the spirit."[3] Or, as Max Beauvoir counsels, "We are all of the same essence as God . . . the same nature as God."[4] Although humans live in the material world and the *lwa* dwell in the unseen realm, their relationship is inextricable, with the seen world being able to influence the unseen world and vice versa. This relationship is facilitated by the earth, its waters, and the cosmos.

The earthquake affected both urban and rural areas of Haiti and its effects reverberated across the ocean to its diasporas. In *Imajine* Claudel Casseus, a young member of Atis Rezistans, recalls arriving home at 4:49 p.m. that Tuesday, after spending the previous day in his mother's hometown of Lascahobas.[5] Edwidge Danticat tells of being in a supermarket in Miami's Little Haiti neighborhood with her two young daughters when her cell phone rang.[6] Dany Laferrière, who lives in Canada but was in Haiti for *Étonnants Voyageurs*, an international festival of books and film, writes in *Tout bouge autour de moi* (*The World Is Moving around Me*) that he was in Hôtel Karibe with his friend Rodney Saint-Éloi waiting for dinner to arrive and "biting into a piece of bread when he heard a terrible explosion."[7] I was in State College, Pennsylvania, making dinner for myself and my son when my friend Nazalima called and asked if I'd heard. We were all involved in the most mundane of activities. We all had plans. Earth and Spirit had other plans. If we do not give they will take.

As several writers, artists, and scholars have proposed about the interrelatedness of history and the events that unfolded that day, while the earthquake might have been natural, the socioeconomic, political, and (lack of) infrastructural conditions that were responsible for so much loss of life (three hundred thousand plus) and its aftermath, were anything but natural. And yet . . . and yet . . . the earthquake was a moment in time followed by several other equally severe moments in time called aftershocks, when Spirit spoke through the earth. Laferrière writes that, upon his experience of the first aftershock, he looked to the elements, the earth, and the gods for guidance. Wondering what form death would take, he asked, "Would the earth gape open and swallow us up? Would the trees fall on us? Fire consume us?"[8] In those ten seconds he knew he "couldn't stay distant from it [death]."[9] He continues: "If an earthquake could shake an entire city, one individual was not going to resist it. That's when we cling to our most archaic beliefs. We think of the gods and the earth."[10] He concludes that in those ten seconds he became one with the earth as well as the forces behind it: "I was a tree, a rock, a cloud, or the earthquake itself. One thing for sure: I wasn't the product of a culture anymore. I had the definite impression of being part of the cosmos."[11] Laferrière characterizes those ten seconds, when he was at one with the earth and the cosmos, as the most precious of his life.

This final chapter of *Istwa across the Water* excavates Haiti's spiritual and oral tradition for explanations for and solutions to the so-called natural disasters that have plagued Haiti in recent years. It discusses Dahomean and Bakôngo antecedents to Haitian beliefs about the relationship between the living and the dead and then traces an initial breaking of the pact between the living and the dead perpetrated during the slave era in Ouidah that resonates in the aftermath of the 2010 earthquake. This tracing is meant to support the work of re-membering Africa to its diaspora in a way that complements the work that Vodou does epistemologically through the Marasa and that Kamau Brathwaite does creatively through his concept of tidalectics. This chapter as part of the larger project is an invocation of the gods/*lwa* and their multiple manifestations both in

Africa and its diaspora to lend themselves to the work of re-pairing the parts to the whole—of repairing ruptures that began with the transatlantic slave trade, continued with the acts of violence that I have discussed in the previous chapters, and persists contemporarily. It is my contention that the rupture both between Haiti's visible and invisible population and between the nation and its sites of origin shifted along with the earth's tectonic plates during *goudougoudou*, creating not only a profound physical opening but also a metaphysical one.[12] Elizabeth McAlister writes in "Voodoo's View of the Quake in Haiti," "In Vodou most ritual is about finding balance, putting yourself into equilibrium with the spirits, with your family, and with yourself. In Haiti things are way out of balance. We might say that spirits of death have launched a coup d'état."[13] For Erol Josué, artist, priest of the spirits, educator, and now director of Bureau d'Ethnologie in Port-au-Prince, *goudougoudou* was "both scientific and symbolic." He related to McAlister that Haitians consider the country a woman, their mother. "'Haïti Chérie,' as the well-known ballad goes. She wants to know, 'who will make me beautiful, put clothes on me, and take care of my children?' When you mistreat her, and uproot her trees, when you give her too much responsibility, she is like a woman with cancer. The tumor metastasizes, and explodes."[14] For Josué,

> the earthquake was mother nature, the land of Haiti, rising up to defend herself against the erosion, deforestation, and environmental devastation that have been ongoing for the last few decades. "Everybody was smashed to the ground," said Erol. "Rich and poor. But look how symbolic this is. The Palace is smashed, the legislative building, the tax office, and the Cathedral. The country is crushed. We are all on our knees."[15]

Indeed, perhaps tellingly, many of the symbols of colonial and postcolonial rule (Western "order") were destroyed in the earthquake, even while the statues of Haiti's founding fathers—Toussaint Louverture, Jean-Jacques Dessalines, and Alexander Pétion as well as *Le Marron inconnu* (The Unknown Maroon), the majority located in downtown Port-au-Prince—remained standing. McAlister rightly interprets Josué's lamentation as "a giant natural rebalancing act, a reaction against human dealings with the ecosystem."[16] In so doing, she understands Josué to be expressing his grief at the massive loss of life through a Vodou episteme that views the relationship between humans, spirits, and nature as inextricable. We have been witnessing Haiti, a wounded mother who, in pain, has been saying "enough" for a number of years.[17]

The repercussions of those tectonic shifts have yet to be fully realized. Nonetheless, as is true for the rest of this book, this chapter, while engaged with historical records, is not dependent upon their reassurance for what I believe to be "Spirit truth-telling" that transcends such "inherited habits of knowing."[18] As such, accessing the meaning in the crises that plague the physical and spirit worlds of Haiti is possible.

As I have discussed several times throughout this text, Vodou strives for equilibrium, centeredness, or balance. Alexander remarks that "the symbols and symbolism of centering—that is, of the concentration of Sacred energies—are numerous. They can be found in the *djevo* (the altar room), the *poto mitan* (the central pole through which the Lwa descend), and the *vèvè* (the Sacred ground etchings on which they come to ceremonial rest, which are not to be displaced once ceremony begins)."[19] Implicit in the concept of equilibrium, centeredness, and balance is its opposite: disequilibrium, off-centeredness, imbalance—a state in which Haiti is caught. This is a critical moment in history; a time when Spirit is telling its truth, calling for a restoration of equilibrium. This is a moment of chaos, manifest most violently and obviously on a physical plane through the hurricanes and floods and the earthquake, again reflecting the inextricable relationship between Spirit, nature, and human.

On the metaphysical plane, the struggle to restore balance began the moment of the first violent separation of Africa from what became its diaspora and has been never-ending, resurfacing periodically, for example, in the revolution of 1804, in that of 1946, and in 1986 through its human agents.[20] It is also what we are witnessing now. This time is also a moment of profound creativity evidenced by not only the work of Atis Rezistans but also by other visual artists like Frantz Zéphirin, who, like a prophet, painted *The Resurrection of the Dead*, depicting three skeletal figures, the Gede, Gran Brijit, and her husband, Bawon Samdi, standing in a doorway in 2007, three years before the earthquake.[21] McAlister offers insight into the image, remarking that the wall surrounding the doorway is filled with

the unblinking faces of the spirits of the recently dead. Just crossed over, they still have eyes, which are the blue and red of the Haitian flag. . . . Below them are the waters, the waters under which lies the country without hats, where the sun rises facing backwards. This is where the dead spend a year and a day. *An ba dlo.* Under the water. Resting. Floating. After that when it is time, they will be lifted out, drawn out, by their living. If they are lucky to have children living and walking on the earth.

The dead are still with us, in the unseen world. They have a space. They have a time. They have company. They are not alone. They will be received. They will hear prayers. They look at us.[22]

Haiti's human, spiritual, and ecological condition are conjoined in the painting and reflected in McAlister's comments about it. Zéphirin was in Haiti at the time of the earthquake, living in a Vodou temple on a mountaintop. Perhaps as a testament to his openness to hearing the voice of Spirit, following the earthquake he set his easel up on the devastated street and began a new painting, *The Cry of the Earth.*[23]

While this study focuses on three particular geographical locations, we must also remember that Haiti as well as the areas known contemporarily as the Congo and Benin Republic—all produced under "the grotesque conditions of slavery"[24]—are also part and parcel of the continent called Africa and the larger diaspora. As we undertake the work of remembering and gathering together, we should hold close Alexander's counsel that "no illness has a manifestation that is only of the individual, this theory of equilibrium applies to the social, that is, to the collective as well. The two are, therefore, entangled."[25] I would also add that many on both sides of the water are entangled.

Tidalectic Disasters

Between the fifteenth and nineteenth centuries about 12 million African people, many of them from the Dahomean major port city of Whydah (Ouidah), were taken from the West Coast of Africa to the "New World," with 80 percent of those people being exiled from the African continent between 1700 and 1850.[26] Ouidah was a major hub of the slave trade from the 1670s through the 1860s, accounting for over 10 percent of all the slave trade, over 1 million people.[27] In the 1690s the trade through Ouidah reached about ten thousand people per year and in the years 1700 and 1713, the number of people disembarked reached approximately fifteen thousand per year, accounting for up to half of the enslaved people who left the continent.[28]

Here I recount one final *istwa* that implicates both King Agadja, who is credited with gaining control of and ritualizing the human commerce in Ouidah, and King Ghezo, who worked closely with the Brazilian slave trader Francisco Félix de Souza, "the Viceroy of Ouidah." According to Robin Law, contemporary local "tradition" asserts that de Souza's barracoon was located in the Zomaï quarter on the west of Ouidah. Zomaï, which means "place where light does not go," was named so because enslaved people "were reportedly brought to the barracoon at night and kept in darkness as a means of control."[29] Law doubts the story because earlier stories explain the name as alluding to the location of de Souza's gunpowder stores. He deduces that the present-day story of Zomaï is probably an authentic tradition of a storehouse being embellished in the recent quest for "'sites of memory' connected to the slave trade."[30] Likewise, the second story—the one that I heard several times—posits that a second place called Zomaï in Zoungbodji, just south of Ouidah, was a barracoon in which captives were lodged before their final departure for the beach. The adjoining site, a memorial erected as part of UNESCO's Slave Route Project and Ouidah '92, is believed to be a communal grave for those who died prior to embarkation.[31]

According to the stories told to me, captives were housed for months in Zomaï in complete darkness while they awaited the future horrors of the transatlantic journey. Because the captives were spending weeks—sometimes months—awaiting transport, the heat and filth of Zomaï made death a close friend. Those captives who succumbed to death were dumped in a mass grave in Zoungbodji. It was only in 1992, when UNESCO undertook the Slave Route Project, that the lives of those who had perished and were left to unrest on the coast of Africa in an unmarked site were commemorated. This monument is the one that Law refers to, and the one he claims that, though not intrinsically implausible, is not corroborated in any contemporary source (Fig. 17).[32]

Not far from the mass grave memorial is the Tree of Return (Fig. 18) where, according to the story told to tourists, slave traders forced those who were destined for the middle passage to circle three times so that their spirits would return to their homeland in death. This ritual followed one in which captives were made to circle the Tree of Forgetting (Fig. 19) so that they would forget their history and culture as well as those who had sold them into slavery.[33] Undoubtedly, some of the people who underwent the ritual did not survive Zomaï. Others did not survive the

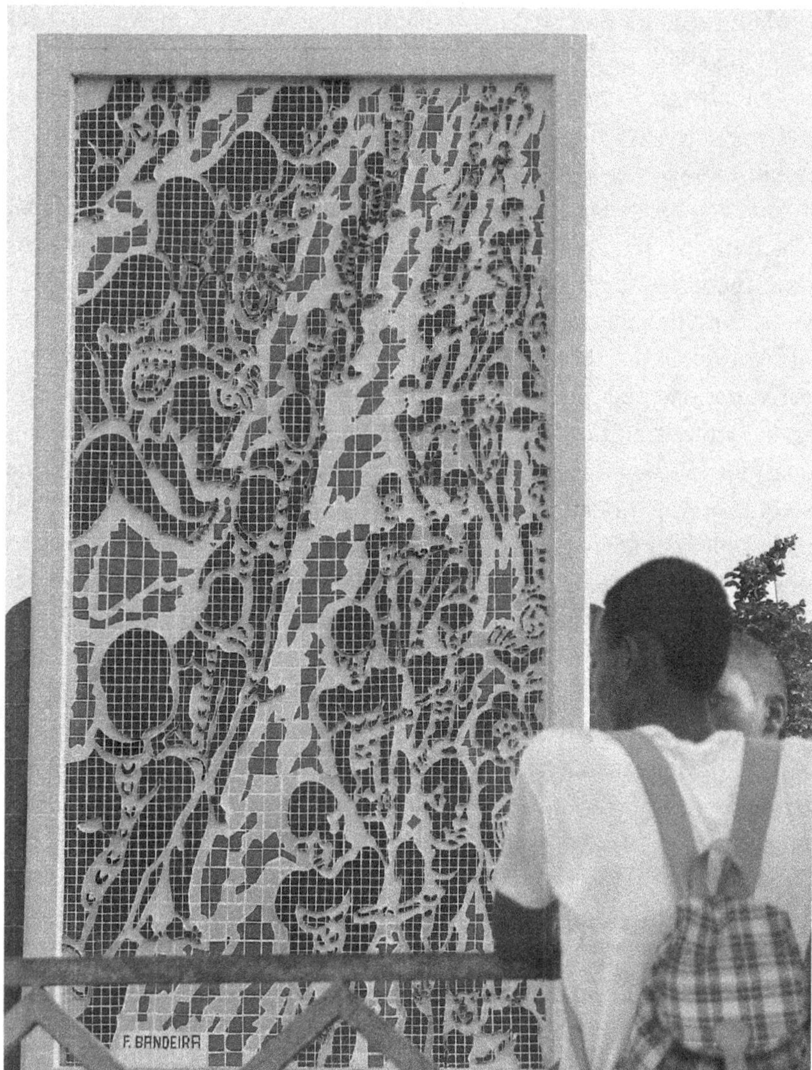

Figure 17. Zoungbodji Memorial. The monument, faced with mosaic tile, is by Cotonou artist Fortuna Bandeira. The memorial is said to be built over the common grave of those who died in the Zomaï Enclosure. Slave Route, Ouidah, Benin Republic. Photo: Toni Pressley-Sanon, 2006.

middle-passage journey. If, as *sèvitè* believe, the soul survives the body and must be remembered and honored by the living, then we must ask ourselves what happened to those souls? Were there new horrors to be faced in death? How was the relationship between the living and the dead affected by this initial violence? Was the ritual successful, so that those

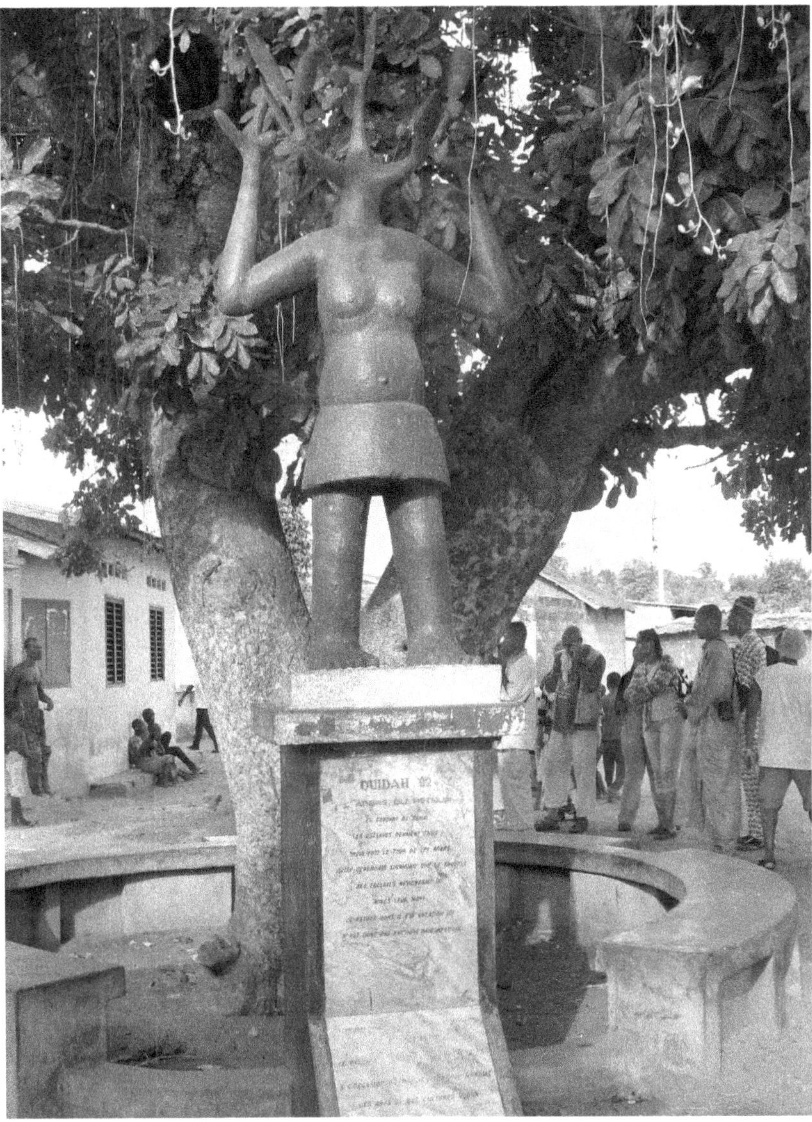

Figure 18. Tree of Return monument sculpture by Cyprien Tokoudagba, Slave Route, Ouidah, Benin Republic. The tree where the sculpture stands is said to be where those destined for the New World were forced to circumambulate three times in order to facilitate their souls' return in death. Photo: Toni Pressley-Sanon, 2005.

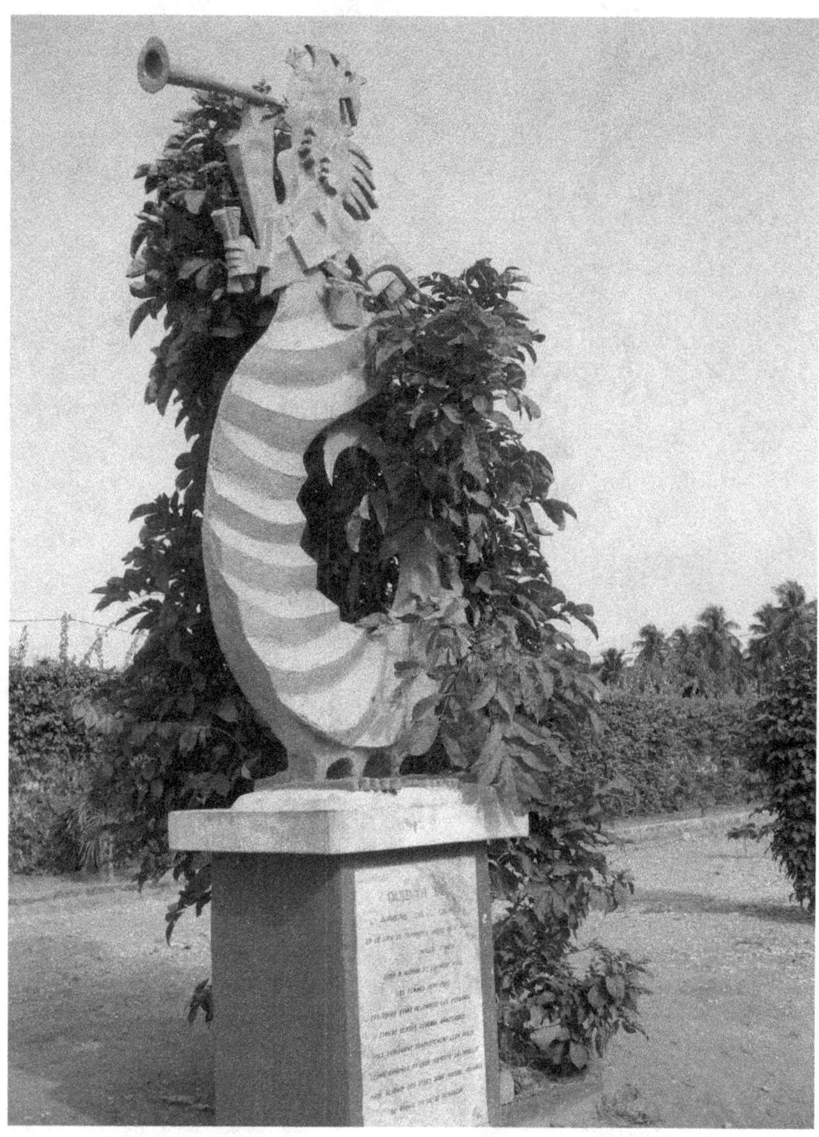

Figure 19. Tree of Forgetting monument with metal Mami Wata sculpture by Porto-Novo artist Dominique Kouas. The memorial marks the site of the Tree of Forgetting on the Slave Route path where captive men were believed to have been made to circumambulate nine times and women seven times to make them forget their pasts. Slave Route, Ouidah, Benin Republic. Photo: Toni Pressley-Sanon, 2005.

souls that returned in death, whether from Zomaï or from abroad, found peace in their land of origin?

According to Martine de Souza, historian, guide, and descendant of Francisco Félix de Souza, King Agadja's ritual was only partly successful. During an interview with me she related the story of being a teenager and accompanying her father and his friend, a foreigner who was also a spiritual medium, to the Tree of Return.[34] She claims that the medium was not able to stand near the tree: "She started screaming, 'Take me out of here! Take me out of here!'"[35] The discord and pain that the medium sensed as she stood at the tree was an indication to de Souza that the souls *did* stay or returned to Ouidah in death as King Agadja had planned. However, they were condemned to an eternity of unrest. According to de Souza, those spirits remain in that tree, unable to pass into the next life.

Law has also written about the rituals of circumambulation that are commonly related to and reenacted by tourists who visit Ouidah.[36] For Law, the stories about the Tree of Forgetting and the Tree of Return encapsulate two contradictory dimensions of the operation of the slave trade:

> its general tendency to obliterate the identity of its victims and, on the other hand, the resistance of the slaves themselves to this process of deracination, while also suggesting some idea of bad conscience (or, at least, fear of retribution) on the part of the African slave-dealers. They have been interpreted as suggesting a conscious policy on the part of the Dahomean kings, beginning with Agadja, who is sometimes credited with planting both trees, to establish "psycho-religious control of the operation" of the slave trade.[37]

However, for Law, similar to his assessment of Zomaï and Zoungbodji, while the Tree of Forgetting and the Tree of Return have their emotional appeal, they were probably not used for their purported purposes. There is no historical evidence to support the belief that they were used during the operation of the slave trade. In fact, there seems to be no record of them before the 1990s. Rather, he speculates that they are contemporary inventions that correspond with Ouidah '92 celebrations.

Although there was a tree called the "Captain's Tree" just south of Ouidah that was reportedly a meeting place for the *yovogan* or viceroy and other local authorities of Ouidah, and certain accounts mention a ceremony of circumambulation, it was the Ouidah chiefs rather than captives who circled the tree three times prior to formally greeting the Europeans.[38] While there is doubt that the rituals that are related actually took place, Law reads the stories about them as mythos that helps explain the origins of the diaspora.

I offer two responses to Law's reading of this history. First, we must remain mindful of the fact that just because something is not part of the historical narrative, this does not mean it does not exist or that an event did not take place, as Hayden White reminds us.[39] The historical narrative is rife with omissions and erasures. Relatedly, all of these stories may be read as *istwa*, which operate in and through history, reaching beyond empirical evidence to memory and story to allow insight into the experience of those who underwent and witnessed the historical event—an extremely traumatic one of enslavement and exile—based on what Stephan Palmié calls their "spiritist doctrines."[40]

As such, the story of the Tree of Forgetting and that of the Tree of Return hold cultural currency not only in Benin Republic but also in the diaspora. How else to explain a mirror of the ritual in Haiti in the "notorious forgetting trees, the *sabliyes*" that, according to Danticat, "our ancestors were told would remove their past from their heads and dull their desire to return home?"[41] While the ritual in Ouidah involved circumambulation, in Haiti one passes under the *sabliye* (that which forgets) tree in order to forget. And probably like their ancestors who underwent the ritual in Ouidah, those in Haiti hold their breath and cross their fingers and toes and hope that the forgetting will not penetrate too deeply into their brains.[42]

After Zomaï

Those who survived Zomaï then had to endure the middle-passage voyage. Of the approximately 12.5 million people exiled to the Americas between 1500 and 1866, about 15 percent died, "most from the accumulation of brutal treatment and inadequate care from the time of their enslavement in the interior of Africa. Others suffocated in the tightly packed holds, while some committed suicide, refused to eat, or revolted."[43] Ship captains also regularly resorted to ordering the jettisoning of their human cargo when pandemics broke out. This was such a common practice that sharks were frequently seen following slave ships. The poet, novelist, and playwright Fred d'Aguiar eloquently depicts the effects of this practice in his novel *Feeding the Ghosts*, based on the events of the slave ship *Zong* in which 131 captives were thrown overboard when a pandemic broke out, some of them still very much alive:

> Soon all those bodies melt down to bones, then the sea begins to treat the bones like rock, there to be shaped over time or ground to dust. Sea does not stop at death. Salt wants to consume every morsel of those bones until the sea becomes them, becomes their memory. So it is from the sea that all 131 souls are to be plucked. From a sea oblivious to time. One hundred and thirty-one dissipated bodies find breath in the wind skimming the surface of the sea and howl. These bodies have their lives written on salt water. The sea current turns pages of memory. One hundred and thirty-one souls roam the Atlantic with countless others. When the wind is heard it is in their breath, their speech.[44]

History blends with memory in creative elegance in d'Aguiar's novel. The Atlantic Ocean holds the bones of thousands of men, women, and children who embarked on the middle-passage voyage. Those fragments of bone formed the coral that would surround the New World's shores and perhaps act as conduits for the metaphysical energy that sustains the dynamic relationship between the diaspora and its sites of origin, as I have discussed throughout this text.[45]

The Dead Remember

Alexander reminds us that "the dead do not like to be forgotten."[46] People's bodies may be gone, but their spirits live on, and if we, the living, do not give, as Morse cautions, "they will take." The sea remembers them, the wind remembers them, and the trees remember them. The souls of the living also remember them.

The *sèvitè*'s belief that the dead do not cease to exist and must be remembered and attended to finds its origins in Africa. John Mbiti writes that if a person is remembered by name, he or she is not really dead, but alive. This person, a "living-dead," is physically dead but alive in the memory of those who knew him or her as well as in the world of the spirits. "So long as the living-dead is thus remembered, he is in the state of *personal immortality*. . . . From the point of view of the survivors, personal immortality is expressed or externalized in acts like respecting the departed, giving bits of food to them, pouring out libation and carrying out instructions given by them either while they lived or when they appear."[47] In Vodou, we also find this belief, as *sèvitè* believe that although the body dies, the soul never really dies, even when "the visual and verbal manifestations of [the person's] transition—the tombstones and mausoleums, the elaborate wakes and church services, the *désounen* prayers that encourage the body to surrender the spirit" fade or cease.[48]

Tidal Dialectics: The Dead and the Living

In Haiti there is the belief that people have several souls. The word "*namn*," from the French word for soul, is only one of the complex forces that constitute a person. It is what animates the human body and leaves soon after death. People also have a *gwo bonanj* and a *ti bonanj*. The *gwo bonanj* is involved in the struggle when a *lwa* mounts a *sèvitè*. It is also the *gwo bonanj* that must be removed from the head of a person shortly after death and then sent *anba dlo* (literally, under the water) for a period of time until it is called up from the water, placed in a *govi* and installed on the family altar.[49] The *ti bonanj* can be characterized as a kind of "spiritual reserve tank. It is an energy or presence within the person that is dimmer or deeper than consciousness, but it is nevertheless there to be called upon in situations of stress and depletion."[50] All three of these forces (*namn*, *gwo bonanj*, *ti bonanj*) that constitute the person along with the *zetwal*, a form of fate, are derivative of what ethnographers call the "multiple soul complex" in West Africa.[51] All of these aspects of the being must be addressed in life and in death.

This belief in several souls means that the community of the Haitian person extends far beyond his immediate family or community as well as his village or city or even his country. It includes not only the various *lwa* but generations of dead relatives and ancestors. Some believe that the dead live in close proximity to the *lwa*, *anba dlo*; others believe that they occupy no special resting place. Some believe that all the dead may eventually become a *lwa* in their own right. There are also African precedents for this belief. Indeed, some of the great *vodun* and *orisha* of the Dahomean and Yorùbá pantheons in West Africa are believed to be deified clan ancestors or kings. An example of this is King Agadja of Dahomey, an historical figure, who is now a *vodun*. More recently, the Daagbo Hounon (the supreme priest of Vodun) proposed making the diaspora the presiding *vodun* of his reign as supreme chief.[52]

The necessity of attending to the dead is also found among the traditional belief systems of the Bapindi and Babunda people of Western Kôngo. The ethnomusicologist Leo Verwilghen commented on this belief, saying, "Towards the dead it is necessary to make offerings as a mark of deference when one wishes to consult them on problems. . . . The dead have the responsibility of protecting their descendants."[53] More importantly, the relationship between the living and the dead is one of interdependence, which is also found among *sèvitè* in Haiti. Karen McCarthy Brown counsels that "in the Vodou view of things the living, the dead, and the spirits are all dependent on one another. No group is, or could be, self-sufficient. The living (*vivan-yo*) need the advice, warning and protection provided by ancestors and the spirits. The ancestor and spirits, in turn, have to be fed and honored if they are to muster the strength and will to protect the living."[54] I contend that this interdependence must be understood as part and parcel of the open and continual dynamic exchange of energies between the dead and the living on both sides of the water if both are to be sustained.

The fear of the repercussions from someone whose rites are not properly carried out is also integral to Haitian cultural belief. First, a person must have his or her *gwo bonanj* removed in death. Otherwise the spirit will be restive and perhaps cause difficulties for her family and descendants. In order to not have the dead wreak havoc on the living, a special rite called *désounen* to remove the *gwo bonanj* from the head of a deceased person must be performed. Second, if a corpse is not taken to a proper graveyard, the *gwo bonanj* can refuse to be buried with the corpse.[55] It instead liberates itself from the corpse and retires *anba dlo*. Then the spirit of the person is no longer a friend and benefactor of the family. He can no longer be inherited by the family and may be angered at the treatment received, returning to harass the family. "Thus, if a family fails to have the maît tête [one's principal protective *lwa*] removed from its family member at death, it may be prosecuted afterward by the spirit of the dead ancestor and the loa as well."[56] In addition to a proper burial, a period of mourning must be observed or "worn" by the deceased's loved ones. By "wearing mourning" the living rid themselves of the souls of the deceased. A peasant woman whom Alfred Métraux interviewed clarified the consequences for the living ignoring their responsibility to the dead when she explained that if they did not mourn the dead, "they would 'seize'" them and try to do them harm.[57]

The Metaphysical Reaches of the Earthquake and Beyond

Everyone is at the mercy of the deceased who feel neglected. The earthquake affected both the urban and rural areas of Haiti. Its vast reach means that it is also no longer mothers and fathers whose wrath the living must face but the huge number of children who perished when grade schools and universities collapsed with students inside. Just as men, women, and children were dumped in the mass grave in Ouidah hundreds of years ago and their descendants have the task of reconciling those restless spirits, so too are the living in Haiti faced with going forward without having been able to properly lay to rest not only the souls of those who grew to adulthood but also those whose lives were just beginning. The mass ocean graves of the past are repeated in the mass graves that now occupy the Haitian landscape. Similar to what Alexander describes about the disrespectful way that African bodies were treated in death under slavery and colonialism, "stacked sometimes ten high in a set of mass graves, the head of one thrown in with the body of another, male becoming female, female becoming male," postearthquake dump trucks scooped up and unceremoniously deposited thousands of bodies in unmarked graves across Haiti's devastated Port-au-Prince as well as Carrefour Feuilles, Léogâne, Petit-Goâve, Miragoâne, and Jacmel.[58] Beauvoir, reflecting on that time, testified, "They grabbed people with cranes. They came and just grabbed everybody together. Your leg was in the hole and your head was somewhere here, and they simply dropped you in the holes. I think it was undignified and I screamed."[59] Also reflecting on that time, Josué has remarked, "When death comes unexpectedly . . . it's confusing to the souls. And now the earthquake has yielded another spiritual tragedy: mass graves. . . . We have to make sure we bury our ancestors. . . . We have to show respect to them. And to put them into a mass grave is no respect for our culture, no respect for our ancestors."[60]   The choice of the deceased's resting place is important to the livings' work of sending off their dead. As in other aspects of the livings' relationship to the dead, the importance of the gravesite in Haitian culture has its roots in Africa. Robert Farris Thompson argues in *Flash of the Spirit* that the importance placed on gravesites in the African diaspora is evidence of continuity from its African roots and identifies Kôngo-Angola influence on the New World in the care that is given to graves in the diaspora. For him, the persistence of tradition is nowhere more profoundly pronounced than

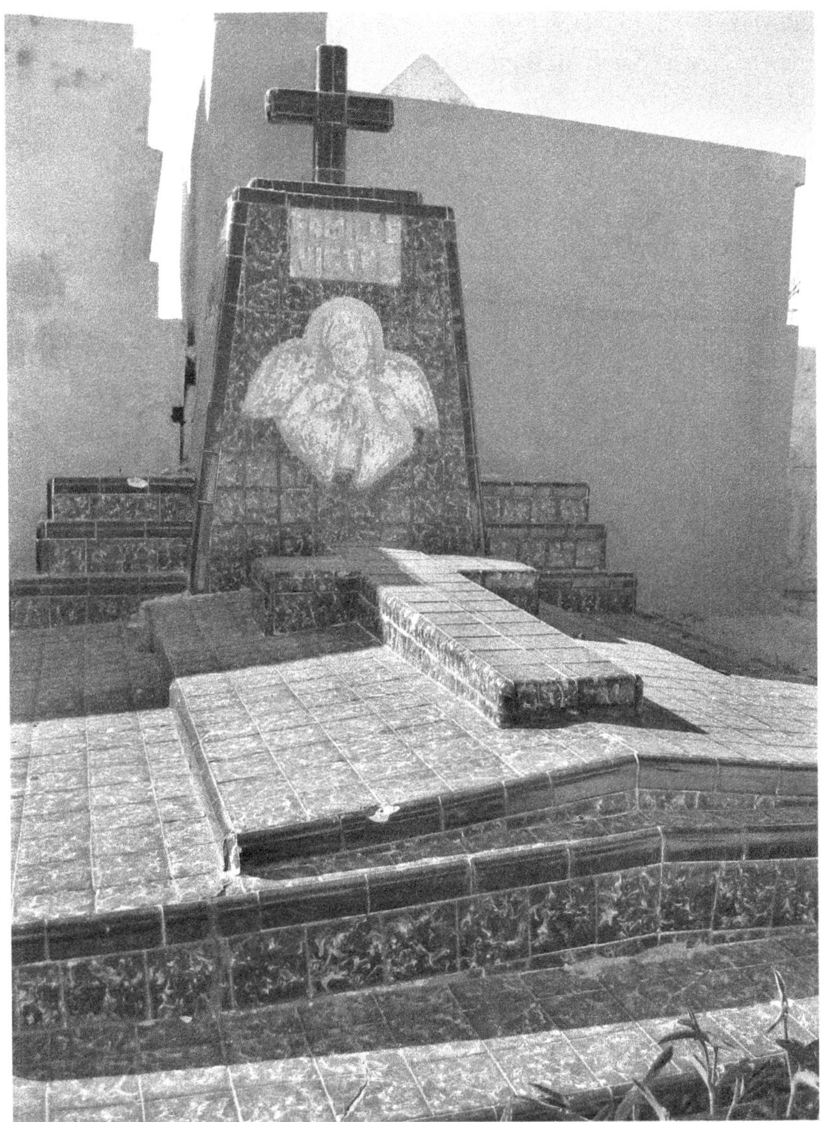

Figure 20. A grave in the National Cemetery, Port-au-Prince. Photo: Toni Pressley-Sanon, 2009.

in black traditional cemeteries in the Southern United States as well as in Haiti and Guadeloupe (Fig. 20). The continuity between Africa and its diaspora might be characterized as a reinstatement of the Kôngo notion of the tomb as a charm for the persistence of Spirit. Like a "container of the Kôngo charm or sacred medicine charged with activating ingredients—a human soul, spirit-embodying and spirit-directing objects," the coffins of Haiti can be seen as the containers and the soul of the deceased, the spark.[61] The decorative objects around a tombstone or crypt honor the spirit on earth, guide it to the other world, and prevent it from wandering or returning to haunt survivors.[62]

The majority of the living population of Haiti could not attend to the traditional ceremonies and rituals postearthquake. Although people tried to bury their loved ones properly, before long, the carpenters who make the coffins behind the National Cemetery, where most of them are built, ran out of wood and had no electricity to make more. People latched wooden coffins to trucks and station wagons and took them to cemeteries where those who had long been resting in family crypts were displaced to make room for strangers. One burial ground in the Delmas area was strewn with coffins that had been dug up and opened and the bones of the original occupants removed so that earthquake victims could be interred. A coffin maker, Pegles Fleurigine, who was overwhelmed with the need for coffins commented, "They bury you like a dog. They don't bury you in caskets."[63] Fleurigine's comment speaks to the incomprehensibility and, thus, the inassimilable nature of the magnitude of loss to human life that the earthquake visited on the country. The living had no choice but to bury the dead as best they could under impossible circumstances. His comment also foretells the metaphysical ramifications of burying the dead without the proper rites. Because the burials were hasty and unorganized, with dump trucks dropping off bodies in Titanyen, a place that used to be a favorite dumping ground for the Tonton Macoutes during the Duvalier era and for the henchmen of Capt. Raoul Cédras' regime, with no one counting, taking pictures, or searching for identification of those left there, many people still have no idea about the fates of their loved ones.

In addition to victims of the earthquake not being properly buried following the disaster, a group of *sèvitè* who tried to guide the souls back to Lan Ginen were attacked by a group of young evangelicals. Journalist Paisley Dodds reported that "some threw rocks while others urinated on

Voodoo symbols. When police left, the crowd destroyed the altars and Voodoo offerings of food and rum."[64] A ceremony that needed to be completed in order to help restore balance was disrupted at the behest of the Protestant missionaries who stepped up their work of proselytizing while demonizing Vodou following the quake.[65] This history of disruption of the relationship between the living and the dead both in Africa and in the diaspora among people for whom that relationship is foundational warrants a consideration of what the absence of respect and proper ritual means for the future physical, metaphysical, and psychological individual and collective health of the island nation as well as its own diaspora.

Reconciliation in Remembrance?

An attempt to ameliorate the effects of that initial dishonoring of the dead can be found in the mural and monument to the victims of the earthquake at the National Cemetery in downtown Port-au-Prince. According to Roginel Pinchinat, the caretaker at the cemetery, over ninety thousand people are buried there. The monument, done by Lionel Saint-Eloi and financed by USAID, is a metal sculpture that depicts an angel watching over the deceased, a globe nestled in her skirts (Fig. 21). The accompanying mural, painted by several local artists, depicts, among other things, the United Nations, government corruption, people helping others emerge from the rubble, Charlemagne Péralte, and technological advancement—snapshots of Haiti's past, present, and envisioned future (Fig. 22).[66]

Shutting Doors on the Dead

During the second anniversary of the earthquake, former Haiti president Michel Martelly held a ceremony at Titanyen with former U.S. president Bill Clinton and former Haiti president Jean-Claude Duvalier in attendance, an oddity that did not go unnoticed by the press and about which Danticat has since written.[67] Danticat's poem, titled "a despot walks into a killing field," draws a connection between the thousands of murdered or left-for-dead "bodies" that were dumped in Titanyen under previous political regimes, including those of the Duvaliers as well as that of Cédras, and those dumped there following the earthquake.[68] Although the living in the audience may behave as if they have no historical memory, Danticat gives the victims a voice with which to contrast the hypocrisy

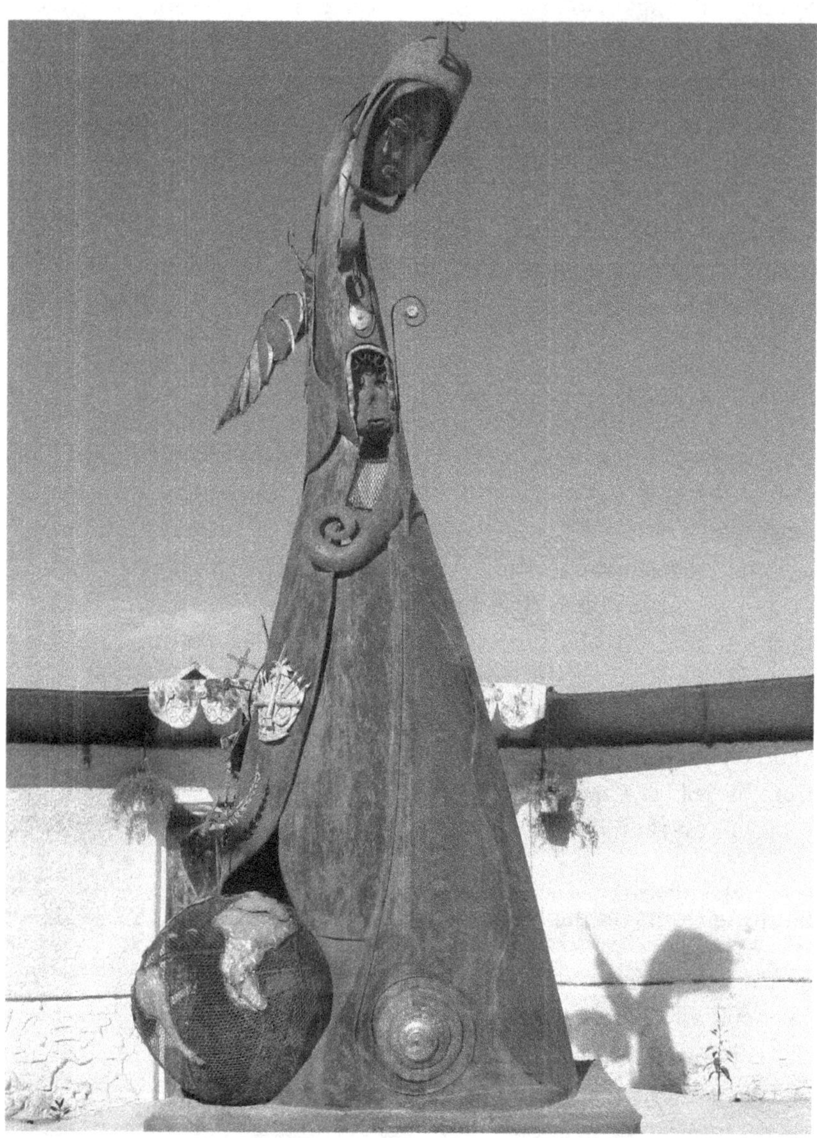

Figure 21. Sculpture by Lionel St. Eloi as part of a monument to commemorate the 2010 earthquake victims, financed by USAID, year unknown. National Cemetery, Port-au-Prince, Haiti. Photo: Toni Pressley-Sanon, 2012.

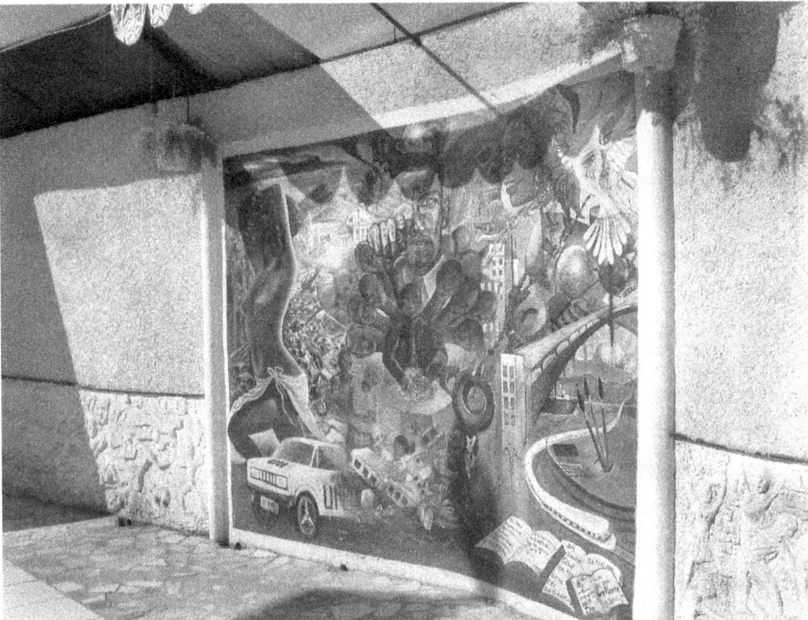

Figure 22. Mural painted by unidentified local artists in monument to commemorate earthquake victims, year unknown. National Cemetery, Port-au-Prince, Haiti. Photo: Toni Pressley-Sanon, 2012.

of those in attendance with the experience of those who are buried there, both following the earthquake and "some thirty years" before under Duvalier's reign:

When the despot arrives
at the ceremony
everyone stands
to greet the despot
and mighty-seeming people
shake his hands

and from the pit of the earth
we
the despot dead
and we the earthquake dead
we scream[69]

The poem also speaks to the haunting that is inevitable in this deliberate forgetting of those whose relationship with the living is never completely broken:

> because it is as if
> the despot were holy
> as if
> we were not here
> as if
> we had never been here
>
> at a ceremony
> where the living
> are meant to remember
> the despot's presence
> tells us they don't
> remember at all[70]

Indeed, if the living truly remembered the exploits of the Duvaliers—many of whom were his victims either directly or indirectly—he would not have been allowed to return to the country after the earthquake, let alone attend the memorial. But while those under the ground ask if those above can hear them, we also know that they will not be silenced. They will make their presence-in-absence known, just as those who were dumped in mass graves in Ouidah because of a similar violence make their presence known if only we listen.

We must ask ourselves how those men, women, and children dumped in Titanyen during Duvalier's and Cédras' reigns mixed in with those more recently with "the head of one thrown in with the body of another" attend to this latest assault on their memory. I believe that the spirits and, as Alexander suggests, the trees, in which spirits live, will whisper remembrances in our ears if we stay still and listen so that the conversations that the Dominican writer Junot Díaz asserts are necessary to understanding what this history means can happen.[71]

In a belief that extends back to points of origin, Dahomey and the Kôngo, the dead continue living. So the question becomes, what kind of spiritual connection is lost when one's spirit departs the body without warning, when the living have no idea whether his or her loved one is alive or dead, or where his or her body lies, and when it is dishonored and desecrated by being left in a field with trash and then further desecrated by the hypocrisy of the living? What happens to the relationship between the living and the ancestors when the living do not give because they are left directionless about where or how to give?

The Way Forward?

While missionaries have been in Haiti for a number of years, their presence increased significantly following the earthquake when Baptists, Catholics, Scientologists, Jehovah's Witnesses, Mormons, and Pentecostals took the crisis of faith that many Haitians suffered in the earthquake's aftermath as an opportunity to step up their efforts to turn the people from their traditional belief systems.[72] *Sèvitè* have reported converting to Christianity not only in order to have access to aid but also to escape the wrath of God that they have been told manifested in the earthquake.[73] As one young woman who had joined the evangelical church two weeks prior to an interfaith ceremony held in February 2010 stated, "The earthquake scared me. . . . Voodoo has been in my family, but the government isn't helping us. The only people giving aid are the Christian churches."[74]

Indeed, this relatively recent encroachment by Protestantism, especially postearthquake, has shifted the balance that *sèvitè* have strived to maintain over the centuries. Protestantism requires abandoning Vodou beliefs and practices. But whereas a few years ago Claudine Michel stated that "few are raised in Protestant families; people typically convert to Protestantism if they decide their religion no longer works for them," and Glenn Smucker saw conversion as a "legitimate means of escaping ritual indebtedness to spirits when they turn a deaf ear or withhold pity in hard times," in postearthquake Haiti the battleground for souls has become fiercer.[75] Protestantism has been in the country long enough for there to be a good number of young people who *were* raised in the church, and they seem to be the most virulent. They were the ones whom Dodds reports pelted the *sèvitè* with rocks during the postearthquake ceremony. And although Michel maintains that "few Haitians stop believing in the spirits and it is not unusual to see people go back to Vodou if Protestantism fails them," Felix Germain notes that "recent developments suggest that the *va et viens* movement between Protestantism and Vodou" is a thing of the past.[76] He attributes this phenomenon to the "increasing material poverty among the majority of the population, the deployment of well-planned Christian crusades, and the financial condition of the churches, which in the context of Haiti is very impressive," a reality that we hear in the explanation of the young convert.[77]

While some may see this assault on Haitian spirituality as a threat to its survival, it could also be seen as a moment when some who claim to have converted are doing what African and African diasporic people have done for centuries when their way of being in the world was threatened. They discerned, adapted, synthesized, assimilated, hid, and revealed their gods within the foreign framework while they continued to do what they needed to do in order to live the way they knew was best for them and theirs.[78] At the same time, they continue to express through various culturally significant ways the myriad means and ways by which they resist their own assimilation. It is this spirit of resistance and the ability to accommodate, assimilate, and mask that will sustain them through this current crisis. It is also a turning toward Nature and Spirit that will guide them through this persistent crisis.

5

Epilogue

Re-Suturing or Joining the Parts to the Whole

In early 2015 Max Beauvoir counseled that Vodou is the soul of the Haitian people, that nothing could be done without that basis.[1] In the spirit of the Marasa who have guided the conceptualization and writing of this text and an orientation born of tidalectics, this epilogue returns to some of the theoretical anchors that have threaded their way throughout this project. It also spirals out, invoking the creative infiniteness that the addition of Dosu/Dosa to form Marasa Twa signify.

In "African Continuity in Haitian Religious Life" Claudine Michel states, "Vodou in Haiti is a means of resistance and organization; it has been employed to re-suture social identity, cultural integration and moral authority in the face of social and historical forces which tended towards annihilation of the slave, and in modern times, the exploitation of the Haitian masses."[2] As I have shown throughout this text, this "re-suturing" about which Michel speaks extends beyond Haiti to encompass Dahomey and the Kôngo as principal contributors to the country's contemporary spiritual orientation and reality. This pull to re-suture takes place in both the visible and invisible realms. The Marasa reigns over it all. As the very essence of completeness, the Marasa Twa affords scholars of Caribbean history and cultural production an important lens through which to understand what they are witnessing in not only oral and written literatures but also visual, dramatic, and musical arts, and to testify. In so doing, they follow the lead of adherents to both African and African diasporic spiritual belief systems and oral and visual artists who have been reflecting and commenting on the continuities and ruptures and imagining an alter/native way of being for centuries.[3] They do so by way of the paradigm shift that an engagement with the history and the *lwa* (the actors in Haiti's "secret history") call for.

Spiritual beliefs affirm moral values. Their efforts to sustain a high sense of humanism and communality both in Africa and abroad support and sustain their supplicants' negotiations with a world that is predicated on physical and spiritual alienation and violence. As I have shown, it can also be useful in fostering the remembering and gathering together of Africa and its diaspora that the Vodou song from the introduction's epigraph summons.

Echoing Beauvoir's pronouncement, Michel writes that Vodou "has been a central thread in the very fabric of the Haitian experience. As such, it is a true measure and expression of national consciousness and of African continuity in the Americas."[4] Vodou insists on these continuities both within and through the ruptures and thus may be the key to re-membering not only the loose seams of Haiti's spiritual systems and its sociopolitical history, as Kate Ramsey suggests, but also those that exist across the ocean in Africa as their own Marasa, both visible and invisible, still struggle with their own memory of the slave trade and its aftermath.[5]

As the gods made their way from Africa into the diaspora via the middle passage—that ultimate liminal space—the physical manifestations of *vodun* power also made their way across the water in the *bociọ* and cakatú, transforming and transfiguring as they went. And while, indeed, it is Legba, Guardian of the Crossroads, who opened the gates and, with the support of the other *lwa*, keep them open, the Marasa Twa, "invoked in the Prière Guinée after Legba, Loko and Ayizan," bridge the multiple divides that I have discussed in this text.[6] They are ever present, showing the way both outward and inward as well as beyond. Their generative power symbolizes the fecundity that is Legba and the rebirth out of death that is Gede.

The *lwa* and the principles they carry with them are needed now more than ever as Haiti is at a crossroads, occupied as it is by an international military force, inundated with international nongovernmental agencies and their workers, and with successive governments that advocate turning the country into a sweatshop haven on one hand and returning it to a playground for foreigners on the other while the Dominican Republic levels a modern-day offensive against Haitian, and inevitably their own, humanity.[7] At the same time, as has always been true, the answers to the way to the other side of the crossroads rests in the culture where one witnesses on a daily basis the Haitian urban masses making beauty out of detritus, painting in the midst of disaster, and the peasantry, the backbone of the Haitian economy, continuing to not only grow food but to organize and raise their voices to those who would prefer they remain silent. They tell their own stories using their own bodies. M. Jacqui Alexander posits, "If healing work is a call to remember and remembering is embodied, then we would want to situate the body centrally in this healing complex."[8] The *lwa* show us the way, as this is precisely what they do when they ride their horses. This project has been about adding my own physical, mental, and spiritual body to the many other bodies—physical, mental, and spiritual—invested in the work of individual and collective healing.

In 2013 Margaret Mitchell Armand published *Healing in the Homeland: Haïtian Vodou Tradition*. Even before I knew about the book's existence, my dear friend who is also a University of Buffalo librarian, Glendora Johnson-Cooper, had already ordered it for me. While this may seem like mere coincidence or the work of a particularly efficient person, it may also be seen as another way that the *lwa* have manifested themselves throughout the researching and writing of this project. Although Armand's work is very different from mine in its execution, the premise behind it and her methodology resonates with my own. She explores how decolonization in Haiti may truly be achieved while deconstructing the *affranchi* bourgeois/elite phenomena in Haiti. Her exploration and understanding of the concomitant exploitation of the poor majority and a way beyond it involve embracing indigenous systems of conducting research as tools for reconnecting with past events and reclaiming knowledge through narratives of people's experiences.[9] Her key methodological tools rest in grounded theory and storytelling.

But while Armand's project stays mainly rooted in Haiti's soil, my project finds meaning in liminality characterized by movement back and forth facilitated by the ocean's tides, from the past to the present to the future and back again and in visible and invisible worlds that impact each other. It is based on a two-ness that spirals out to a third infinitely creative space that is not bound by geography. It takes the position that, while what is can be useful in understanding what has gone before and vice versa, and while what will be uses the past and the present as a blueprint, the possibilities for a different liberative future are limitless. The African diaspora in its many rhizomatic iterations teaches us that. Vodou, with its origins in Africa and Europe and born of and in the diaspora, echoes and reinforces these teachings.

Like *Healing in the Homeland*, my work also deploys storytelling, an ancient tradition that has sustained generations and helped people reflect and comment on their realities while showing the way to something different. These stories use memory to reveal histories that may not find their way into traditional historical narratives. As I have shown, they are not only transmitted orally or in written text but also bodily and visually. They are embodied in rituals that teach people how to experience a world that was conceived in violence, dehumanization, alienation, and, ultimately, zombification.

The belief systems that began in Africa and made their way into the diaspora keep open the lines of communication that the systems of power that are built on the suppression of the body, mind, and spirit try to disrupt. These systems are deployed through rituals in the diaspora that use the trauma of the past to survive and perhaps even thrive in the present and the future. The recognition and activation of ancient belief systems account for and incorporate methods of social disruption in, for example, the *bociọ* and *bo*. They can be recognized, although transformed, because of the trials of the diasporic experience across the ocean. These systems can also be witnessed in mechanisms for establishing social control and maintaining harmony, such as the *cakatú* and individual and collective healing systems such as the *nkisi* as well as rituals that will enable the move beyond liminality to (re)aggregation in a new society founded on equity and balance. The hope for reconciliation and, ultimately, healing between Africa and its diaspora toward a return to equilibrium can be found in the contemporary artwork of artists from Haiti who call upon ancient wisdoms while remaining firmly rooted in the here and now of contemporary Haiti, drawing on international influences.

Gina Ulysse has called for new narratives of Haiti. It is true that Haitians "as subjects of research and representation have often been portrayed historically as fractures, as fragments—bodies without minds, heads without bodies, or roving spirits. These disembodied beings have always been in need of an intermediary. They never spoke for themselves."[10] This is not only true of Haitians but of people from the continent and other African diasporic peoples. Ulysse's work calls for Haitians, as part of Africa and the larger African diaspora, to speak for themselves. The ability for them to speak on their own terms, from within their own sense(s) of the world necessitates a putting back together that which has been torn apart. Only then will new truly liberating narratives emerge.

It seems to me that these new narratives will be driven, at least in part, by a looking back to ancient epistemes and ontologies that are constantly transforming and evolving to understand what is happening on the ground and that will facilitate movement beyond the current moment of crisis. A rejoining of the past and the present, the mind with the spirit with the body, and all of them to the natural and supernatural world will not only counter but will also go beyond the fragmented native that is the stuff of mainstream journalists' wet dreams (perhaps under the auspices of the Gede) to a creative regeneration that is built on balance and harmony. The formation of the resultant new narratives will be a collective process, even though there are, by necessity, moments of solitary reflection, within it.

The work of multiple physical and metaphysical ruptures that the transatlantic slave trade engendered was a collective process even as it divided. The work of uncovering multiple histories is also a collective process. Ultimately, the way toward a metaphysical wholeness that Ngũgĩ wa Thiong'o instructs constituted Africa before the transatlantic slave trade or a restoration of equilibrium through a Vodou episteme is also a collective process. It must account for and incorporate the different epistemologies and ontologies that have gone into Vodou and make the world what it is in order to see a way out of its current crisis of Spirit. I see this recent addition to the scholarship by Armand as part of that collective process. I also see my own work as part of the process, joining with the work of people like Joan (Colin) Dayan, one of several scholars from whom I take my cues. Other scholars such as Patrick Bellegarde-Smith and Claudine Michel, whose multiple delineations of Vodou coalesce into a ritual that spans several years and volumes, illustrate the importance of the "repetition of the repetition." Karen McCarthy Brown's ability to condense profound and intricate philosophies into digestible and assimilable wisdoms is a testament to her own commitment to attaining the mind/body unification that she explained so well. Michel-Rolph Trouillot's *Ti Dife Boule Sou Istwa Ayiti*, which Natalie Pierre rightly argues would be an ideal text for civic engagement and politicization among Kreyòl speaking citizens, paved the way for a more inclusive way of conceptualizing Haitian history, one that invited Haiti's "secret history" to announce itself.[11] Kamau Brathwaite's insistence on making the connections between body, spirit, mind, prose, poetry, earth, water, and the cosmos that for centuries were denied have made this current work possible. Kitsimba and Tomás, who made themselves known to those who listened—M. Jacqui Alexander and Stephan Palmié—invite all of us to do so that we may profit from their wisdom. (Not) finally, the many practitioners on both sides of the water who, despite the current assaults against their way of being in and of the world, keep the faith and tradition alive form the *poto-mitan* of this *travay* (work) that demands the full investment of the mind, body, and spirit.

Haiti is at a sociopolitical crossroads. More importantly, it is at a spiritual crossroads. But, like the creativity within the chaos and the continuity within the rupture that characterizes the African diasporic experience, there is hope within the despair. The Marasa reigns over it all. I add my own voice to the "ritualistic invocation to the forces that rule human destiny" to aid in the realization of the hope.[12] As such, I chant,
The Marasa reigns over it all.
The Marasa reigns over it all.
The Marasa reigns over all.
And so it is.

Notes

Groundings: Tidalectics, Marasa, and *Istwa*

1. "The Haitian Flag," in *Ancestral Rays: Journey Through Haitian History and Culture*, ed. Claudine Michel (Santa Barbara: Center for Black Studies, University of California, 2005), 7.

2. Patrick Bellegarde-Smith, "The Spirit of the Thing: Religious Thought and Social/Historical Memory," in *Fragments of Bone: Neo-African Religions in a New World*, ed. Patrick Bellegarde-Smith, 52–70 (Chicago: University of Illinois Press, 2005), 54.

3. André Pierre, qtd. in "A World Created by Magic: Excerpts from a Conversation with André Pierre," in *Sacred Arts of Haitian Vodou*, ed. Donald Cosentino, xx–xxiii (Los Angeles: UCLA Fowler Museum of Cultural History), xxiii.

4. During spirit possession, the person who is possessed is said to be ridden by a spirit like a horse.

5. A *pakèt kongo* is filled with Haitian spiritual objects and used in spiritual ceremonies.

6. Leah Gordon, "Gede: The Poster Boy for Vodou," in *In Extremis: Life and Death in 21st Century Haitian Art*, ed. Donald Cosentino, 101–14 (Los Angeles: Fowler Museum at UCLA, 2012), 111.

7. Leslie Desmangles, *The Faces of the Gods: Vodou and Roman Catholicism in Haiti* (Chapel Hill: University of North Carolina Press, 1992), 115.

8. Bell, qtd. in Gordon, "Gede," 111. Smartt Bell's assertion echoes that of Carolyn E. Fick, in *The Making of Haiti: The Saint Domingue Revolution from Below* (Knoxville: University of Tennessee Press, 1990), 26–17.

9. John K. Thornton, "African Soldiers in the Haitian Revolution," *Journal of Caribbean History* 25 (1991): 61.

10. Boisrond-Tonnerre, qtd. in Gordon, "Gede," 113.

11. Sibylle Fischer, *Modernity Disavowed: Haiti and the Cultures of Slavery in the Age of Revolution* (Durham, N.C.: Duke University Press, 2004), 201.

12. Ibid.

13. Fischer, *Modernity Disavowed*, 202. I understand "black" here to be a politicized term in the way that James Cone uses it in *A Black Theology of Liberation*, 2nd ed. (Maryknoll, N.Y.: Orbis, 1987). As such, native peoples, as an oppressed group, would be considered "black."

14. Alfred Métraux, *Voodoo in Haiti*, trans. Hugo Charteris (New York: Schocken Books, 1972), 11.

15. Schmidt, in Sidney Mintz, Introduction to *Voodoo in Haiti*, Métraux, 23.

16. See Bellegarde-Smith, "Spirit of the Thing," 53. Throughout this text I make a distinction here between "enslaved," a condition to which people are subjected, as opposed to a "slave," a condition that someone internalizes or becomes.

17. Donald Cosentino, "Aristocrats: Themes in the Photographs and Films of Leah Gordon, Diane Arbus and Maya Deren," in *Kanaval: Vodou, Politics and Revolution on the Streets of Haiti*, ed. Leah Gordon (Soul Jazz Publishing: London, 2010), 49.

18. M. Jacqui Alexander, *Pedagogies of Crossing: Meditations on Feminism, Sexual Politics, Memory and the Sacred* (Durham, N.C.: Duke University Press, 2005), 293.

19. Marasa spelled with a capital "m" refers to the *lwa*, while "*marasa*" with a small "m" may either be the Kreyòl term for twins or refer to the concept developed by literary critic Vèvè Clark.

20. See Ngũgĩ wa Thiong'o's *Something Torn and New: An African Renaissance* (New York: Basic Civitas Books, 2009); Abiola Félix Iroko's *La Côte des Esclaves et la Traite Atlantique: Les faites et le jugement de l'histoire* (Cotonou, Bénin: Nouvelle presse publications, 2003); Anne Bailey's *African Voices of the Atlantic Slave Trade: Beyond the Silence and the Shame* (Boston: Beacon Press, 2005); and Sandra Greene's *West African Narratives of Slavery: Texts from Late Nineteenth and Early Twentieth Century Ghana* (Bloomington: Indiana University Press, 2011), to name a few.

21. See, for example, *The Interesting Narrative of the Life of Olaudah Equiano or Gustavas Vassa the African, Written by Himself*, published in 1789, or *Mohammah G. Baquaqua, a Native of Zoogoo* (Djougou), published in 1854. For collected testimonies, see Philip D. Curtin's *Africa Remembered: Narratives by West Africans from the Era of the Slave Trade* (Madison: University of Wisconsin Press, 1967); and John Blassingame's *Slave Testimony: Two Centuries of Letters, Speeches, Interviews, and Autobiographies* (Baton Rouge: Louisiana State University Press, 1977).

22. Guy Endore's *Babouk: Voices of Resistance* (New York: Monthly Review Press, 1991); *Ama: A Story of the Atlantic Slave Trade* by Manu Herbstein (New York: Open Road Integrated Media, 2000); Lawrence Hill's *The Book of Negroes (Someone Knows My Name)* (New York: Norton, 2007); and Daniel Black's *The Coming* (New York: St. Martin's Press, 2015) are a few examples of texts that imaginatively treat the slave trade from the perspective of those who were exiled. While these stories may not be "true," they reflect the historical reality and comment upon the impact of that reality on their protagonists as representative of the larger experience.

23. These include Akinwumi Ogundiran and Paula Saunders' edited volume, *Materialities of Ritual in the Black Atlantic* (Bloomington: Indiana University Press, 2014); and Isidore Okpewho, Carole Boyce Davies, and Ali A. Mazrui's *The African Diaspora: African Origins and New World Identities* (Bloomington: Indiana University Press, 2001).

24. See George Brandon's *Santeria from Africa to the New World: The Dead Sell Memories* (Bloomington: Indiana University Press, 1997); Linda Heywood's edited volume, *Central Africans and Cultural Transformations in the African Diaspora* (New York: Cambridge University Press, 2002); Joseph Murphy and Mei-Mei Sanford's *Osun Across the*

Waters: A Yoruba Goddess in Africa and the Americas (Bloomington: Indiana University Press, 2001); Jacob Olupona and Terry Rey's edited volume, *Òrìsà Devotion as World Religion: The Globalization of Yorùbá Religious Culture* (Madison: University of Wisconsin Press, 2008); Stephan Palmié's *Wizards and Scientists: Exploration in Afro-Cuban Modernity and Tradition* (Durham, N.C.: Duke University Press, 2002); and Rosalind Shaw's *Memories of the Slave Trade: Ritual and the Historical Imagination in Sierra Leone* (Chicago: University of Chicago Press, 2002).

25. See Ogundiran and Saunders, *Materialities of Ritual in the Black Atlantic*; Cosentino, *Sacred Arts of Vodou*; Suzanne Preston Blier, *African Vodun: Art, Psychology and Power* (Chicago: University of Chicago Press, 1995); Suzanne Preston Blier, "Vodun: West African Roots of Vodou," in *Sacred Arts of Haitian Vodou*, edited by Donald Cosentino, 60–87 (Los Angeles: UCLA Fowler Museum of Cultural History, 1995); Robert Farris Thompson, *Flash of the Spirit: African and Afro-American Art and Philosophy* (New York: Random House, 1983); Robert Farris Thompson, *Aesthetic of the Cool: Afro-Atlantic Art and Music* (Pittsburgh: Periscope, 2011); Robert Farris Thompson and Joseph Cornet, *The Four Moments of the Sun: Kongo Art in Two Worlds* (Washington, D.C.: National Gallery of Art, 1981); and Susan Cooksey, Robin Poyner, and Hein Vanhee, eds., *Kongo across the Waters* (Gainesville: University Press of Florida, 2013).

26. See Okpewho, Davies, and Mazrui, *African Diaspora*; and Naana Opku-Agyemang, Paul E. Lovejoy and David V. Trotman, eds. *Africa and Trans-Atlantic Memories: Literary and Aesthetic Manifestations of Diaspora and History* (Trenton: Africa World Press, 2008).

27. See LeGrace Benson, "A Long Bilingual Conversation Concerning Paradise Lost: Landscapes in Haitian Art," in *Caribbean Literature and the Environment: Between Nature and Culture*, ed. DeLoughrey, Elizabeth M., Renee K. Gosson, and George B. Handley (Charlottesville: University of Virginia Press, 2005), 100.

28. Ibid., 100–101.

29. Ibid., 99.

30. For examples of my writings on the influence of the deities and *lwa* on the lives of people in the earthly realm, see Toni Pressley-Sanon, "Exile, Return, Ouidah, and Haiti: Vodun's Workings on the Art of Edouard Duval-Carrié" in *African Arts Journal* 46, no. 3 (August 2013): 40–53; and "One Plus One Equals Three: Marasa Consciousness, the Lwa and Three Stories" Research in African Literatures 44, no. 3 (Fall 2013):118–37.

31. I undertake this project in the tradition of historian Thomas Madiou, who used the oral tradition in his *Histoire d'Haïti* in 1848; anthropologist Michel-Rolph Trouillot, whose *Ti Dife Boule Sou Istwa Ayiti* (1977; repr. Port-au-Prince: Inivèsite Karayib, 2012) is actually framed as a storytelling session to relate the little-known revolutionary history of Haiti as a blueprint for Haiti's way forward vis-à-vis the Haitian peasantry; and anthropologists Rachel Beauvoir and Didier Dominique, whose *Savalou E* (Montreal: Les Éditions du CIDIHCA, 2003) is a collection of stories that they culled around the Seremoni Bwa Kayiman (Bois Caïman Ceremony).

32. Desmangles, *Faces of the Gods*, 1. Sèvitè are also called Vodouists and Vodouizans. The first mention of the term "Vaudoux" is found in 1797 in *Description topographique, physique, civile, politique et historique de la partie française de l'isle Saint-Domingue* writ-

ten by Moreau de St. Méry. He wrote about it as a dance that was popular in the west province. While there are now Haitians who use the terms (Vodouists, Vodouiszans), most Haitians still prefer to say they "serve the spirits." Karen McCarthy Brown, "Serving the Spirits: The Ritual Economy of Haitian Vodou," in *Sacred Arts of Haitian Vodou*, ed. Donald Cosentino, 205–23 (Los Angeles: UCLA Fowler Museum of Cultural History, 1995), 205.

33. Desmangles, *Faces of the Gods*, 3.

34. Joan Dayan, *Haiti, History and the Gods* (Berkeley: University of California Press, 1998), xvii.

35. I use the fragmented spelling of "history" (hi/story) to draw attention to the sacred history behind the history that is written in the historical narrative. It reflects the fragmentary nature of history when the sacred aspect is excluded from the totality of the narrative. I am riffing off of Joan Dayan's brilliant delineation and interpretation of Mintz's introduction to Métraux's *Voodoo in Haiti* when she says that what most haunted her about the introduction was "the sense of thought pressing down on the mind and in the spirit" (xvii). Mintz "supplies what he meant by a 'core of belief': '—one might almost say a series of philosophical postulates about reality" (xvii). In Dayan's words, "the idea of philosophy, of thought thinking itself through history, compelled me. I began to consider not only the historical functions of vodou—its preservation of pieces of history ignored, denigrated, of exoticized by the standard 'drum and trumpet' histories of empire—but the project of thought, the intensity of interpretation and dramatization that it allowed" (xvii).

36. See, for example, Thompson, *Flash of the Spirit*; Blier, *African Vodun*; Donald Cosentino's edited volume, *Sacred Arts of Haitian Vodou* (Los Angeles: UCLA Fowler Museum of Cultural History, 1995); and the numerous articles about power objects that appear regularly in arts journals such as *African Arts*, some of which I discuss in the text.

37. wa Thiong'o, *Something Torn and New*, 5.

38. Ibid.

39. Mackandal in *Monsieur Toussaint, A Play*, by Edouard Glissant, translated by J. Michael Dash and Edouard Glissant (Boulder, Colo.: Lynn Reinner, 2005).

40. Kamau Brathwaite and Nathaniel Mackey, *ConVERSations with Nathaniel Mackey* (Staten Island, N.Y.: We Press, 1999), 32–34.

41. Elizabeth DeLoughrey's whole project in *Routes and Roots: Navigating Caribbean and Pacific Island Literatures* (Honolulu: University of Hawai'i Press, 2007) builds upon Brathwaite's feminized vision of history as destabilizing to the myth of island isolation and as a way of engaging the island as a world as well as a worldliness of islands (2). Brathwaite's reliance on the peasant woman to carry the metaphor forward is important and, I believe, points to the role of women as carriers of culture. At the same time, I would suggest that under the conditions of the transatlantic slave trade, mothering was not solely the work of women. With the need to create life out of death, both women *and* men became facilitators and nurturers of both the individual and the collective transformation that was intrinsic to the experience. In other words, both men and women gave birth to new ways of being in the world.

42. Brathwaite, qtd. in Elizabeth DeLoughrey, "Routes and Roots: Tidalectics in Ca-

ribbean Literature," in *Caribbean Culture: Soundings on Kamau Brathwaite*, ed. Annie Paul (Jamaica: University of the West Indies Press, 2007), 164.

43. DeLoughrey, *Routes and Roots*, 2.

44. Ibid.

45. The term "bodily epistemology" is used by Lisa Woolfolk to discuss bodily memory and the working through of trauma through the body. See Lisa Woolfolk, *Embodying American Slavery in Contemporary Culture* (Urbana: University of Illinois Press, 2009).

46. Brown, "Serving the Spirits," 216.

47. Alexander, *Pedagogies of Crossing*, 316.

48. Ibid.

49. I discuss Legba extensively in chapter 1.

50. Brown, "Serving the Spirits," 222.

51. Ibid.

52. See Max Beauvoir's comments in *Black in Latin America with Henry Louis Gates, Jr.*, Henry Louis Gates Jr. and Ricardo Pollack (PBS Distribution, 2011. http://www.pbs.org/wnet/black-in-latin-america/); and see Erol Josué's comments in his interview with Elizabeth McAlister, "Voodoo's View of the Quake in Haiti," *On Faith*, January 15, 2010, http://www.faithstreet.com/onfaith/2010/01/15/voodoos-view-of-the-quake-in-haiti/2118.

53. Brown, "Serving the Spirits," 223.

54. Claudine Michel, "Of Worlds Seen and Unseen: The Educational Character of Haitian Vodou," in *Haitian Vodou: Spirit, Myth and Reality*, eds. Patrick Bellegarde-Smith and Claudine Michel (Bloomington: Indiana University Press, 2006), 33.

55. Michael Lambek, qtd. in Palmié, *Wizards and Scientists*, 6.

56. Alexander, *Pedagogies of Crossing*, 6.

57. Ibid., 313–15.

58. DeLoughrey, "Routes and Routes."

59. While these scholars relegate their discussion to the African diaspora and, more specifically, the Caribbean, I extend the concept to Africa, which the Atlantic Ocean also conjoins and which also constitutes the original physical root and route for the African diaspora.

60. See Jana Evans Braziel, *Duvalier's Ghost: Race, Diaspora and U.S. Imperialism in Haitian Literatures* (Gainesville: University Press of Florida, 2010), 70–71.

61. Ibid., 70.

62. Ibid. I put "adopting" in quotation marks to call attention to the fact that even though members of the African diaspora occupy countries other than the ones they originate from, very rarely are they actually adopted by the country to which they emigrate. They are, by and large, perpetual "others."

63. Edouard Glissant, *Poetics of Relation*, trans. Betsy Wing (Ann Arbor: University of Michigan Press, 1997), 6.

64. Grace Nichols, "One Continent / To Another," in *i is a long memoried woman* (London: Karnak House, 1983), 5.

65. Glissant, *Poetics of Relation*, 6.

66. Ibid.

67. Bridget Jones makes this point in "'The Unity Is Submarine': Aspects of a Pan-

Caribbean Consciousness in the Work of Kamau Brathwaite, in *The Art of Kamau Brathwaite*, ed. Stewart Brown (Mid Glamorgan, Wales: Seren, 1995), 97, although in a slightly different context.

68. Kamau Brathwaite, *Contradictory Omens: Cultural Diversity and Integration in the Caribbean* (Mona: Savacou Publications, 1974), 6.

69. For a discussion of the relationship between rupture and continuity, see Stuart Hall's essay "Cultural Identity and Diaspora," in *Identity: Community, Culture and Difference*, ed. Jonathan Rutherford (London: Lawrence and Wishart, 1990).

70. Glissant, *Poetics of Relation*, 7.

71. Ibid., 8.

72. Harold Courlander, *The Drum and the Hoe: Life and Lore of the Haitian People* (Berkeley: University of California Press, 1960), 32.

73. Ibid.

74. Ibid.; I have updated the orthography.

75. Marilyn Houlberg, "Magique Marasa: The Ritual Cosmos of Twin and Other Sacred Children," in *Sacred Arts of Haitian Vodou*, ed. Donald Cosentino (Los Angeles: UCLA Fowler Museum of Cultural History, 1995), 268.

76. Ibid.

77. Claudine Michel, "African Continuity in Haitian Religious Life," in *Ancestral Rays: Journey through Haitian History and Culture*, ed. Claudine Michel, 18–19 (Santa Barbara: Center for Black Studies, University of California, 2005).

78. Wyatt MacGaffey, "Twins, Simbi Spirits and Lwas in Kongo and Haiti," in *Central Africans and Cultural Transformations in the American Diaspora*, ed. Linda M. Heywood (New York: Cambridge University Press, 2002), 214.

79. Ibid., 213.

80. Paul Mercier, "The Fon of Dahomey," in *African Worlds: Studies in the Cosmological Ideas and Social Values of African Peoples*, ed. Daryll Forde (New York: Oxford University Press, 1965), 219.

81. Melville J. Herskovits and Francis S. Herskovits, *Dahomean Narrative: A Cross-Cultural Analysis* (Evanston: Northwestern University Press, 1958), 30–31.

82. Edna Bay, *Wives of the Leopard: Gender, Politics, and the Culture of the Kingdom of Dahomey* (Charlottesville: University of Virginia Press, 1998), 216.

83. Mercier, "Fon of Dahomey," 219. "Worldsense" is defined as a more inclusive way of describing the conception of the world that privileges senses other than the visual or even a combination of senses as part of a cultural continuum that "interferes with the neatness of ideological arguments and an official stance that subscribes to the 'two sides' view of reality." See Oyèrónké Oyêwùmí, "Visualizing the Body: Western Theories and African Subjects," in *African Gender Studies: A Reader*, edited by Oyèrónké Oyêwùmí, 3–21 (New York: Palgrave MacMillan, 2005), 4.

84. Ibid.

85. Herskovits, in Métraux, *Voodoo in Haiti*, 150.

86. MacGaffey, "Twins, Simbi Spirits," 214.

87. Herskovits, in Métraux, *Voodoo in Haiti*, 150.

88. In *Life in a Haitian Valley* (1937; repr., New York: Alfred A. Knopf, 2007), Her-

skovits claims that it is not necessary for a family to actually have twins in their generation or to have a memory of them for them to be worshipped. It is sufficient that twins are part of the family lineage. Some families worship twins because an *oungan* has divined that their unknown ancestors in Ginen had included them (203).

89. Houlberg, *Magique Marasa*, 269.

90. Marilyn Houlberg, "Magique Marasa: The Ritual Cosmos of the Twins and Other Sacred Children," in *Fragments of Bone: Neo-African Religions in a New World*, ed. Patrick Bellegarde-Smith, 13–31 (Chicago: University of Illinois Press, 2005), 15.

91. MacGaffey, "Twins, Simbi Spirits," 224.

92. Dayan, *Haiti, History and the Gods*, 36.

93. I do not confine my discussion to the Fon because I am aware, as Robert Farris Thompson reminds us, that "the deities of the Yoruba had made their presence felt in Dahomey over hundreds of years. Yoruba deities were served under different manifestations in Allada before 1659 . . . transforming them into Ewe and Fon local spirits." See Thompson, *Flash of the Spirit*, 166.

94. Courlander, *Drum and the Hoe*, 32.

95. See Beverly Bell, *Walking on Fire: Haitian Women's Stories of Survival and Resistance* (Ithaca, N.Y.: Cornell University Press, 2001), for a discussion of this term and her use of it to collect and discuss Haitian women's stories.

96. Edouard Glissant, *Caribbean Discourse: Selected Essays*, trans. J. Michael Dash (Charlottesville: University Press of Virginia, 1989), 156.

97. Ibid., 155.

98. Paul Connerton, *How Societies Remember* (New York: Cambridge University Press, 1989), 18.

99. Ibid., 18–19.

100. Elizabeth Isichei, *Voices of the Poor in Africa: Moral Economy and the Popular Imagination* (Rochester, N.Y.: University of Rochester Press, 2002), 2.

101. Ibid.

102. Ibid.

103. bell hooks, *Art on My Mind: Visual Politics* (New York: New Press, 1995), 64.

104. Derek Walcott, "The Sea Is History," in *Collected Poems: 1948–1084* (New York: Farrar, Straus & Giroux, 1986), 364–67.

105. Alexander, *Pedagogies of Crossing*, 290.

106. Omise'eke Natasha Tinsley, "Black Atlantic, Queer Atlantic: Queer Imaginings of the Middle Passage," *GLQ: A Journal of Lesbian and Gay Studies* 14, nos. 2–3 (2008): 194.

107. Ibid.

108. Bridget Jones raises the critical question, "what values have been created, what emerges to guide and strengthen a scatter of struggling post-colonial societies?" See Jones, "Unity Is Submarine," 86.

109. Joseph M. Murphy, *Working the Spirit: Ceremonies of the African Diaspora* (Boston: Beacon Press, 1994), ix–xi.

110. Antonio Benítez-Rojo, *The Repeating Island: The Caribbean and the Postmodern Perspective*, 2nd ed., trans. James E. Maraniss (Durham, N.C.: Duke University Press, 2006).

111. Dayan, *Haiti, History, and the Gods*, xv.

112. Brown, "Serving the Spirits," 205.

113. Ibid.

114. Dayan, *Haiti, History and the Gods*, xi.

115. See Gina Ulysse, *Why Haiti Needs New Narratives: A Post-Earthquake Chronicle* (Middleton, Conn.: Wesleyan University Press, 2015).

116. Dayan, *Haiti, History and the Gods*, xv.

117. Dayan makes this point about Vodou in "Dread and Dispossession: An Interview with Colin Dayan," *The Public Archive*, September 23, 2013, http://thepublicarchive. com/?p=3988.

118. I borrow this phrase from LeGrace Benson, who uses it in relation to Wilson Bigaud's *Paradis terrestre* (Earthly Paradise) and which I take to refer to his looking to the motherlands for inspiration. Again, where for Benson the motherlands are Africa and Europe, for me, while I acknowledge Europe's, and for that matter the United States' influence on Haiti as well as indigenous and other African cultures that were imported during the slave trade, for the purposes of this project, I refer to the motherlands as Dahomey and the Kôngo.

119. In her essay "The Site of Memory," in *Inventing the Truth: The Art and Craft of Memoir*, 2nd ed., edited by William Zinsser, 83–102 (1987; repr. Boston: Houghton Mifflin, 1995), Toni Morrison explores the challenges to African American authors' expression of their interior lives under slavery. The limits on it ultimately blocked a deep understanding of the black experience. She talks of fiction (a form of cultural production) by authors who are members of marginalized groups as a way of overcoming the challenge.

Chapter 1. The Changing Same: Bokǫfíó across the Sea

1. Omise'eke Natasha Tinsley, "Black Atlantic, Queer Atlantic: Queer Imaginings of the Middle Passage," *GLQ: A Journal of Lesbian and Gay Studies* 14, nos. 2–3 (2008): 194.

2. Ibid.

3. Harold Scheub, *The Poem in the Story: Music, Poetry and Narrative* (Madison: University of Wisconsin Press, 2002), xiii.

4. Edward Said's *Culture and Imperialism* (New York: Knopf, 1993), in which he reads several European novels contrapuntally, is an example of work that has explored such erasures or rather, presence-in-absences.

5. See Toni Morrison, "The Site of Memory" in *Inventing the Truth: The Art and Craft of Memoir*, 2nd ed., ed. William Zinsser (Boston: Houghton Mifflin, 1995), 91.

6. See Anne Bailey, *African Voices of the Atlantic Slave Trade: Beyond the Silence and the Shame* (Boston: Beacon Press, 2005); Rosalind Shaw, *Memories of the Slave Trade: Ritual and the Historical Imagination in Sierra Leone* (Chicago: University of Chicago Press, 2002); and Elizabeth Isichei, *Voices of the Poor in Africa: Moral Economy and the Popular Imagination* (Rochester, N.Y.: University of Rochester Press, 2002).

7. Françoise Pfaff, "Sembene, A Griot of Modern Times" in *Cinemas of the Black Diaspora: Diversity, Dependence, and Oppositionality*, ed. Michael T. Martin, 118–28 (Detroit: Wayne State University Press, 1995), 119.

8. Melville J. Herskovits, *Dahomey: An Ancient West African Kingdom,* vol. 2 (Evanston: Northwestern University Press, 1967), 241–43.

9. See Heather Russell, *Legba's Crossing: Narratology in the African Atlantic* (Athens: University of Georgia Press, 2011).

10. See, for example, S. Y. Boadi-Siaw's "Brazilian Returnees of West Africa," in *Global Dimensions of the African Diaspora,* edited by Joseph E. Harris, 421–39 (Washington, D.C.: Howard University Press, 1979), which I discuss later in this chapter.

11. Stuart Hall, "Cultural Identity and Diaspora," in *Identity: Community, Culture and Difference,* ed. Jonathan Rutherford, 222–37 (London: Lawrence and Wishart, 1990).

12. I refer here to the Vodou song from the "Groundings" section.

13. See, for example, the documentary series *Wonders of the African World* (by Henry Louis Gates Jr., Arlington, Va.: PBS, 1999) and *Family across the Sea* (by Tim Carrier, Columbia, S.C.: SCETV, 1990). I also heard such explanations when I was conducting field research in Ouidah.

14. UNESCO had planned for the gathering of African and African diasporic people to focus on scientific evidence. Instead the organizers on the ground thought that an artistic commemoration of Ouidah's history would be more appropriate. Thus, Ouidah '92 was born to facilitate memory as well as celebrate the rich history of the religion and its diaspora.

15. Boadi-Siaw, "Brazilian Returnees of West Africa," 422.

16. Ibid. Note the period of trial or testing as an allusion to the rites-of-passage ritual in which an initiate is exiled and undergoes a series of trials or tests before being welcomed back into the community as a valued member.

17. Ibid., 422–23.

18. Edna Bay, "Protection, Political Exile, and the Atlantic Slave Trade: History and Collective Memory in Dahomey," in *Rethinking the African Diaspora: The Making of a Black Atlantic World in the Bight of Benin and Brazil,* eds. Kristin Mann and Edna Bay, 42–60 (Portland: Frank Cass, 2001), 56.

19. Henry Louis Gates Jr., *Wonders of the African World* (New York: Knopf, 1999), 207.

20. Ibid., 50.

21. Herskovits, *Dahomey,* 240.

22. Ibid.

23. John S. Mbiti, *African Religions and Philosophy* (London: Heinemann, 1971), 121.

24. Herskovits, *Dahomey,* 244.

25. Harold Courlander, *The Drum and the Hoe: Life and Lore of the Haitian People* (Berkeley: University of California Press, 1960), 21.

26. The issue of magic is also built into the story in the first lines when Bokǫfíó hears a whistling in his ear just before he finds himself in the large clearing tied with a rope. The use of magic to enslave is a recurring theme in African diasporic myth. One of the most extensive studies of the metaphor of magic to describe the enslavement process is *Exchanging Our Country Marks: The Transformation of African Identities in the Colonial Antebellum South* (Chapel Hill: University of North Carolina Press, 1998) by historian Michael Angelo Gomez. Gomez, who analyzes stories from the slave narratives collected during the WPA project, recounts stories of red cloth being used to lure people to the

ocean shores, rivers being crossed similar to that in the story from Dahomey, and the use of magic to ensorcell captives.

27. Paul Mercier, "The Fon of Dahomey," in *African Worlds: Studies in the Cosmological Ideas and Social Values of African Peoples*, ed. Daryll Forde, 210–34 (New York: Oxford University Press, 1965), 220.

28. Herskovits, *Dahomey*, 248.

29. Ibid., 220–21.

30. Herskovits does not mention the source of the myth.

31. Herskovits, *Dahomey*, 250.

32. Herskovits, *Dahomey*, 249. Sogbó is one of the children of Mawú-Lísa, the original god who was at the same time both male and female. "Sib" refers to the patrilineal relationship groupings that existed in Dahomey. As Herskovits explains, Aido Hwedo is Dan, and Dan represents riches.

33. Ibid.

34. Mercier, " Fon of Dahomey," 221.

35. Ibid.

36. Bernard Maupoil, *La Géomancie à l'Ancienne Côte des Esclaves* (Paris: Institut d'Ethnologie, 1943), 74.

37. Paul Hazoumé, "*La Conquête du royaume houédah par les Dahomeens au XVIIIe siècle*," *Bulletin de l'enseignement de l'Afrique occidentale française*, 45 (January–February 1921): 41–45; Paul Hazoumé, "*Aperçu historique sur les origines de Ouidah*," *La reconnaisance africaine*, 10–11 (1926); and Robin Law, "The Atlantic Slave Trade in Local History Writing in Ouidah," in *Africa and Trans-Atlantic Memories: Literary and Aesthetic Manifestations of Diaspora and History*, ed. Naana Opku-Agyemang, Paul E. Lovejoy and David V. Trotman, 257–74 (Trenton, N.J.: Africa World Press, 2008), 261.

38. Law, "Atlantic Slave Trade," 261.

39. Courlander, *Drum and the Hoe*, 20.

40. Maya Deren, *Divine Horsemen Divine Horsemen: The Living Gods of Haiti* (New York: McPherson and Company, 1970), 115.

41. Ibid.

42. The other two shrines are Legba and Dan. See Herskovits, *Dahomey*, 300–303.

43. Ibid., 303.

44. Deren, *Divine Horsemen*, 146.

45. Agasou, another god, is described as a sacred ancestor and founder of a royal Dahomean sib, according to Herskovits, and ranks close to Loko and Aizan in importance and shares many of their functions and characteristics. See Deren, *Divine Horsemen*, 310n95.

46. The deities Silibo-Gweto and Nana-Bouclou are Dahomean in origin.

47. Deren, *Divine Horsemen*, 148–49.

48. See Karen McCarthy Brown, "Serving the Spirits: The Ritual Economy of Haitian Vodou," in *Sacred Arts of Haitian Vodou*, ed. Donald Cosentino, 205–23 (Los Angeles: UCLA Fowler Museum of Cultural History, 1995), 223.

49. Roger Bastide, *African Civilisations in the New World*, trans. Peter Green (1967; repr. London: C. Hurst and Company, 1971), 142.

50. See Deren, *Divine Horsemen*, 47.

51. Bastide, *African Civilisations*, 143; and Brown, "Serving the Spirits," 205.

52. Hayden White, *Metahistory: The Historical Imagination in Nineteenth Century Europe* (Baltimore: John Hopkins University Press, 1973), 7.

53. Ibid., 2.

54. Hayden White, *Tropics of Discourse: Essays in Cultural Criticism* (Baltimore: Johns Hopkins University Press, 1978), 51.

55. Stephan Palmié, *Wizards and Scientists: Exploration in Afro-Cuban Modernity and Tradition* (Durham, N.C.: Duke University Press, 2002), 8–9.

56. I refer here to Edouard Glissant's quarrel with "History" (with a capital H) in opposition to the multiple histories of the Caribbean in *Caribbean Discourse: Selected Essays*, trans. J. Michael Dash (Charlottesville: University Press of Virginia, 1989). As Glissant avers, "Because the collective memory was too often wiped out, the Caribbean writer must 'dig deep' into this memory, following the latent signs that he has picked up in the everyday world" (64).

57. See Palmié's *Wizards and Scientists*, 9, for this discussion.

58. M. Jacqui Alexander, *Pedagogies of Crossing: Meditations on Feminism, Sexual Politics, Memory and the Sacred* (Durham, N.C.: Duke University Press, 2005), 289.

59. Ibid., 309.

60. Mercier, " Fon of Dahomey," 211.

61. "Social disorder" is a term Blier uses to describe the psychological effect that the slave trade and, later, the demand for palm oil had on those who were subjected to the sociopolitical and economic demands of the markets in both precolonial and postcolonial Dahomey. Blier, *African Vodun: Art, Psychology and Power* (Chicago: University of Chicago Press, 1995), 27.

62. Bay, "Protection, Political Exile," 51.

63. Ibid., 52.

64. Ibid.

65. She borrows the terms from Michael Taussig, *Shamanism, Colonialism, and the Wild Man: A Study in Terror and Healing* (Chicago: University of Chicago Press, 1987), 6.

66. Blier, *African Vodun*, 1.

67. Bakhtin, qtd. in ibid., 18.

68. Maupoil, *La Géomancie*; Edna Bay, *Asen, Ancestors, and Vodun: Tracing Change in African Art* (Urbana: University of Illinois Press, 2008); and Dana Rush, "Ephemerality and the 'Unfinished' in Vodun Aesthetics," *African Arts* 43, no. 1 (2010): 60–75.

69. Dana Rush, "Contemporary Vodun Arts of Ouidah, Benin," *African Arts* 34, no. 4 (2001): 62.

70. Bay, *Asen, Ancestors, and Vodun*, 3.

71. Rush, "Ephemerality and the 'Unfinished,'" 62.

72. Dana Rush, "In Remembrance of Slavery: Tchamba Vodun Arts," *African Arts* 44, no.1 (Spring 2011): 50.

73. Ibid.

74. Sidney Mintz and Michel-Rolph Trouillot, "The Social History of Haitian Vodou,"

in *Sacred Arts of Haitian Vodou*, ed. Donald Cosentino, 123–47 (Los Angeles: UCLA Fowler Museum of Cultural History, 1995), 126.

75. Ibid.

76. Ibid.

77. Elizabeth McAlister, "A Sorcerer's Bottle: The Visual Art of Magic in Haiti," in *Sacred Arts of Haitian Vodou*, ed. Donald Cosentino, 305–21 (Los Angeles: UCLA Fowler Museum of Cultural History, 1995), 305.

78. See my discussion of the *zonbi* in chapter 2.

79. Blier, *African Vodun*, 11.

80. Ibid., 13. I say "seems" because, as I discuss later, the *zonbi* is not as bereft of power as he or she is normally depicted.

81. Herskovits, *Dahomey*, 244.

Chapter 2. Of *Bociọ, Bo, Cakatú, Zonbi, Nkisi,* and *Pakèt Kongo*

Epigraph source: "Closing Event," Rachel Beauvoir-Dominique and Didier Dominique, Université d'Etat d'Haïti, presented at the KOSANBA Conference, Harvard University, Cambridge, Mass., October 18–20, 2013.

1. Descourtilz, in Hein Vanhee, "Central African Popular Christianity and the Making of Haitian Vodou Religion," in *Central Africans and Cultural Transformation in the American Diaspora*, edited by Linda M. Heywood, 243–64 (New York: Cambridge University Press, 2002), 254.

2. Althéa de Peuch Parham, ed. and trans., *My Odyssey: Experience of a Young Refugee from Two Revolutions, by a Creole from Saint Domingue* (Baton Rouge: Louisiana State University Press, 1959), 32.

3. Ibid., 34.

4. Ibid.

5. See Franck Degoul, "*Du Passé Faisons Table d'Hôte: Le mode entretien des zombi dans l'imaginaire haïtien et ses filiations historiques*," *Ethnologies* 28, no. 1 (2006): 242.

6. Maya Deren, *Divine Horsemen: The Living Gods of Haiti* (New York: McPherson and Company, 1970), 113.

7. *Bo* (empowered object) and *ciọ* (cadaver); Suzanne Preston Blier, *African Vodun: Art, Psychology and Power* (Chicago: University of Chicago Press, 1995), 2.

8. Ibid., 28.

9. Ibid., 5.

10. Ibid., 23–24.

11. Ibid., 26, 31.

12. Leah Gordon, ed. *Kanaval: Vodou, Politics, and Revolution on the Streets of Haiti* (London: Soul Jazz Records, 2010), n.p.

13. Gordon, Introduction to *Kanaval*, n.p.

14. Elizabeth McAlister, *Rara! Vodou, Power, and Performance in Haiti and Its Diaspora* (Berkeley: University of California Press, 2002), 7.

15. As Mimi Sheller writes in *Citizenship from Below: Erotic Agency and Caribbean Freedom* (Durham, N.C.: Duke University Press, 2012), "The patterns of highly uneven distribution of human suffering, poverty and violence found in many parts of the Carib-

bean and the wider Americas are closely related to the histories of colonialism, slavery, and exclusion that formed the contemporary world" (1).

16. Karen McCarthy Brown, "Serving the Spirits: The Ritual Economy of Haitian Vodou," in *Sacred Arts of Haitian Vodou*, ed. Donald Cosentino, 205–23 (Los Angeles: UCLA Fowler Museum of Cultural History, 1995), 220.

17. Ibid.

18. Ibid. Tying is also used in love magic according to Brown; ibid., 220.

19. Dana Rush, "Contemporary Vodun Arts of Ouidah, Benin," *African Arts* 34, no.4 (2001): 38.

20. By "distant past," he means before the transatlantic trade.

21. Rémi Seglonou, personal interview, January 2006, Ouidah, Benin Republic.

22. Rush, "Contemporary Vodun Arts," 38–39.

23. Ibid.

24. Ibid., 94.

25. Nancy Scheper-Hughes and Margaret M. Lock, "The Mindful Body: A Prolegomenon to Future Work in Medical Anthropology," *Medical Anthropology Quarterly*, New Series 1, no. 1 (March 1987): 23.

26. Ibid., 24.

27. Ibid.

28. Wade Davis, *Passage of Darkness: The Ethnobiology of the Haitian Zombie* (Chapel Hill: University of North Carolina Press, 1988), 274. I am aware of the problem with using Davis' work with the questions that linger about how he collected his information as well as his misrepresentation of Haiti and its cultural practices. However, I use his work here primarily because the reason given for zombification echoes the reason told to me in Ouidah and that Dana Rush gives for the enactment of the *cakatú*. It is also Max Beauvoir, a well-known *oungan*, who is credited with providing Davis with the explanation. See Hans-W Ackermann and Jeanine Gauthier, "The Ways and Nature of the Zombi," *Journal of American Folklore* 104, no. 414 (Autumn 1991): 475.

29. Davis, *Passage of Darkness*, 275.

30. Ibid., 276.

31. Ibid., 278. Rachel Beauvoir offers a similar explanation in Laënnec Hurbon, *Le Barbare imaginaire* (Paris: Cerf, 1988), 190–91.

32. Davis, *Passage of Darkness*, 278.

33. Edna Bay, "Protection, Political Exile, and the Atlantic Slave Trade: History and Collective Memory in Dahomey," in *Rethinking the African Diaspora: The Making of a Black Atlantic World in the Bight of Benin and Brazil*, eds. Kristin Mann and Edna Bay, 42–60 (Portland: Frank Cass, 2001), 53.

34. Ibid.

35. Melville J. Herskovits, *Dahomey: An Ancient West African Kingdom*, vol. 2 (Evanston: Northwestern University Press, 1967), 63.

36. Claudine Michel, "African Continuity in Haitian Religious Life," in *Ancestral Rays: Journey through Haitian History and Culture*, ed. Claudine Michel, 18–19 (Santa Barbara: Center for Black Studies, University of California, 2005), 18.

37. Ibid.

38. Ackermann and Gauthier, " Ways and Nature of the Zombi," 467.

39. Doris Garraway, *The Libertine Colony: Creolization in the Early French Caribbean* (Durham, N.C.: Duke University Press, 2005), 179.

40. See Ackerman and Gauthier, "Ways and Nature of the Zombi," 475, who attribute the rationale to Ati Max Beauvoir in Wade Davis, *Serpent and the Rainbow* (New York: Simon and Schuster, 1985); and Davis, *Passage of Darkness*. A similar explanation has been offered by Laënnec Hurbon in *Le Barbare imaginaire*, 191.

41. There are several possible etymologies of the word "zonbi." One possible origin is "*jumbie*," the West Indian term for "ghost." Another is "*nzambi*," the Kôngo word meaning "spirit of a dead person." A *zonbi* is a person who is believed to have died and been brought back to life without speech or free will. It is akin to the Kimbundu *nzúmbe* ghost. These words are approximately from 1871.

42. The concept of the *zonbi* was first introduced to the American public by journalist William Seabrook in *The Magic Island* (New York: Harcourt, Brace, 1929), published during the first American Occupation. Since that time, it has been associated with Vodou.

43. Laënnec Hurbon, *Voodoo: Search for the Spirit*, trans. Lory Frankel (New York: H.N. Abrams, 1995), 192–93; and Alfred Métraux, *Voodoo in Haiti*, trans. Hugo Charteris (New York: Schocken Books, 1972), 282.

44. Zora Neale Hurston, *Tell My Horse: Voodoo and Life in Haiti and Jamaica* (New York: Harper and Row, 1990), 62.

45. Ibid., 183; Hurston also claims that *zonbi* do not have the power of speech unless given salt.

46. Hurbon, *Le Barbare imaginaire*, 193 (my translation).

47. Her description is based on a story that she heard while conducting field research. I am aware of the scholarship that has interrogated Hurston's relationship with her work in the Caribbean. As Gwendolyn Mikell notes in "When Horses Talk: Reflections on Zora Neale Hurston's Haitian Anthropology," *Phylon* 43, no. 3 (1982): 218–30, "Hurston's Haitian ethnography . . . is a delicate balance between the calm insider's and the agitated outsider's perspectives" (222), and while the Caribbean required more explanation than her work from the United States, "Haiti required more: explanation and justification" (224). Some of the judgments that she passes about Haitian society mark her as a product of her time. She was, according to Mikell, "the embodiment of all the contradictions inherent in a racist society, and as such, she instinctively reacted to many aspects of Caribbean society" (229). Ifeoma Kiddoe Nwankwo reads Hurston more critically in "Insider and Outsider, Black and American: Rethinking Zora Neale Hurston's Caribbean Ethnography," *Radical History Review* 87 (Fall 2003): 49–77, arguing that while Hurston was accused of primitivization of blacks in *Mules and Men*, her "negative approach is magnified when she encounters Caribbean blacks. Her treatment of the Caribbean results from/reflects both the exoticization of the other inherent in the anthropological gaze, the U.S. imperialist gaze, and . . . the binaristic black weltanschauung" (73). These criticisms may be true, but I find the story that she relates valuable as an example of a story that sheds light on a story that I heard while conducting field research in Benin Republic in terms of the enslavement process and the memories and myths surrounding it.

48. Hurston, *Tell My Horse*, 183.

49. Robin Law discusses the probable recentness of the story in *Ouidah: The Social History of a West African Slaving Port 1727–1892* (Athens: Ohio University Press, 2004). I tell the story here because it has become part of the popular culture as part of the push to memorialize the slave past and is told regularly to visitors to UNESCO's Slave Route Project. I thus read it as an example of *istwa*.

50. Law also tells the story in *Ouidah*.

51. My translation.

52. I use "slaves" here to distinguish them from "enslaved" workers, perhaps a semantic difference but one that I think is important as it points to the failure of the ritual in Ouidah. If the ritual had been successful we would not have the numerous histories of revolts with the one in Saint-Domingue culminating in the first Black Republic in the Western world.

53. Hurston, *Tell My Horse*, 183.

54. The only time that I have read that salt is not a liberatory element for the *zonbi* is in Hamilton Morris, "I Walked with a Zombie: Travels among the Undead," *Harper's*, November 2011, http://harpers.org/archive/2011/11/i-walked-with-a-zombie/. His informant is his fixer, a kind of guide who makes appointments and arrangements for researchers and clues them in to the social norms.

55. Métraux, *Voodoo in Haiti*, 283. Wade Davis' text *Passage of Darkness* tries to decipher the cause and cure for the *zonbi*. He provides several theories about how *zonbi* are made, the most popular being the administration of poison from a puffer fish. The antidote to the poison is not so straightforward, and he spends several chapters going around the subject asserting various theses and then pointing out their weaknesses.

56. Hurbon, *Le Barbare imaginaire*, 193.

57. The story of Joseph Cinqué of the slave ship *Amistad* is a famous example of one of those who returned to a devastated community. When Cinqué returned to his native land of Sierra Leone in 1842, he encountered a civil war. His wife and three children had been killed while he was in the United States fighting for his own freedom.

58. Orlando Patterson, *Slavery and Social Death: A Comparative Study* (Cambridge, Mass.: Harvard University Press, 1982), 38.

59. Ibid.

60. Hurbon, *Le Barbare imaginaire*, 192.

61. John Mbiti, *African Religions and Philosophy* (London: Heinemann, 1971), 121; and Victor Turner, *The Forest of Symbols: Aspects of Ndembu Ritual* (Ithaca, N.Y.: Cornell University Press, 1967), 96.

62. Turner, *Forest of Symbols*, 96.

63. Ibid.

64. Ibid.

65. Hurbon, for example, does not relate the ultimate fates of the *zonbi* who were freed from *Rozanfe*, though he does say that those who had been gone a long time had trouble remembering their families. In one of the best literary explorations of zombification, Lilas Desquiron, *Les Chemins de Loco-Miroir* (1990), trans. Robin Orr Bodkin, *Reflections of Loko Miwa* (Charlottesville: University Press of Virginia, 1998), the fate of the protagonist is also ambivalent.

66. Hurbon, *Le Barbare imaginaire*, 201.

67. Achille Mbembe, "Necropolitics," trans. Libby Meintjes, *Public Culture* 15, no. 1(2003): 21.

68. Ibid.

69. Ibid.

70. Karen McCarthy Brown, *Tracing the Spirit: Ethnographic Essays on Haitian Art* (Davenport, Iowa: Davenport Museum of Art, 1995), 25.

71. René Depestre, "Change," *Violence II*, no. 9 (Paris: Seuil, 1971), 20.

72. See, for example, Haiti Grassroots Watch's discussion of what this invitation to foreign businesses and vacationers means to the poor in Haiti Grassroots Watch's "Haiti—Open for Business," http://haitigrassrootswatch.squarespace.com/haiti-grass-roots-watch-engli/2011/11/29/haiti-open-for-business.html.

73. Maximilien Laroche, "La Lutte du héros contre sa victimisation," *Tanbou*, Spring 1994, http://www.tanbou.com/1994/Spring/Lutte.htm.

74. Ibid.

75. Kaiama Glover, *Haiti Unbound: A Spiralist Challenge to the Postcolonial Canon* (Liverpool: Liverpool University Press, 2010), 59. Franck Degoul offers an interesting take on the *zonbi* and zombification, arguing that it has been interiorized and embraced by the Haitian population and turned into a source of power against outsiders. See Degoul, *"Du Passé Faisons Table d'Hôte."*

76. Hurston, *Tell my Horse*, 191.

77. Joan Dayan, *Haiti, History and the Gods* (Berkeley: University of California Press, 1998), 36.

78. Thomas Madiou, qtd. in ibid., 36.

79. Ibid.

80. Haitian *lwa* are divided into *nachon* (nations), with some being considered cool (Rada) and others considered hot (Petwo). Karen McCarthy Brown delineates the *nachon* and the *lwa* in her essay "Systematic Remembering, Systematic Forgetting," in *Ogun: Old World and New*, ed. Sandra T. Barnes, 65–89 (Bloomington: Indiana University Press, 1997).

81. Dayan, *Haiti, History, and the Gods*, 36.

82. Roger Bastide, *African Civilisations in the New World*, trans. Peter Green (1967; repr. London: C. Hurst and Company, 1971), 140.

83. Ibid.

84. Other scholars have argued for the African diasporic birth of the Petwo rite claiming that the Petwo nation was developed under the guidance of a "Negro of Spanish origin" named Don Pedro in 1768. Bastide, *African Civilisations in the New World*, 141. Don Pedro was said to have introduced a dance called Dom Pèdre in the south in Petit Goâve. The dance was said to have been more violent than the already known Vaudoux dance, with dancers mixing gunpowder in the *tafia* that they drank while dancing. Vanhee, "Central African Popular Christianity," 247. Still others, such as filmmaker and writer Luc de Heusch, have argued for an African source of the rites pointing to linkages to the Kôngo kings Pedro I, III, and IV and the content of Petwo belief to Kôngo beliefs. Luc de Heusch, "Kongo in Haiti: A New Approach to Religious Syncretism," *Man* 24, no. 2

(June 1989): 292–93. This is a point that anthropologist Hein Vanhee takes up extensively in his writing about the Central African influence in Haitian Vodou. He cites the work of Descourtilz, who wrote that he had attended a ceremony led by "an almighty priest" named *Dompète* who often used poison to punish "the uncertain," people believed to be witches. Vanhee notes Moreau de Saint Méry also mentioned *Dompète* in his writings. Vanhee, "Central African Popular Christianity," 247).

85. Deren, *Divine Horsemen*, 62.

86. René Depestre, *A Rainbow for the Christian West*, trans. Joan Dayan (Amherst: University of Massachusetts Press, 1977), 83.

87. Garraway, *Libertine Colony*, 180. Garraway uses the French spelling of *zonbi*.

88. Ibid.,182; and Dayan, *Haiti, History, and the Gods*, 36.

89. Hurbon briefly relates the story in *Le Barbare imaginaire*, 201.

90. William Seabrook, in Kate Ramsey, *The Spirits and the Law: Vodou and Power in Haiti* (Chicago: University of Chicago Press, 2011), 172.

91. Ibid. Apparently, *tablette*, a kind of local peanut brittle.

92. See Karen Richman, *Migration and Vodou* (Gainesville: University Press of Florida, 2005), 100–102.

93. Ibid., 99.

94. Laurent Dubois, *Haiti: The Aftershocks of History* (New York: Metropolitan Books, 2012), 208; and Richman, *Migration and Vodou*, 104.

95. Richman, *Migration and Vodou*, 104.

96. Ramsey, *Spirits and the Law*, 173.

97. The *Caco* rebellion was led by Charlemagne Péralte, a landowner from the province of Hinche in the Central Plateau region. The rebellion consisted of a loose band of peasant insurgents who waged war against the U.S. Marines.

98. Although Turner was writing about rites-of-passage rituals among Ndembu, it is this state of liminality that he describes that interests me here for the point of my argument around the state of in-betweenness that the *zonbi* inhabits. As Turner notes in delineating the different states that he envisions for his discussion of the "rites of passage," he concurs with J. S. Mill, who has written that rather than simply signifying status or office, state may refer to "any type of stable or recurrent condition that is culturally recognized." Turner, *Forest of Symbols*, 96.

99. Glover, *Haiti Unbound*, 60.

100. Ibid. Emphasis mine.

101. Mbembe, "Necropolitics," 22.

102. Stuart Hall, "Cultural Identity and Diaspora," in *Identity: Community, Culture and Difference*, ed. Jonathan Rutherford, 222–37 (London: Lawrence and Wishart, 1990), 222.

103. Ibid., 226–27.

104. Kamau Brathwaite, and Nathaniel Mackey, *ConVERSations with Nathaniel Mackey* (Staten Island: We Press, 1999), 32; and Brown, "Serving the Spirits," 205.

105. Glover, *Haiti Unbound*, 60

106. Ibid.; and Métraux, *Voodoo in Haiti*, 283.

107. Dayan, *Haiti, History, and the Gods*, xii; and Michel-Rolph Trouillot, *Haiti, State*

against Nation (New York: Monthly Review Press, 1990), 106. Although some of the *oungan* who were affiliated with the Duvaliers were killed there were also many innocent victims of mob violence. Rachel Beauvoir and Didier Dominique recount several news stories about *oungan* who, along with their *ounfò* and drums, were burned and their possessions stolen in Okap (Cap Haitian), 1000 "young Christians" in Gonaïves who murdered several other people in Pòdpe (Port-de-Paix), as well as massacres in Bariadelle and a woman, "known and loved by practitioners of Vodou" having her throat slit. Rachel Beauvoir and Didier Dominique, *Savalou E* (Montreal: Les Éditions du CIDIHCA, 2003), 17–18.

108. For a discussion of these interventions and their ideological and discursive underpinnings, see Toni Pressley-Sanon, "Haitian (Pre)Occupations: Ideological and Discursive Repetitions, 1915–1934 and 2004 to Present," *Caribbean Studies Journal* 42, no. 2 (2014): 115–53.

109. For example, in the 1990s the terms "voodoo politics" and "voodoo economics" were coined to denote any political or economic system that was backward or that did not serve its constituents from a Western point of view.

110. Haitians have migrated to the Dominican Republic, Cuba, Jamaica, the Bahamas, and Guadeloupe for a number of decades, working on sugar cane plantations, as gardeners, and domestic workers. More recently, postearthquake and with the summer Olympics in Brazil in 2016, a sizable number of Haitians migrated there in search of construction work.

111. Robin Poyner, "The Western Congo Basin," in *A History of Art in Africa*, eds. Monica Blackmun Visonà, Robin Poyner, Herbert M. Cole, Suzanne Preston Blier, and Rowland Abiodun, 366–411 (Upper Saddle River, N.J.: Pearson/Prentice Hall, 2008), 376.

112. Robert Farris Thompson, *Flash of the Spirit: African and Afro-American Art and Philosophy* (New York: Random House, 1983), 117.

113. Nsemi Isaki, qtd. in ibid.

114. Author observation, September 17, 2013, Washington, D.C. The role of the *minkisi* has changed contemporarily as the card continues: " . . . now these strategies are used to tie members of these communities to their land and its healing properties. Both gourds and the more rare figures used in healing arts are wrapped, bound and tied with cords, hide and string."

115. Stephan Palmié, *Wizards and Scientists: Exploration in Afro-Cuban Modernity and Tradition* (Durham, N.C.: Duke University Press, 2002), 179–80, 25.

116. Ibid., 1.

117. Ibid., 168.

118. Thompson, *Flash of the Spirit*, 117–18.

119. Poyner, "Western Congo Basin," 376.

120. Ibid.

121. Ibid., 377.

122. Ibid.

123. Zdenka Volavkova, "Nkisi Figure of the Lower Congo," *African Arts* 5, no. 2 (Winter 1972): 56.

124. Marilyn Houlberg, "*Pakèt Kongo*: Spirit Bundles," in *Vodou: Visions and Voices of Haiti*, ed. Phyllis Galembo (Berkeley, Calif.: Ten Speed Press, 2005), 66.

125. Thompson, *Flash of the Spirit*, 125.

126. Métraux, *Voodoo in Haiti*, 301.

127. Blier, *African Vodun*, 74.

128. Métraux, *Voodoo in Haiti*, 312.

129. Ibid.

130. Thompson, *Flash of the Spirit*, 126.

131. See Volavkova, "Nkisi Figures," 54.

132. Houlberg, "*Pakèt Kongo*," 66. See also those included in Thompson's *Flash of the Spirit*, 126.

133. Thompson, *Flash of the Spirit*, 127; and Donald J. Cosentino, "On Looking at a Vodou Altar," *African Arts* 29, no. 2 (1996): 96.

134. See Ramsey, *Spirits and the Law*, 43–44.

135. Ibid.

136. Boston, *Independent Chronicle and the Universal Advertiser*, September 29, 1791.

137. Michel-Etienne Descourtilz, *Voyages d'un naturaliste, et ses observations* (Paris, 1809), 3:206.

138. Ibid.

139. Thompson, *Flash of the Spirit*, 127.

140. Brown, "Serving the Spirits," 208; and Katherine Smith, "Gede Rising: Haiti in the Age of *Vagabondaj*" (PhD diss., University of California Los Angeles, 2010), 22.

141. Leah Gordon, "Gede: The Poster Boy for Haitian Vodou," in *In Extremis: Life and Death in 21st Century Haitian Art*, ed. Donald Cosentino, 101–14 (Los Angeles: Fowler Museum at UCLA, 2012), 111.

142. Brown, "Serving the Spirits," 208.

Chapter 3. *Bociọ*, *Nkisi*, Legba, Ogun, and Ghede across the Water

Epigraph source: LeGrace Benson, remarks at KOSANBA Conference, Harvard University, Cambridge, Mass., October 18–20, 2013.

1. The work produced by the artists of Grand Rue can be found in several galleries and private collections both in Haiti and abroad.

2. LeGrace Benson, "Habits of Attention: Persistence of Lan Ginée in Haiti," in *The African Diaspora: African Origins and New World Identities*, ed. Isidore Okpewho, Carole Boyce Davies, and Ali A. Mazrui, 428–38 (Bloomington: Indiana University Press, 2001), 428.

3. Robert Farris Thompson, in *The Four Moments of the Sun: Kongo Art in Two Worlds* (Washington, D.C.: National Gallery of Art, 1981), 27.

4. LeGrace Benson, "Gédé: Transmogrifications; Sex, Death and Resurrection on Grand Rue," http://www.atis-rezistans.com/downloads/GrandRueFeb07.pdf, accessed November 2, 2015.

5. All of the art that I discuss herein is public, the majority of which is in an open-air gallery of André Eugene, one of the founders of Atis Rezistan's atelier and *lakou*. In its most basic expression, a *lakou* is a cluster of homes that share a common yard.

6. Benson, "Gédé."

7. There is an award-winning film about the artists, *Atis-Rezistans: The Sculptors of Grand Rue* by Leah Gordon, and a website dedicated to the Ghetto Biennale Conference, http://www.ghettobiennale.org. Guyodo has since left the collective, but other artists have also joined, including Papa Da, featured in Gordon's film.

8. Leah Gordon, "The Sculptors of Grand Rue: Reinterpreting Slavery," in *Dazed and Confused* (March 2007), previously available at http://www.atis-rezistans.com.

9. Suzanne Preston Blier, *African Vodun: Art, Psychology and Power* (Chicago: University of Chicago Press, 1995), 1.

10. Ibid.

11. Suzanne Preston Blier, "Vodun: West African Roots of Vodou," in *Sacred Arts of Haitian Vodou*, ed. Donald Cosentino, 60–87 (Los Angeles: UCLA Fowler Museum of Cultural History, 1995), 74–75.

12. Ezio Bassani, Michael Bockemühl, and Patrick R. McNaughton, "*Mangaaka*," in *The Power of Form: African Art from the Horstmann Collection* (Milan: Skira Editore, 2002), 140.

13. Patrick Bellegarde-Smith, "The Gede: Vignettes of Life, Death, the Dead and Rebirth," *Journal of Haitian Studies* 10, no. 2 (2004): 162–67.

14. Bruno Gilli, *Hevioso et le bon ordre du monde: Approche d'une religion africaine* (Paris: Memoire, EHESS-Ecoles des Hautes Etudes des Science Sociales, 1976), 7.

15. Benson, "Habits of Attention," 429.

16. Personal interview with André Eugene, Port-au-Prince, Haiti, April 2010.

17. Thompson, *Four Moments of the Sun*, 27.

18. Ibid.

19. Blier, "Vodun," 67.

20. Similarly, *minkisi* were mistakenly associated with Christianity. Because of the nails driven through their bodies, they were thought to symbolize the suffering of Christ. Zdenka Volavkova, "Nkisi Figures of the Lower Congo," *African Arts* 5, no. 2 (Winter 1972): 55. Interestingly, Jacques Maquet, in Irving Penn's *Photographs of Dahomey* (1967; repr. Houston: Museum of Fine Arts, 2004), speculates that by identifying Legba with the devil, the Christian mission helped make Legba an especially popular figure of Dahomean lore.

21. For stories about the origin of Fa, see Melville J. Herskovits and Francis S. Herskovits' *Dahomean Narrative: A Cross-Cultural Analysis* (Evanston, Ill.: Northwestern University Press, 1958), 173–93; Paul Mercier, "The Fon of Dahomey," in *African Worlds: Studies in the Cosmological Ideas and Social Values of African Peoples*, edited by Daryll Forde, 210–34 (New York: Oxford University Press, 1965), 214; and Robert D. Pelton, *The Trickster in West Africa: A Study of Mythic Irony and Sacred Delight* (Berkeley: University of California Press, 1980), 85–87.

22. Robert Farris Thompson, "From the Isle Beneath the Sea: Haiti's Africanizing Vodou Art," in *Sacred Arts of Haitian Vodou*, ed. Donald Cosentino, 91–119 (Los Angeles: UCLA Fowler Museum of Cultural History), 98–99.

23. He is, in fact, larger than all the other statues in the forest and faces the entrance of the forest, so he is one of the first figures people see upon entering.

24. Pelton, *Trickster in West Africa*, 126.

25. Bellegarde-Smith, "Gede," 165.

26. Joan Dayan, Introduction to *A Rainbow for the Christian West*, by René Depestre (Amherst: University of Massachusetts Press, 1977), 59.

27. Elizabeth McAlister, "Love, Sex, and Gender Embodied: The Spirits of Haitian Vodou" (Division II Faculty Publications. Paper 14. Oxford, 2000, http://wesscholar.wesleyan.edu/div2facpubs/14), 129.

28. Ibid.

29. Ibid.

30. Donald Cosentino, "Gede Rising," in *In Extremis: Life and Death in 21st Century Haitian Art*, ed. Donald Cosentino, 25–75 (Los Angeles: UCLA Fowler Museum of Cultural History, 2012), 56. Even after the earthquake, Papa Legba was still standing. He swayed, but he did not fall. He finally fell in a tornado in July 16, 2012, but has since been repositioned in his rightful place as guardian over the *lakou*.

31. Ibid.

32. Dayan, Introduction to *Rainbow for the Christian West*, 60.

33. Ibid.; and Maya Deren, *Divine Horsemen: The Living Gods of Haiti* (New York: McPherson and Company, 1970), 99.

34. Leslie Desmangles, *The Faces of the Gods: Vodou and Roman Catholicism in Haiti* (Chapel Hill: University of North Carolina Press, 1992), 109.

35. Dayan, Introduction to *Rainbow for the Christian West*, 62.

36. Karen McCarthy Brown "Serving the Spirits: The Ritual Economy of Haitian Vodou," in *Sacred Arts of Haitian Vodou*, ed. Donald Cosentino (Los Angeles: UCLA Fowler Museum of Cultural History, 1995), 206.

37. I discuss the *boko* and *bòkò* in chapter 2.

38. Karen McCarthy Brown, "Systematic Remembering, Systematic Forgetting," in *Ogun: Old World and New*, ed. Sandra T. Barnes, 65–89 (Bloomington: Indiana University Press, 1997), 65; and Deren, *Divine Horsemen*, 130.

39. Deren, *Divine Horsemen*, 130.

40. Ibid.,132.

41. Ibid.

42. Ibid., 102.

43. On the epiphany of Gede, see Dayan, *Rainbow for the Christian West*, 61.

44. Blier, "Vodun," 83.

45. Ibid.

46. Ibid.

47. Roger Bastide, *African Civilisations in the New World*, trans. Peter Green (London: C. Hurst and Company, 1971), 140.

48. Melville J. Herskovits, *Dahomey: An Ancient West African Kingdom*, vol. 2 (Evanston: Northwestern University Press, 1967); Emmanuel C. Paul, *Panorama du folklore haïtien*, 3rd ed. (1962; repr., Port-au-Prince: Présence Africaine en Haïti, 2014); Paul Hazoumé, *Le Pacte du sang au Dahomey* (Paris: *Institut d'ethnologie*, 1956); and Desmangles, *Faces of the Gods*.

49. Herskovits, *Dahomey*, 63.

50. Ibid.

51. Ibid.

52. Herskovits does not actually say that the story was told to him. He simply launches into it and references the version from Hazoumé's text.

53. Desmangles, *Faces of the Gods*, 119.

54. Herskovits, *Dahomey*, 2:64.

55. Hazoumé, *Le Pacte*, 32n1.

56. Herskovits, *Dahomey*, 2:64; and Desmangles, *Faces of the Gods*, 120.

57. Blier, "Vodun."

58. It is also known as "Kennedy" because it was President John F. Kennedy who started having Americans' used clothing sent to Haiti.

59. A good example of this is my personal experience of walking in the outdoor market in Port-au-Prince in Summer 2011 and seeing a teenage boy wearing a t-shirt that read, "The South Shall Rise Again" complete with a picture of a Confederate flag. I doubt the boy had any idea what the shirt said or the historical significance of it.

60. Jean Hérard Celeur, another member of Atis Rezistans, created a sculpture made entirely of high heels and winter boots to comment on the inanity of sending such shoes to a country without winter and where wearing high heels could very possibly lead to broken bones because of the conditions of the roads and sidewalks in Port-au-Prince.

61. Personal interview with André Eugene, Port-au-Prince, Haiti, April 2010.

62. Kimbwandende Kia Bunseki Fu-Kiau, *African Cosmology of the Bântu-Kôngo: Principles of Life and Living* (Brooklyn, N.Y.: Athelia Henrietta Press, 2001), 35.

63. Charles Kenny, "Haiti Doesn't Need Your Old T-Shirt." *Foreign Affairs*, October 11, 2011, http://foreignpolicy.com/2011/10/11/haiti-doesnt-need-your-old-t-shirt/.

64. *Haiti's Pepe Trade*, Reason.TV, 2013, https://www.youtube.com/watch?v=h2ZD1EQu7_U.

65. A *peristil* is a large covered area partially open at the sides where most Vodou services are held.

66. Personal interview with André Eugene, Port-au-Prince, Haiti, April 2010.

67. Alfred Métraux, *Le Vaudou haïtien* (Paris: Editions Gallimard, 1958), 323. In Métraux's *Voodoo in Haiti* (New York: Schocken Books, 1972), translated by Hugo Charteris, the phrase is translated as "It is too often forgotten that Voodoo, for all its African heritage belongs to the modern world and is part of our own civilization."(365).

68. Stephan Palmié, *Wizards and Scientists: Exploration in Afro-Cuban Modernity and Tradition* (Durham, N.C.: Duke University Press, 2002), 41–42.

69. Cosentino, "Gede Rising," 55.

70. Gordon, " Sculptors of Grand Rue," n.p.

71. Paget Henry, *Caliban's Reason: Introducing Afro-Caribbean Philosophy* (New York: Routledge, 2000), 26.

72. Thompson, *Four Moments*, 27.

73. Ibid.

74. Sentius, qtd. in Leah Gordon, dir. *Atis-Rezistans: The Sculptors of Grand Rue* (2010), in *Iron in the Soul: The Haiti Documentary Films of Leah Gordon*, DVD (Boston, Mass.: Soul Jazz Films and Soul Jazz Records, 2015).

75. Ibid. The person who is possessed by the *lwa* is said to be ridden by the *lwa*, as one rides a horse.

76. Veerle Poupeye, *Caribbean Art* (New York: Thames and Hudson, 1998), 144.

77. Ibid., 145.

78. See, for example, the work of visual artists, Gerard Fortune, Pierre Maxo, and Jean Edner Cadet.

79. Brown, "Systematic Remembering," 84.

80. Ibid.

81. Ibid.

82. Poupeye, *Caribbean Art*, 183.

83. Desmangles, *Faces of the Gods*, 143.

Chapter 4. Tidalectical Dishonor

Epigraph source: Claudine Michel and Patrick Bellegarde-Smith, remarks at KO-SANBA Conference, Harvard University, Cambridge, Mass., October 18–20, 2013.

1. M. Jacqui Alexander, *Pedagogies of Crossing: Meditations on Feminism, Sexual Politics, Memory and the Sacred* (Durham, N.C.: Duke University Press, 2005), 309.

2. Ibid.

3. Pierre, qtd. in Elizabeth McAlister, "Voodoo's View of the Quake in Haiti," *On Faith*, January 15, 2010. http://www.faithstreet.com/onfaith/2010/01/15/voodoos-view-of-the-quake-in-haiti/2118.

4. "Five Years after Earthquake, Interview with the Supreme Leader of Haitian Voodoo," Thomas Reuters Foundation, January 12, 2015, https://www.youtube.com/watch?v=fwdXmaxhEEE.

5. Claudel Casseus, *Imajine* (London: Penkiln Burn Book Fourteen, 2011), 11.

6. Edwidge Danticat, "Lòt Bò Dlo: The Other Side of the Water," in *Haiti after the Earthquake*, ed. Paul Farmer, 249–58 (New York: Public Affairs, 2011), 249.

7. Casseus, *Imajine*, 14.

8. Dany Laferrière, *The World Is Moving around Me: A Memoir of the Haiti Earthquake*, trans. David Homel (Vancouver, B.C.: Arsenal Pulp Press, 2011), 86.

9. Ibid.

10. Ibid.

11. Ibid.

12. Goudougoudou is an onomatopoeic approximation of the sound the earth made when it shifted position on that fateful day.

13. McAlister, "Voodoo's View of the Quake in Haiti."

14. Josué, qtd. in ibid.

15. Ibid.

16. Ibid.

17. Immediately following the earthquake, Josué made the following statement: "Haitians believe Haiti, she's a woman. . . . We believe she's a mother, and [when] that woman got that pain, she [said], 'Enough.'" See Barbara Bradley Hagerty, "Voodoo Brings Solace to Grieving Haitians," on "All Things Considered," NPR, January 20, 2010, http://www.npr.org/templates/story/story.php?storyId=122770590.

18. Alexander, *Pedagogies of Crossing*, 301.

19. Ibid., 311.

20. As a result of the failure of SHADA (the *Société Haïtiano-Américaine de Développement Agricole*), which displaced hundreds of families and sacrificed locally produced foodstuff for the cultivation of rubber trees, the revolution of 1946 was sparked by leftist activists and students who took to the streets in January 1946 shouting anti–Elie Lescot slogans and singing the national anthem. They were joined by workers and state employees as they headed for the national palace. After the Garde d'Haïti killed two people during one of the ensuing protests, crowds stormed police stations and ransacked houses and stores of government ministers. Several government-owned factories were also burned to the ground in the provinces. With Lescot's exile, parliament elected Dumarsais Estimé to office. Estimé launched a number of progressive initiatives to support unions, the environment, and agriculture while also expanding educational opportunities for poor Haitians, implementing a social security system, increasing the minimum wage, and instituting new labor laws.

21. Blake Eskin, "Cover Story: The Resurrection of the Dead," *New Yorker Magazine*, January 18, 2010, http://www.newyorker.com/online/blogs/newsdesk/2010/01/cover-story-frantz-zephirin.html. Bawon Samdi is head of the Gede family of spirits, and Gran Brijit, his wife.

22. McAlister, in ibid.

23. McAlister, in ibid.

24. Alexander, *Pedagogies of Crossing*, 293.

25. Ibid., 312.

26. Paul Lovejoy, "The Volume of the Atlantic Slave Trade: A Synthesis," *Journal of African History* 23, no. 4 (1982): 473–501.

27. Robin Law, *Ouidah: The Social History of a West African Slaving Port: 1727–1892* (Athens: Ohio University Press, 2004), 1–2.

28. Ibid.

29. Ibid., 137.

30. Ibid.

31. Ibid., 138.

32. Ibid.

33. I discuss this ritual in chapter 2.

34. Author interview with Martine de Souza, October 2005, in Ouidah, Benin Republic.

35. Personal interview, Ouidah, Benin Republic, January 2006.

36. I attended one such tour led by Martine de Souza, who suggested to those gathered that they reenact the ritual that their ancestors had undergone as a way of reversing its hold. Several people took her up on the offer.

37. Law, *Ouidah*, 153.

38. Ibid.

39. See chapter 1 for my discussion of history writing as Hayden White explains it.

40. Stephan Palmié, *Wizards and Scientists: Exploration in Afro-Cuban Modernity and Tradition* (Durham, N.C.: Duke University Press, 2002), 1.

41. Edwidge Danticat, *Create Dangerously: The Immigrant Artist at Work* (Princeton, N.J.: Princeton University Press, 2010), 65.

42. Ibid.

43. Brendan Wolfe, "Slave Ships and the Middle Passage," *Encyclopedia Virginia*, http://www.encyclopediavirginia.org/Slave_Ships_and_the_Middle_Passage.

44. Fred d'Aguiar, *Feeding the Ghosts* (Hopewell, N.J.: Ecco Press, 1999), 4.

45. I am riffing off of the title of Patrick Bellegarde-Smith's collection of essays on Haitian Vodou: *Fragments of Bone: Neo-African Religions in a New World* (Chicago: University of Illinois Press, 2005).

46. Alexander, *Pedagogies of Crossing*, 290.

47. John Mbiti, *African Religions and Philosophy* (London: Heinemann, 1971), 25–26.

48. Edwidge Danticat, "A Year and a Day," *New Yorker*, January 17, 2011, http://www.newyorker.com/talk/comment/2011/01/17/110117taco_talk_danticat.

49. A *govi* is an earthenware vessel used to hold spirits.

50. Karen McCarthy Brown, "Afro-Caribbean Spirituality: A Haitian Case Study," in *Vodou in Haitian Life and Culture: Invisible Powers*, ed. Claudine Michel and Patrick Bellegarde-Smith, 1–26 (New York: Palgrave Macmillan, 2006), 9.

51. Ibid.

52. Peter Sutherland, "In Memory of the Slaves: An African View of the Diaspora in the Americas," in *Representations of Blackness and the Performance of Identities*, ed. Jean Muteba Rahier, 195–211 (Westport, Conn.: Bergen and Garvey, 1999), 204.

53. Verwilghen, qtd. in Harold Courlander, *The Drum and the Hoe: Life and Lore of the Haitian People* (Berkeley: University of California Press, 1960), 31.

54. Karen McCarthy Brown, "Serving the Spirits: The Ritual Economy of Haitian Vodou," in *Sacred Arts of Haitian Vodou*, ed. Donald Cosentino205–23 (Los Angeles: UCLA Fowler Museum of Cultural History, 1995), 206.

55. Examples of improper burials can be found in the case for those who died at Zomaï or during the middle passage; or Toussaint Louverture, who died in France; those massacred in the Dominican Republic in 1937 during Operación Perejil; during the first American Occupation; or murdered during the Duvalier era; and overwhelmingly in the crisis following the 2010 earthquake.

56. Courlander, *Drum and the Hoe*, 33.

57. Alfred Métraux, *Voodoo in Haiti*, trans. Hugo Charteris (New York: Schocken Books, 1972), 256.

58. Alexander, *Pedagogies of Crossing*, 289.

59. "Five Years after Earthquake, Interview with the Supreme Leader of Haitian Voodoo."

60. Hagerty, "Voodoo Brings Solace to Grieving Haitians."

61. Thompson, *Flash of the Spirit*, 132.

62. Ibid.

63. Qtd. in Damien Cave, "As Haitians Flee, the Dead Go Uncounted: Earthquake Robs Victims and Mourners of Even the Most Basic Funeral Rites," *New York Times*, January 19, 2010.

64. Paisley Dodds, "Voodoo Practitioners Attacked at Ceremony for Haiti Earth-

quake Victims," *Huffington Post*, www.nola.com/religion/index.ssf/2010/02/voodoo-ists_attacked_at_ceremony_for_haiti_earthquake_victims.html.

65. See Felix Germain, "The Earthquake, the Missionaries and the Future of Vodou," *Journal of Black Studies* 42, no. 2 (2011) : 247–63.

66. Charlemagne Péralte led a resistance movement against the first American occupation of Haiti from 1915–34.

67. See "Haitians Pay Tribute on Second Anniversary of Devastating Earthquake," *Telegraph*, January 13, 2012, http://www.telegraph.co.uk/news/worldnews/centralamericaandthecaribbean/haiti/9011990/Haitians-pay-tribute-on-second-anniversary-of-devastating-earthquake.html.

68. See Danticat's essay on Alèrte Bélance, a victim of Cédras' killing squads in *Create Dangerously* (2010).

69. Edwidge Danticat, "a despot walks into a killing field," *Progressive*, 76, no. 5 (May 2012): 37.

70. Ibid.

71. I take this concept from a line in M. Jacqui Alexander's text, *Pedagogies of Crossing*, in which she says, "Trees remember and will whisper remembrances in your ear, if you stay still and listen" (263). The trees whispering can be seen as what happened in the story that Martine de Souza tells about the medium who stood at the Tree of Return. See "Dominica/Africa: Junot Díaz on Writing Disasters." *One on One. http://www.bombasticelement.org/2010/08/dominica-africa-junot-diaz-on-writing.html*. Monday, August 23, 2010. Accessed January 27, 2012.

72. Felix Germain argues in "The Earthquake, the Missionaries and the Future of Vodou" (2011) that, "during the past three decades Christian missionaries from various U.S.-based Protestant and Pentecostal churches have been swarming to Haiti, and unlike the Haitian Catholic Church, which somewhat 'tolerates' the presence of Vodou in society, they condemn the Afro-Haitian belief system labeling it a satanic cult" (248).

73. See Germain, "The Earthquake," for a discussion of this history.

74. "Haitians Hold Day of Mourning One Month after Devastating Earthquake." *New York Daily News*, February 12, 2010. http://www.nydailynews.com/news/world/haitians-hold-day-mourning-month-devastating-earthquake-article-1.197247.

75. Claudine Michel, "Of Worlds Seen and Unseen: The Educational Character of Haitian Vodou," in *Haitian Vodou: Spirit, Myth and Reality*, ed. Patrick Bellegarde-Smith and Claudine Michel, 32–45 (University of Indiana Press, 2006), 35; and Smucker, qtd. in ibid.

76. Michel, "Of Worlds Seen and Unseen"; and Germain, "The Earthquake, the Missionaries," 252.

77. Germain, "The Earthquake, the Missionaries."

78. An interesting development around this issue is the "protestantization" of Vodou that Elizabeth McAlister is currently researching. She discussed this phenomenon in a paper, "The New Self-Presentation of Public Vodou in Haiti," that she gave at the KOSANBA conference in Montreal, Canada, in October 2015.

Chapter 5. Epilogue: Re-Suturing or Joining the Parts to the Whole

1. Max Beauvoir, "Five Years after Earthquake, Interview with the Supreme Leader of Haitian Voodoo," Thomas Reuters Foundation. January 12, 2015. https://www.youtube.com/watch?v=fwdXmaxhEEE.

2. Claudine Michel, "African Continuity in Haitian Religious Life," in *Ancestral Rays: Journey Through Haitian History and Culture*, ed. Claudine Michel, 18–19 (Santa Barbara: Center for Black Studies, University of California, 2005), 19. Emphasis mine.

3. See Toni Pressley-Sanon, "One Plus One Equals Three: Marasa Consciousness, the Lwa, and Three Stories in *Research in African Literatures* 44, no. 3 (Fall 2013): 118–37, for a discussion of the work of literary artists and the Marasa.

4. Michel, "African Continuity," 19.

5. Kate Ramsey, *The Spirits and the Law: Vodou and Power in Haiti* (Chicago: University of Chicago Press, 2011), 44.

6. Vèvè Clark, "Developing Literacy and *Marasa* Consciousness," *Theatre Survey* 50, no. 1 (May 2009): 43. In "A Sacred Space for the Resolution of Haiti's Age Old Antimonies" (2005) Marc A. Christophe asserts that the Marasa are invoked propitiously at the beginning of Vodou ceremonies. See "A Sacred Space for the Resolution of Haiti's Age Old Antimonies," in *Ancestral Rays: Journey through Haitian History and Culture*, ed. Claudine Michel, 22–24 (Santa Barbara: Center for Black Studies, University of California, 2005), 23.

7. See Ramon Sahmkow's article, "Haiti Is a Future Tourist Destination, Says President," *Yahoo*, December 5, 2011, https://au.finance.yahoo.com/news/haiti-future-tourist-destination-says-062231495.html; and Haiti Grassroots Watch's "Martelly Government Betting on Sweatshops: Open for Business" *Haiti Liberte*, 6, no. 34, http://www.haiti-liberte.com/archives/volume5-21/Martellygovernment.asp.

8. M. Jacqui Alexander, *Pedagogies of Crossing: Meditations on Feminism, Sexual Politics, Memory and the Sacred* (Durham, N.C.: Duke University Press, 2005), 316.

9. Margaret Mitchell Armand, *Healing in the Homeland* (Lanham, Md.: Lexington Books, 2013), xvii.

10. Gina Ulysse, "Why Haiti Needs New Narratives Now More than Ever," in *Tectonic Shifts: Haiti Since the Earthquake*, ed. Mark Schuller and Pablo Morales, 240–45 (Sterling: Kumarian Press, 2012), 241. Ulysse has since published a trilingual collection of essays under a similar title: *Why Haiti Needs New Narratives: A Post-Earthquake Chronicle* (Middleton, Conn.: Wesleyan University Press, 2015).

11. Natalie Pierre, "*Ti Dife Boule Sou Istwa Ayiti* as Haitian Civic Education," *Cultural Dynamics* 26, no. 2 (2014): 209–17.

12. Marc A. Christophe makes this observation about Hërsza Barjon's painting *Table of Deliverance* in "A Sacred Space for the Resolution of Haiti's Age Old Antimonies" and is a fitting end to the ritualistic work that inspires this narrative.

Bibliography

Ackermann, Hans-W, and Jeanine Gauthier. "The Ways and Nature of the Zombi." *Journal of American Folklore* 104, no. 414 (Autumn 1991): 466–94.

Alexander, M. Jacqui. *Pedagogies of Crossing: Meditations on Feminism, Sexual Politics, Memory and the Sacred*. Durham, N.C.: Duke University Press, 2005.

Armand, Margaret Mitchell. *Healing in the Homeland*. Lanham, Md.: Lexington Books, 2013.

Bailey, Anne. *African Voices of the Atlantic Slave Trade: Beyond the Silence and the Shame*. Boston: Beacon Press, 2005.

Bassani, Ezio, Michael Bockemühl, and Patrick R. McNaughton. *The Power of Form: African Art from the Horstmann Collection*. Milan: Skira Editore, 2002.

Bastide, Roger. *African Civilisations in the New World*. Translated by Peter Green. 1967. Reprint, London: C. Hurst, 1971.

Bay, Edna. *Asen, Ancestors, and Vodun: Tracing Change in African Art*. Urbana: University of Illinois Press, 2008.

———. "Protection, Political Exile, and the Atlantic Slave Trade: History and Collective Memory in Dahomey." In *Rethinking the African Diaspora: The Making of a Black Atlantic World in the Bight of Benin and Brazil*, edited by Kristin Mann and Edna Bay, 42–60. Portland: Frank Cass, 2001.

———. *Wives of the Leopard: Gender, Politics, and the Culture of the Kingdom of Dahomey*. Charlottesville: University of Virginia Press, 1998.

Beauvoir, Rachel, and Didier Dominique. *Savalou E*. Montreal: Les Éditions du CIDIHCA, 2003.

Bell, Beverly. *Walking on Fire: Haitian Women's Stories of Survival and Resistance*. Ithaca, N.Y.: Cornell University Press, 2001.

Bellegarde-Smith, Patrick. "The Gede: Vignettes of Life, Death, the Dead and Rebirth." *Journal of Haitian Studies* 10, no. 2 (2004): 162–67.

———. *Haiti: The Breached Citadel*, 2nd ed. Toronto: Canadian Scholar's Press, 2004.

———. "The Spirit of the Thing: Religious Thought and Social/Historical Memory." In *Fragments of Bone: Neo-African Religions in a New World*, edited by Patrick Bellegarde-Smith, 52–70. Chicago: University of Illinois Press, 2005.

Bellegarde-Smith, Patrick, and Claudine Michel. "Danbala/Ayida as Cosmic Prism: The Lwa as Trope for Understanding Metaphysics in Haitian Vodou and Beyond." *Journal of Africana Religions* 1, no. 4 (2013): 458–87.

Benítez-Rojo, Antonio. *The Repeating Island: The Caribbean and the Postmodern Perspective*, 2nd ed. Translated by James E. Maraniss. Durham, N.C.: Duke University Press, 2006.

Benson, LeGrace. "Gédé: Transmogrifications; Sex, Death and Resurrection on Grand Rue." http://www.atis-rezistans.com/downloads/GrandRueFeb07.pdf. Accessed November 2, 2015.

———. "Habits of Attention: Persistence of Lan Guinee in Haiti." In *The African Diaspora: African Origins and New World Identities*, edited by Isidore Okpewho, Carole Boyce Davies, and Ali A. Mazrui, 428–38. Bloomington: Indiana University Press, 2001.

———. "A Long Bilingual Conversation Concerning Paradise Lost: Landscapes in Haitian Art." In *Caribbean Literature and the Environment: Between Nature and Culture*, edited by Elizabeth M. DeLoughrey, Renee K. Gosson, and George B. Handley, 99–109. Charlottesville: University of Virginia Press, 2005.

Black, Daniel. *The Coming*. New York: St. Martin's Press, 2015.

Black in Latin America with Henry Louis Gates, Jr. Henry Louis Gates Jr. and Ricardo Pollack. PBS Distribution, 2011. http://www.pbs.org/wnet/black-in-latin-america/.

Blassingame, John. *Slave Testimony: Two Centuries of Letters, Speeches, Interviews, and Autobiographies*. Baton Rouge: Louisiana State University Press, 1977.

Blier, Suzanne Preston. *African Vodun: Art, Psychology and Power*. Chicago: University of Chicago Press, 1995.

———. "Vodun: West African Roots of Vodou." In *Sacred Arts of Haitian Vodou*, edited by Donald Cosentino, 60–87. Los Angeles: UCLA Fowler Museum of Cultural History, 1995.

Boadi-Siaw, S. Y. "Brazilian Returnees of West Africa." In *Global Dimensions of the African Diaspora*, edited by Joseph E. Harris, 421–39. Washington, D.C.: Howard University Press, 1979.

Brandon, George. *Santeria from Africa to the New World: The Dead Sell Memories*. Bloomington: Indiana University Press, 1997.

Brathwaite, Kamau. *Contradictory Omens: Cultural Diversity and Integration in the Caribbean*. Mona: Savacou Publications, 1974.

Brathwaite, Kamau, and Nathaniel Mackey. *ConVERSations with Nathaniel Mackey*. Staten Island, N.Y.: We Press, 1999.

Braziel, Jana Evans. *Duvalier's Ghost: Race, Diaspora and U.S. Imperialism in Haitian Literatures*. Gainesville: University Press of Florida, 2010.

Brown, Karen McCarthy. "Afro-Caribbean Spirituality: A Haitian Case Study." In *Vodou in Haitian Life and Culture: Invisible Powers*, edited by Claudine Michel and Patrick Bellegarde-Smith, 1–26. New York: Palgrave Macmillan, 2006.

———. "Serving the Spirits: The Ritual Economy of Haitian Vodou." In *Sacred Arts of Haitian Vodou*, edited by Donald Cosentino, 205–23. Los Angeles: UCLA Fowler Museum of Cultural History, 1995.

———. "Systematic Remembering, Systematic Forgetting." In *Ogun: Old World and New*, edited by Sandra T. Barnes, 65–89. Bloomington: Indiana University Press, 1997.

———. *Tracing the Spirit: Ethnographic Essays on Haitian Art*. Davenport, Iowa: Davenport Museum of Art, 1995.

Bunseki Fu-Kiau, Kimbwandende Kia, *African Cosmology of the Bântu-Kôngo: Principles of Life and Living*. Brooklyn, N.Y.: Athelia Henrietta Press, 2001.

Carrier, Tim. *Family across the Sea*. VHS. Columbia, S.C.: SCETV, 1990.

Casseus, Claudel. *Imajine*. London: Penkiln Burn Book Fourteen, 2011.

Cave, Damien. "As Haitians Flee, the Dead go Uncounted: Earthquake Robs Victims and Mourners of Even the Most Basic Funeral Rites." *New York Times*, January 19, 2010.

Christophe, Marc A. "A Sacred Space for the Resolution of Haiti's Age Old Antimonies." In *Ancestral Rays: Journey through Haitian History and Culture*, edited by Claudine Michel, 22–24. Santa Barbara: Center for Black Studies, University of California, 2005.

Clark, Vèvè A. "Developing Diaspora Literacy and *Marasa* Consciousness." *Theatre Survey* 50, no. 1 (May 2009): 9–18.

Cooksey, Susan, Robin Poynor, and Hein Vanhee, eds. *Kongo across the Waters*. Gainesville: University Press of Florida, 2013.

Cone, James. *A Black Theology of Liberation*, 2nd ed. Maryknoll, N.Y.: Orbis, 1987.

Connerton, Paul. *How Societies Remember*. New York: Cambridge University Press, 1989.

Cosentino, Donald J. "Aristocrats: Themes in the Photographs and Films of Leah Gordon, Diane Arbus and Maya Deren." In *Kanaval: Vodou, Politics and Revolution on the Streets of Haiti*, edited by Leah Gordon, 43–57. Soul Jazz Publishing: London, 2010.

———. "Gede Rising." In *In Extremis: Life and Death in 21st Century Haitian Art*, edited by Donald Cosentino, 25–75. Los Angeles: UCLA Fowler Museum of Cultural History, 2012.

———. "On Looking at a Vodou Altar." *African Arts* 29, no. 2 (1996): 67–70.

———, ed. *Sacred Arts of Haitian Vodou*. Los Angeles: UCLA Fowler Museum of Cultural History, 1995.

Courlander, Harold. *The Drum and the Hoe: Life and Lore of the Haitian People*. Berkeley: University of California Press, 1960.

Curtin, Philip D. *Africa Remembered: Narratives by West Africans from the Era of the Slave Trade*. Madison: University of Wisconsin Press, 1967.

d'Aguiar, Fred. *Feeding the Ghosts*. Hopewell, N.J.: Ecco Press, 1999.

Danticat, Edwidge. *Create Dangerously: The Immigrant Artist at Work*. Princeton, N.J.: Princeton University Press, 2010.

———. "a despot walks into a killing field." *Progressive* 76, no. 5 (May 2012): 37.

———. "*Lòt Bò Dlo*: The Other Side of the Water." In *Haiti after the Earthquake*, edited by Paul Farmer, 249–58. New York: Public Affairs, 2011.

———. "A Year and a Day." *New Yorker*. January 17, 2011. http://www.newyorker.com/talk/comment/2011/01/17/110117taco_talk_danticat.

Davies, Carole Boyce. "African Diaspora Culture." In *Ancestral Rays: Journey Through Haitian History and Culture*, edited by Claudine Michel, 10. Santa Barbara: Center for Black Studies, University of California, 2005.

Davis, Wade. *Passage of Darkness: The Ethnobiology of the Haitian Zombie.* Chapel Hill: University of North Carolina Press, 1988.

———. *Serpent and the Rainbow.* New York: Simon and Schuster, 1985.

Dayan, Colin. "Dread and Dispossession: An Interview with Colin Dayan." *The Public Archive.* September 23, 2013. http://thepublicarchive.com/?p=3988.

Dayan, Joan. *Haiti, History and the Gods.* Berkeley: University of California Press, 1998.

———. Introduction to *A Rainbow for the Christian West,* by René Depestre. Amherst: University of Massachusetts Press, 1977.

Degoul, Franck. "*Du Passé Faisons Table d'Hôte: Le mode entretien des zombi dans l'imaginaire haïtien et ses filiations historiques.*" *Ethnologies* vol. 28, no. 1 (2006): 241–78.

de Heusch, Luc. "Kongo in Haiti: A New Approach to Religious Syncretism." *Man* 24, no. 2 (June 1989): 290–303.

DeLoughrey, Elizabeth M. *Routes and Roots: Navigating Caribbean and Pacific Island Literatures.* Honolulu: University of Hawai'i Press, 2007.

———. "Routes and Roots: Tidalectics in Caribbean Literature." In *Caribbean Culture: Soundings on Kamau Brathwaite,* edited by Annie Paul, 163–75. Jamaica: University of the West Indies Press, 2007.

Depestre, René. "Change." *Violence II,* no. 9: Paris: Seuil, 1971.

———. *A Rainbow for the Christian West.* Translated with an introduction by Joan Dayan. Amherst: University of Massachusetts Press, 1977.

de Peuch Parham, Althéa, ed. and trans. *My Odyssey: Experiences of a Young Refugee from Two Revolutions, by a Creole of Saint Domingue.* Baton Rouge: Louisiana State University Press, 1959.

Deren, Maya. *Divine Horsemen: The Living Gods of Haiti.* New York: McPherson and Company, 1970.

Descourtilz, Michel-Etienne. *Voyages d'un naturaliste, et ses observations,* 3 vols. (Paris, 1809).

Desquiron, Lilas. *Les Chemins de Loco-Miroir* (1990). Translated by Robin Orr Bodkin, *Reflections of Loko Miwa.* Charlottesville: University Press of Virginia, 1998.

Desmangles, Leslie. *The Faces of the Gods: Vodou and Roman Catholicism in Haiti.* Chapel Hill: University of North Carolina Press, 1992.

Díaz, Junot. "Apocalypse: What Disasters Reveal." *Boston Review.* May 2, 2011. http://www.bostonreview.net/junot-diaz-apocalypse-haiti-earthquake.

Dodds, Paisley. "Voodoo Practitioners Attacked at Ceremony for Haiti Earthquake Victims." *Huffington Post.* www.nola.com/religion/index.ssf/2010/02/voodooists_attacked_at_ceremony_for_haiti_earthquake_victims.html.

Dubois, Laurent. *Avengers of the New World: The Story of the Haitian Revolution.* Cambridge: Harvard University Press. 2004.

———. *Haiti: The Aftershocks of History.* New York: Metropolitan Books, 2012.

Endore, Guy. *Babouk: Voices of Resistance.* New York: Monthly Review Press, 1991.

Eskin, Blake. "Cover Story: The Resurrection of the Dead." *New Yorker.* January 15, 2010. http://www.newyorker.com/online/blogs/newsdesk/2010/01/cover-story-frantz-zephirin.html.

Fick, Carolyn E. *The Making of Haiti: The Saint Domingue Revolution from Below*. Knoxville: University of Tennessee Press, 1990.

Fischer, Sibylle. *Modernity Disavowed: Haiti and the Cultures of Slavery in the Age of Revolution*. Durham, N.C.: Duke University Press, 2004.

Garraway, Doris. *The Libertine Colony: Creolization in the Early French Caribbean*. Durham, N.C.: Duke University Press, 2005.

Gates, Henry Louis, Jr. *Wonders of the African World*. New York: Knopf, 1999.

———. *Wonders of the African World*. DVD. Arlington, Va: PBS, 1999.

Germain, Felix. "The Earthquake, the Missionaries and the Future of Vodou." *Journal of Black Studies* 42, no. 2 (2011): 247–63.

Gilli, Bruno. *Hevioso et le bon ordre du monde: Approche d'une religion africaine*. Paris: Memoire, EHESS-Ecoles des Hautes Etudes des Science Sociales, 1976.

Glissant, Edouard. *Caribbean Discourse: Selected Essays*. Translated by J. Michael Dash. Charlottesville: University Press of Virginia, 1989.

———. *Monsieur Toussaint, A Play*. Translated by J. Michael Dash and Edouard Glissant. Boulder, Colo.: Lynn Reinner, 2005.

———. *Poetics of Relation*. Translated by Betsy Wing. Ann Arbor: University of Michigan Press, 1997.

Glover, Kaiama. *Haiti Unbound: A Spiralist Challenge to the Postcolonial Canon*. Liverpool: Liverpool University Press, 2010.

Gomez, Michael Angelo. *Exchanging Our Country Marks: The Transformation of African Identities in the Colonial Antebellum South*. Chapel Hill: University of North Carolina Press, 1998.

Gordon, Leah, dir. *Atis-Rezistans: The Sculptors of Grand Rue* (2010), in *Iron in the Soul: The Haiti Documentary Films of Leah Gordon*. Boston, MA: Soul Jazz Films and Soul Jazz Records, 2015. DVD.

———. "Gede: The Poster Boy for Vodou." In *In Extremis: Life and Death in 21st Century Haitian Art*, edited by Donald Cosentino, 101–14. Los Angeles: UCLA Fowler Museum of Cultural History, 2012.

———. "The Sculptors of Grand Rue: Reinterpreting Slavery." *Dazed and Confused* (March 2007) http://www.atis-rezistans.com/downloads/final.pdf. Accessed November 7, 2015.

———, ed. *Kanaval: Vodou, Politics, and Revolution on the Streets of Haiti*. London: Soul Jazz Records, 2010.

Greene, Sandra E. *West African Narratives of Slavery: Texts from Late Nineteenth and Early Twentieth Century Ghana*. Bloomington: Indiana University Press, 2011.

Hagerty, Barbara Bradley. "Voodoo Brings Solace to Grieving Haitians." On "All Things Considered," NPR. January 20, 2010. http://www.npr.org/templates/story/story.php?storyId=122770590. Accessed March 14, 2013.

Haiti Grassroots Watch. "Martelly Government Betting on Sweatshops: Open for Business." *Haiti Liberte* 6, no. 34. http://www.haiti-liberte.com/archives/volume5-21/Martellygovernment.asp.

"Haitians Pay Tribute on Second Anniversary of Devastating Earthquake." *Telegraph*. January 13, 2012. http://www.telegraph.co.uk/news/worldnews/centralamericaandthecaribbean/haiti/9011990/Haitians-pay-tribute-on-second-anniversary-of-devastating-earthquake.html.

Hall, Stuart. "Cultural Identity and Diaspora." In *Identity: Community, Culture and Difference*, edited by Jonathan Rutherford, 222–37. London: Lawrence and Wishart, 1990.

Hazoumé, Paul. "*Aperçu historique sur les origins de Ouidah*," *La reconnaisance africaine*, nos. 4–5, 7–8 (1925), 10–11 (1926).

———. "La Conquête du royaume houédah par les Dahoméens au XVIIIe siècle." *Bulletin de l'enseignement de l'Afrique occidentale française*, 45 (January–February 1921): 41–45.

———. *Le Pacte du sang au Dahomey*. Paris: Institut d'ethnologie, 1956.

Henry, Paget. *Caliban's Reason: Introducing Afro-Caribbean Philosophy*. New York: Routledge, 2000.

Herbstein, Manu. *Ama: A Story of the Atlantic Slave Trade*. New York: Open Road Integrated Media, 2000.

Herskovits, Melville J. *Dahomey: An Ancient West African Kingdom*, Vols. 1 and 2. Evanston: Northwestern University Press, 1967.

———. *Life in a Haitian Valley*. 1937. Reprint, New York: Alfred A. Knopf, 2007.

Herskovits, Melville J., and Francis S. Herskovits. *Dahomean Narrative: A Cross-Cultural Analysis*. Evanston, Ill.: Northwestern University Press, 1958.

Heywood, Linda, ed. *Central Africans and Cultural Transformations in the African Diaspora*. New York: Cambridge University Press, 2002.

Hill, Lawrence. *The Book of Negroes (Someone Knows My Name)*. New York: Norton, 2007.

hooks, bell. *Art on My Mind: Visual Politics*. New York: New Press, 1995.

Houlberg, Marilyn. "Magique Marasa: The Ritual Cosmos of the Twins and Other Sacred Children." In *Fragments of Bone: Neo-African Religions in a New World*, edited by Patrick Bellegarde-Smith, 13–31. Chicago: University of Illinois Press, 2005.

———. "Magique Marasa: The Ritual Cosmos of the Twins and Other Sacred Children." In *Sacred Arts of Haitian Vodou*, edited by Donald Cosentino, 267–83. Los Angeles: UCLA Fowler Museum of Cultural History, 1995.

———. "*Pakèt Kongo*: Spirit Bundles." In *Vodou: Visions and Voices of Haiti*, edited by Phyllis Galembo, 66. Berkeley, Calif.: Ten Speed Press, 2005.

Hurbon. Laënnec. *Le Barbare imaginaire*. Paris: Cerf, 1988.

———. *Voodoo: Search for the Spirit*. Translated by Lory Frankel. New York: H.N. Abrams, 1995.

Hurston, Zora Neale. *Tell My Horse: Voodoo and Life in Haiti and Jamaica*. New York: Harper and Row, 1990.

Iroko, Abiola Félix. *La Côte des Esclaves et la Traite Atlantique: Les faits et le jugement de l'histoire*. Cotonou, Bénin: Nouvelle presse publications, 2003.

Isichei, Elizabeth. *Voices of the Poor in Africa: Moral Economy and the Popular Imagination*. Rochester, N.Y.: University of Rochester Press, 2002.

Jones, Bridget. "'The Unity Is Submarine': Aspects of a Pan-Caribbean Consciousness in the Work of Kamau Brathwaite." In *The Art of Kamau Brathwaite*, edited by Stewart Brown, 86–100. Mid Glamorgan, Wales: Seren, 1995.

Kenny, Charles. "Haiti Doesn't Need Your Old T-Shirt." *Foreign Affairs*, October 11, 2011. http://foreignpolicy.com/2011/10/11/haiti-doesnt-need-your-old-t-shirt/.

Laferrière, Dany. *The World Is Moving around Me: A Memoir of the Haiti Earthquake*. Translated by David Homel. Vancouver, B.C.: Arsenal Pulp Press, 2011.

Laroche, Maximilien. "*La Lutte du héros contre sa victimisation*." *Tanbou*. Spring, 1994. http://www.tanbou.com/1994/Spring/Lutte.htm.

Law, Robin. "The Atlantic Slave Trade in Local History Writing in Ouidah." In *Africa and Trans-Atlantic Memories: Literary and Aesthetic Manifestations of Diaspora and History*, edited by Naana Opku-Agyemang, Paul E. Lovejoy, and David V. Trotman, 257–74. Trenton, N.J.: Africa World Press, 2008.

———. *Ouidah: The Social History of a West African Slaving Port 1727–1892*. Athens: Ohio University Press, 2004.

Lovejoy, Paul. "The Volume of the Atlantic Slave Trade: A Synthesis." *Journal of African History* 23, no. 4 (1982): 473–501.

MacGaffey, Wyatt. "Twins, Simbi Spirits and Lwas in Kongo and Haiti." In *Central Africans and Cultural Transformations in the American Diaspora*, edited by Linda M. Heywood, 211–26. New York: Cambridge University Press, 2002.

Maupoil, Bernard. *La Géomancie à l'Ancienne Côte des Esclaves*. Paris: Institut d'Ethnologie, 1943.

Mbembe, Achille. "Necropolitics." Translated by Libby Meintjes. *Public Culture* 15, no. 1 (2003): 11–40.

Mbiti, John S. *African Religions and Philosophy*. London: Heinemann, 1971.

McAlister, Elizabeth. "Love, Sex, and Gender Embodied: The Spirits of Haitian Vodou." Division II Faculty Publications. Paper 14. Oxford, 2000. http://wesscholar.wesleyan.edu/div2facpubs/14.

———. *Rara! Vodou, Power, and Performance in Haiti and Its Diaspora*. Berkeley: University of California Press, 2002.

———. "A Sorcerer's Bottle: The Visual Art of Magic in Haiti." In *Sacred Arts of Haitian Vodou*, edited by Donald Cosentino, 305–21. Los Angeles: UCLA Fowler Museum of Cultural History, 1995.

———. "Voodoo's View of the Quake in Haiti." *On Faith*, January 15, 2010. http://www.faithstreet.com/onfaith/2010/01/15/voodoos-view-of-the-quake-in-haiti/2118.

Mercier, Paul. "The Fon of Dahomey." In *African Worlds: Studies in the Cosmological Ideas and Social Values of African Peoples*, edited by Daryll Forde, 210–34. New York: Oxford University Press, 1965.

Métraux, Alfred. *Le Vaudou haïtien*. Paris: Editions Gallimard, 1958.

———. *Voodoo in Haiti*. Translated by Hugo Charteris. New York: Schocken Books, 1972.

Michel, Claudine. "African Continuity in Haitian Religious Life." In *Ancestral Rays: Journey through Haitian History and Culture*, edited by Claudine Michel, 18–19. Santa Barbara: Center for Black Studies, University of California, 2005.

———. "Of Worlds Seen and Unseen: The Educational Character of Haitian Vodou."

In *Haitian Vodou: Spirit, Myth and Reality*, edited by Patrick Bellegarde-Smith and Claudine Michel, 32–45. Bloomington: Indiana University Press, 2006.

Mikell, Gwendolyn. "When Horses Talk: Reflections on Zora Neale Hurston's Haitian Anthropology." *Phylon* 43, no. 3 (1982): 218–30.

Mintz, Sidney. Introduction to *Voodoo in Haiti*. By Alfred Métraux. Translated by Hugo Charteris. New York: Schocken Books, 1972.

Mintz, Sidney, and Michel-Rolph Trouillot. "The Social History of Haitian Vodou." In *Sacred Arts of Haitian Vodou*, edited by Donald Cosentino, 123–47. Los Angeles: UCLA Fowler Museum of Cultural History, 1995.

Morris, Hamilton. "I Walked with a Zombie: Travels among the Undead." *Harper's*, November 2011, http://harpers.org/archive/2011/11/i-walked-with-a-zombie/.

Morrison, Toni. "The Site of Memory." In *Inventing the Truth: The Art and Craft of Memoir*, 2nd ed., edited by William Zinsser, 83–102. Boston: Houghton Mifflin, 1995.

Murphy, Joseph M. *Working the Spirit: Ceremonies of the African Diaspora*. Boston: Beacon Press, 1994.

Murphy, Joseph, and Mei-Mei Sanford, *Osun across the Waters: A Yoruba Goddess in Africa and the Americas*. Bloomington: Indiana University Press, 2001.

Nichols, Grace. *i is a long-memoried woman*. London: Karnak House, 1983.

Nwankwo, Ifeoma Kiddoe. "Insider and Outsider, Black and American: Rethinking Zora Neale Hurston's Caribbean Ethnography." *Radical History Review* 87 (Fall 2003): 49–77.

Ogundiran, Akinwumi, and Paula Saunders, eds. *Materialities of Ritual in the Black Atlantic*. Bloomington: Indiana University Press, 2014.

Okpewho, Isidore, Carole Boyce Davies, and Ali A. Mazrui, eds. *The African Diaspora: African Origins and New World Identities*. Bloomington: Indiana University Press, 2001.

Olupona, Jacob, and Terry Rey, eds. *Òrìsà Devotion as World Religion: The Globalization of Yorùbá Religious Culture*. Madison: University of Wisconsin Press, 2008.

Opku-Agyemang, Naana, Paul E. Lovejoy and David V. Trotman, eds. *Africa and Trans-Atlantic Memories: Literary and Aesthetic Manifestations of Diaspora and History*. Trenton, N.J.: Africa World Press, 2008.

Oyêwùmí, Oyèrónké. "Visualizing the Body: Western Theories and African Subjects." In *African Gender Studies: A Reader*, edited by Oyèrónké Oyêwùmí, 3–21. New York: Palgrave MacMillan, 2005.

Palmié, Stephan. *Wizards and Scientists: Exploration in Afro-Cuban Modernity and Tradition*. Durham, N.C.: Duke University Press, 2002.

Patterson, Orlando. *Slavery and Social Death: A Comparative Study*. Cambridge, Mass.: Harvard University Press, 1982.

Paul, Emmanuel C. *Panorama du folklore haïtien*. 3rd ed. 1962. Port-au-Prince: Présence Africaine en Haïti, 2014.

Pelton, Robert D. *The Trickster in West Africa: A Study of Mythic Irony and Sacred Delight*. Berkeley: University of California Press, 1980.

Penn, Irving. *Photographs of Dahomey*. 1967. Reprint, Houston: Museum of Fine Arts, 2004.

Pfaff, Françoise. "Sembene, A Griot of Modern Times." In *Cinemas of the Black Diaspora: Diversity, Dependence, and Oppositionality*, edited by Michael T. Martin, 118–28. Detroit: Wayne State University Press, 1995.

Pierre, Natalie. "*Ti Dife Boule Sou Istwa Ayiti* as Haitian Civic Education." *Cultural Dynamics* 26, no. 2 (2014): 209–17.

Poupeye, Veerle. *Caribbean Art*. New York: Thames and Hudson, 1998.

Poynor, Robin. "The Western Congo Basin." In *A History of Art in Africa*, edited by Monica Blackmun Visonà, Robin Poynor, Herbert M. Cole, Suzanne Preston Blier, and Rowland Abiodun, 366–411. Upper Saddle River, N.J.: Pearson/Prentice Hall, 2008.

Pressley-Sanon, Toni. "Exile, Return, Ouidah and Haiti: Vodun's Workings on the Art of Edouard Duval-Carrié." *African Arts Journal* 46, no. 3 (August 2013): 40–53.

———. "Haitian (Pre)Occupations: Ideological and Discursive Repetitions, 1915–1934 and 2004 to Present." *Caribbean Studies Journal* 42, no. 2 (2014): 115–53.

———. "One Plus One Equals Three: Marasa Consciousness, the Lwa, and Three Stories." *Research in African Literatures* 44, no. 3 (Fall 2013): 118–37.

Ramsey, Kate. *The Spirits and the Law: Vodou and Power in Haiti*. Chicago: University of Chicago Press, 2011.

Richman, Karen. *Migration and Vodou*. Gainesville: University Press of Florida, 2005.

Rush, Dana. "Contemporary Vodun Arts of Ouidah, Benin." *African Arts* 34, no. 4 (2001): 32–47.

———. "Ephemerality and the 'Unfinished' in Vodun Aesthetics." *African Arts* 43, no. 1 (2010): 60–75.

———. "In Remembrance of Slavery: Tchamba Vodun Arts." *African Arts* 44, no. 1 (Spring 2011): 40–51.

Russell, Heather. *Legba's Crossing: Narratology in the African Atlantic*. Athens: University of Georgia Press, 2011.

Sahmkow, Ramon. "Haiti Is a Future Tourist Destination, Says President." *Yahoo*, December 5, 2011. https://au.finance.yahoo.com/news/haiti-future-tourist-destination-says-062231495.html.

Said, Edward. *Culture and Imperialism*. New York: Knopf, 1993.

Scheper-Hughes, Nancy, and Margaret M. Lock. "The Mindful Body: A Prolegomenon to Future Work in Medical Anthropology." *Medical Anthropology Quarterly*, New Series 1, no. 1 (March 1987): 6–41.

Scheub, Harold. *The Poem in the Story: Music, Poetry and Narrative*. Madison: University of Wisconsin Press, 2002.

Seabrook, William. *The Magic Island*. New York: Harcourt, Brace, 1929.

Shaw, Rosalind. *Memories of the Slave Trade: Ritual and the Historical Imagination in Sierra Leone*. Chicago: University of Chicago Press, 2002.

Sheller, Mimi. *Citizenship from Below: Erotic Agency and Caribbean Freedom*. Durham, N.C.: Duke University Press, 2012.

Smith, Katherine. "Gede Rising: Haiti in the Age of *Vagabondaj*." PhD diss., University of California Los Angeles, 2010.

Sutherland, Peter. "In Memory of the Slaves: An African View of the Diaspora in the

Americas." In *Representations of Blackness and the Performance of Identities*, edited by Jean Muteba Rahier, 195–211. Westport, Conn.: Bergen and Garvey, 1999.

Thompson, Robert Farris. *Aesthetic of the Cool: Afro-Atlantic Art and Music*. Pittsburgh: Periscope, 2011.

———. *Flash of the Spirit: African and Afro-American Art and Philosophy*. New York: Random House, 1983.

———. "From the Isle Beneath the Sea: Haiti's Africanizing Vodou Art." In *Sacred Arts of Haitian Vodou*, edited by Donald Cosentino, 91–119. Los Angeles: UCLA Fowler Museum of Cultural History, 1995.

Thompson, Robert Farris, and Joseph Cornet. *The Four Moments of the Sun: Kongo Art in Two Worlds*. Washington, D.C.: National Gallery of Art, 1981.

Thornton, John K. "African Soldiers in the Haitian Revolution." *Journal of Caribbean History* 25 (1991): 58–80.

Tinsley, Omise'eke Natasha. "Black Atlantic, Queer Atlantic: Queer Imaginings of the Middle Passage." *GLQ: A Journal of Lesbian and Gay Studies* 14, nos. 2–3 (2008): 191–215.

Trouillot, Michel-Rolph. *Haiti, State against Nation: The Origins and Legacy of Duvalierism*. New York: Monthly Review Press, 1990.

———. *Ti Difé Boule Sou Istwa Ayiti*. 1977. Port-au-Prince: Inivèsite Karayib, 2012.

Turner, Victor. *The Forest of Symbols: Aspects of Ndembu Ritual*. Ithaca, N.Y.: Cornell University Press, 1967.

Ulysse, Gina Athena. *Why Haiti Needs New Narratives: A Post-Earthquake Chronicle*. Middleton, Conn.: Wesleyan University Press, 2015.

———. "Why Haiti Needs New Narratives Now More than Ever." In *Tectonic Shifts: Haiti since the Earthquake*, edited by Mark Schuller and Pablo Morales, 240–45. Sterling: Kumarian Press, 2012.

Vanhee, Hein. "Central African Popular Christianity and the Making of Haitian Vodou Religion." In *Central Africans and Cultural Transformation in the American Diaspora*, edited by Linda M. Heywood, 243–64. New York: Cambridge University Press, 2002.

Volavkova, Zdenka. "Nkisi Figure of the Lower Congo." *African Arts* 5, no. 2 (Winter 1972): 52–59.

Walcott, Derek. *Collected Poems: 1948–1984*. New York: Farrar, Straus & Giroux, 1986.

wa Thiong'o, Ngũgĩ. *Something Torn and New: An African Renaissance*. New York: Basic Civitas Books, 2009.

White, Hayden. *Metahistory: The Historical Imagination in Nineteenth Century Europe*. Baltimore: John Hopkins University Press, 1973.

———. *Tropics of Discourse: Essays in Cultural Criticism*. Baltimore: Johns Hopkins University Press, 1978.

Woolfolk, Lisa. *Embodying American Slavery in Contemporary Culture*. Urbana: University of Illinois Press, 2009.

"A World Created by Magic: Excerpts from a Conversation with André Pierre." In *Sacred Arts of Haitian Vodou*, edited by Donald Cosentino, xx–xxiii. Los Angeles: UCLA Fowler Museum of Cultural History, 1995.

Index

Toni Pressley-Sanon is associate professor of Africology and African American Studies at Eastern Michigan University.